SOCIAL AND PSYCHOLOGICAL
CONSEQUENCES OF
VIOLENT
VICTIMIZATION

*To my mother, Mary P. Ruback, and
the memory of my father, Norman Ruback.*
                    —*Barry*

*To my husband, Kip Kingree,
and my son, Jack Kingree.*
                    —*Martie*

SOCIAL AND PSYCHOLOGICAL CONSEQUENCES OF
VIOLENT
VICTIMIZATION

R. BARRY RUBACK ◆ MARTIE P. THOMPSON

Sage Publications
International Educational and Professional Publisher
Thousand Oaks ■ London ■ New Delhi

For information:

 Sage Publications, Inc.
2455 Teller Road
Thousand Oaks, California 91320
E-mail: order@sagepub.com

Sage Publications Ltd.
6 Bonhill Street
London EC2A 4PU
United Kingdom

Sage Publications India Pvt. Ltd.
M-32 Market
Greater Kailash I
New Delhi 110 048 India

Printed in the United States of America

Library of Congress Cataloging-in-Publication Data

Ruback, R. Barry, 1950-
   Social and psychological consequences of violent victimization / by
   R. Barry Ruback and Martie P. Thompson.
       p.   cm.
Includes bibliographical references and index.
   ISBN 10: 0-7619-1040-9 ISBN 13: 978-0-7619-1040-4 (cloth: alk. paper)
   ISBN 10: 0-7619-1041-7 ISBN 13: 978-0-7619-1041-1 (pbk.: alk. paper)
   1. Victims of crimes—United States.   2. Violent crimes—
United States.   I. Thompson, Martie P.   II. Title.
   HV6250.3.U5 R8   2001
   362.88' 0973—dc21   00-012406

07 08 09 10 11 12   10 9 8 7 6 5 4 3

Acquiring Editor:	Nancy Hale
Editorial Assistant:	Vonessa Vondera
Production Editor:	Denise Santoyo
Editorial Assistant:	Kathryn Journey
Typesetter:	Janelle LeMaster
Cover Designer:	Michelle Lee

Contents

Preface

A violent crime is more than a single incident affecting a single person along a single dimension of injury. Rather, it is typically the beginning of a series of actions that the victim, the victim's family, and the victim's friends have to take in order to cope with the physical injury, emotional distress, and economic costs that result from the violence. These actions include having to decide whether or not to call the police, seek medical care, and obtain counseling. Making these decisions is often more problematic when the victim and offender have a prior relationship, because questions of perceived blame may be difficult to answer.

The purpose of this book is to examine the impact of violent crime on individuals, families, and communities. To do so, we have used the literature from several disciplines, because the issues transcend levels of analysis (i.e., individuals, groups, and communities) and they cross traditional boundaries (e.g., between research and clinical practice and between criminology and public health). One of our primary goals in writing this book is to emphasize the need for multiple research methods and multiple theoretical perspectives for understanding the effects and implications of violent crime.

This book is primarily a product of our own thinking and research over the past few years about the consequences of victimization. However, at a more fundamental level, the book reflects our conversations and collaborations with several individuals during the past 20 years. Ruback first became interested in the topic through research conducted with Martin Greenberg at the University of Pittsburgh, much of which is summarized in this book. Since then, his research collaborators (particularly Deborah Ivie, Kim Ménard, and Jennifer Shaffer) and the students in his courses on victimization have sharpened his focus on questions of psychological impact and public policy. Thompson first became interested in the effects of violent crime through her doctoral research with Fran Norris in the community psychology program at Georgia State University. Thereafter, her postdoctoral work with Nadine Kaslow at Emory University School of Medicine, and her experiences as a scientist, working primarily with Linda Saltzman and Jim Mercy in the Division of Violence Prevention at the Centers for Disease Control and Prevention, have expanded her thinking on the causes and consequences of violent crime.

We would like to thank the National Institute of Justice and the National Institute of Mental Health, which have funded our research and encouraged our thinking about the effects of victimization. We would also like to thank our institutions, Pennsylvania State University and Emory University, for their support. Thanks also to Neil Weiner at the University of Pennsylvania for initially suggesting the need for this book. At Sage we would like to thank Terry Hendrix, who was supportive of the book from the beginning, and Nancy Hale, who shepherded us through the publication process.

Violent crimes can have profound effects on individuals, neighborhoods, and society in general. Our hope is that this book will encourage readers to think more broadly about how these consequences can be measured, understood, ameliorated, and prevented.

1

Introduction and Overview

Kathy, a 47-year-old married woman, related the following assault:

My daughter and I usually run together in the early evening. On that day, at about 5:30, she called to say that her husband had just called, and he was held up at work, and I was a bit leery of going alone as by 5:30 it was already getting dark, and I knew that the area wasn't the safest place for women. But I was in a good routine, and I wanted to keep up my momentum so that I'd be in form for the Bonnie Bell race. I left a note for my husband and drove over to the jogging track. There was hardly anyone in the parking lot, and I thought that maybe I should just not go, but I thought to myself that I was just being an old fogy. So I warmed up and went down the open stretch at the beginning of the track where the streetlights flooded the path. Then I turned the curve. I saw the outline of the woman's form painted on the path, which was the place where a woman was raped, and which the Women's Center had painted there as a reminder.

I was a bit taken aback, more so than usual. But again, I chided myself for being silly. I ran a bit faster. It's a 5-mile course, and as I passed the 3-mile marker I felt that I'd have been foolish to stay home. It felt good to be moving. That's when he got me. He must have been hiding in the bushes by the golf course, as all

1

of a sudden he was in front of me. He pulled me off the path, and as I began to yell, he clamped a hand over my mouth and told me that he had a knife. He said that I had better do what he wanted. I did. I lay down. He raped me. I was sobbing. My eyes were wide open—startled. Finally, he let me go. I was terrified!

I ran away for a few minutes, and then I stopped. I was too frightened to go on, thinking someone else was waiting for me further ahead. I stood there immobile. Finally, another runner appeared—a woman—and I started wailing. She walked me the rest of the way back to the parking lot and drove me to the hospital. She called the rape crisis center, and I called my husband. He came right away, as did a woman from the center. She stayed with me throughout all of the tests they did. My husband was gentle but confused.

Now I have stopped running—there is nowhere safe in the city to run. I'm seeing a woman counselor in an attempt to overcome my fears of being alone outside at night. It's even hard to go for an evening stroll with my family.

Therapist's case summary:

Initially, Kathy was seen by a rape crisis center advocate who helped her through the medical exams and police investigation. Treatment was clearly crisis oriented. The advocate referred Kathy to a woman's therapy collective. The development of rape-related fears led Kathy to seek therapy approximately one month after her rape.

Therapy focused on affirming Kathy's strengths and encouraging her to become involved in projects that would put her in a position of controlling her environment. She became active in a "green light" project in her neighborhood as a result of this suggestion. The therapy also centered on learning some assertive, self-defense maneuvers. An attempt was made to validate Kathy's fears and at the same time to help her put them into perspective. She continued therapy for four months.[1]

This true incident, taken from a book about rape victims by Koss and Harvey (1991, pp. 60-61, 193), illustrates eight issues that we will discuss in this book. First, the incident shows how *fear of crime* affects potential victims' behavior, particularly whether they take precautions or avoid going to some places altogether. Second, it suggests that victims, even when facing lethal weapons, consider *whether or not to resist* the offender. Third, it shows the important roles of *social support and social influence* on crime victims. That is, victims commonly seek out others after the crime, even strangers, and these strangers can influence how well victims cope with the trauma. Fourth, it suggests that although victims commonly seek help from others, this does not always involve *reporting the crime to the police.* Indeed, in crimes like rape, it is more common for victims not to report the crime. Fifth, it shows that after a violent crime like rape, victims commonly experience *stress that may require both crisis-oriented and longer-term therapy.* Sixth, it shows that others, particularly close relatives, are also affected by a violent crime. In this incident, Kathy's husband's *indirect victimization* produced emotional reactions such as confusion, anger, and fear. Seventh, it shows how violent crimes *affect the general community* in terms of residents' fears, willingness to venture outside their homes, and decisions to stay or move away. Finally, the incident shows that violent crime often prompts individuals and groups to become involved in crime awareness and *crime prevention.* In this case, the Women's Center had painted the outline of a woman's form to indicate where a woman had previously been raped, and after the crime, Kathy herself became involved in a neighborhood prevention project and learned self-defense.

THE VIOLENT CRIME PROBLEM

Directly or indirectly, violent crime touches everyone. In any given year, about 10 million violent victimizations take place in the United States, and about 7% of all households contain at least one person who is a victim of violent crime (U.S. Bureau of Justice Statistics, 1997). Over the course of their lifetimes, about 5 of every 6 persons will be victims of attempted or completed violent crimes (U.S. Bureau of Justice Statistics, 1987). Public opinion polls consistently reveal that crime is perceived to be one of this country's most serious domestic problems. In a nationally representative public opinion survey, 82% reported being very concerned about violence, and 54% said that violent crime was more problematic in their neighborhoods than it was a decade ago (Kilpatrick, Seymour, & Boyle, 1991).

Victims of violent crimes suffer psychologically, physically, and financially. Less obvious is the fact that victims' relatives and friends are also likely to suffer—from increased fear and from tangible costs such as having to help victims pay medical and other expenses. Communities are also damaged by violent crime. Residents who can afford to move will try to leave a dangerous environment. Those who cannot leave are likely to change their behavior, interacting less with their neighbors and going outside less, particularly at night. In addition to their impact on individuals, high rates of violent crime often force businesses to leave communities because of the danger of future crime, greater costs associated with higher insurance rates, and the need for private security. Finally, violent crime affects the level and allocation of criminal justice resources, especially law enforcement, and of community treatment and mental health services.

This book is about the social and psychological effects of violent victimizations. We discuss the effects on many aspects of individual victims' lives—their emotions, cognitions, and behaviors—and show how the impact varies across time. However, a violent crime is not an isolated incident affecting only the person who was directly harmed; we also discuss the impact on victims' friends and families, their neighborhoods, and the larger society. In our multilevel discussion of the effects of violent crime, we draw on research and theory from a number of academic disciplines, including psychology, sociology, criminology, economics, and geography.

In this first chapter, we summarize the growth of interest in violent victimization and the scope of violent crime in the United States. We also look at methodological issues involved in measuring violent victimization and at theoretical issues related to its causes and correlates.

GROWTH OF INTEREST IN VICTIMS

Beginning in the late 1960s, people in the United States became more interested in crime victims for several reasons (Greenberg & Ruback, 1992). They became concerned at the societal level when the victimization surveys initiated in the 1970s, which examined nationally representative samples and intensive samples of particular cities, revealed large numbers of individuals and households affected by crime. (The research continues today as the National Crime Victimization Survey.) Similar surveys conducted in other countries (e.g., the Canadian Violence Against Women Survey) provided additional information about factors related to victimization and the reporting of crime, and they also provided additional support for theories incorporating these factors. At the same time, studies of police agencies indicated that citizens, especially victims, were crucial in dealing with the crime problem because virtually all police investigations were the product of reports by citizens rather than of police surveillance (Black, 1970).

The growth of the victims' movement was another factor leading to increased interest in crime victims. The movement had been spurred by a general concern for victims of injustice, a rising crime rate, and a perception that the criminal justice system was more concerned with criminals than it was with victims. The report of the President's Task Force on Victims of Crime (1982) reflected this concern and led to the Comprehensive Crime Control Act of 1984. This legislation increased federal funding for state victim compensation programs. It also established the National Office of Victim Assistance (NOVA) within the U.S. Department of Justice as the primary vehicle for developing and supporting agencies to serve crime victims. Two years after the President's Task Force report, the Attorney General's Task Force on Family Violence (1984) focused attention on the problems of violence against partners and children. Also during the 1980s, the National Institute of Mental Health (NIMH) and the National Institute of Justice (the primary research agency within the Department of Justice) sponsored several research projects and evaluations that examined causes of, and recovery from, criminal victimization. The studies were concerned with both individuals and communities and provided the basis for several policy recommendations regarding crime prevention and treatment services for crime victims.

In addition to increased emphasis on crime victims at the federal level, state governments also began to give more attention to crime victims. Since 1985, 49 states have passed victims' bills of rights, and 22 have added constitutional amendments guaranteeing the provision of certain services (Tomz & McGillis, 1997). Across the United States today, about 10,000 victim assistance programs provide a wide array of services, including crisis counseling and support during the criminal justice processing of the case (e.g., police investigation, prosecution, and settlement).

Aside from, and in some cases the cause of, these state and federal programs, numerous private organizations have addressed victims' rights. NOVA was one of the first, and it remains one of the best known and most active. Among the others are Mothers Against Drunk Driving (MADD) and Parents of Murdered Children.

In addition to these societal factors, methodological and theoretical advances also facilitated interest in crime victims. The primary methodological advance was the development of the victimization survey, which is described in more detail below. The primary theoretical advance was the creation of the diagnostic category *posttraumatic stress disorder* (PTSD). The theory was based on the premise that crime victimizations can produce the same emotional reactions as other highly traumatic events, such as war. The measurement and effects of PTSD are described more fully in Chapters 2, 4, and 5.

These advances in research were reflected by an increase in the number of research studies and the creation of journals that focused specifically on crime victims. Among the latter were *Violence and Victims,* the *Journal of Interpersonal Violence,* the *International Review of Victimology, Child Abuse and Neglect,* and *Violence Against Women.* Increased research interest was reflected in studies of crime victims by the Task Force of the American Psychological Association (Frieze, Hymer, & Greenberg, 1987).

VIOLENCE IN THE UNITED STATES

Violent crimes are "behaviors by individuals that intentionally threaten, attempt, or inflict physical harm on others" (Reiss & Roth, 1993). Thus, violence includes both attempted and completed simple assault, aggravated assault, robbery, rape, and murder. In other words, violent crimes are the ones that people judge to be the most serious and of which they are the most afraid.

There is more violent crime in the United States than in most other countries (Reiss & Roth, 1993), although recent evidence suggests that serious violent crimes have become more prevalent in some countries of the former Soviet Union such as Estonia, Kazakhstan, and Kyrgyzstan (van Dijk & Kangaspunta, 2000). The United States has the highest homicide rate of any industrialized nation. Among 16 countries, it has the highest rates for sexual assaults and assaults involving threats of physical harm. The closest cross-national comparison may be made with Canada; the United States and Canada are similar in several dimensions, including geography and culture. In every measure of violent crime, the United States has much higher rates than Canada. However, the characterization of the United States as the world's most violent industrialized nation may no longer be true. Violent crime rates fell in the United States in the 1990s and increased in other countries. For example, although the homicide rate in the United States is still about 6 times higher than the rate in England, robbery and assault rates are now higher in England than in the United States (Langan & Farrington, 1998). But even if the United States is not the most violent industrialized country in every category, it still has very high rates of violence.

Firearm usage is one factor related to the high rates of violence in the United States. About 1.1 million violent crimes per year are committed with firearms (U.S. Bureau of Justice Statistics, 1997, table 66). Firearm-related injuries are the eighth leading cause of death for the population as a whole and the leading cause of death for blacks between the ages of 15 and 34 (Mercy, 1993). In 1985, more than 65,000 people were hospitalized as a result of firearms-related injuries, and more than 170,000 were injured but not hospitalized. About 100,000 people are treated in hospital emergency departments every year for nonfatal firearm-related injuries (Annest, Mercy, Gibson, & Ryan, 1995).

Rates of violence are high in the United States, and the media present stories about violent crimes and violent individuals at rates even higher than their actual occurrence. It is important to put contemporary crime rates in perspective. Historically, they have been much higher. For example, rates of violent crime in medieval England were probably 10, and perhaps 20, times higher than those in 20th-century England (Gurr, 1989). In the United States, interpersonal violence showed upsurges in 1850, 1900, and 1960 (Gurr, 1989) and a large increase in the 1980s, especially violence linked to handguns. In the 1990s, there was a decrease in violent crimes, including homicide (Fox & Zawitz, 2000), due to greater police involvement in tracking illegal weapons, a drop in new crack cocaine users, a stronger economy, and higher rates of incarceration (Blumstein & Rosenfeld, 1999).

According to the best estimates, about one quarter of all crimes in the United States involve violence. In 1995, this number was about 9.6 million violent crimes of 38 million total. However, relative to the total number of violent crimes, there are few very serious ones. Analyses of violent crimes indicate that of every 1,000, there are about 500 simple assaults (e.g., hitting, slapping, or punching), 300 aggravated assaults (involving weapons or serious nonfatal injury), 176 robberies, 20 rapes, and 4 homicides (Reiss & Roth, 1993). In general, the more serious a crime is, the less likely it is to occur. For example, there are more simple assaults than aggravated assaults, and within each type of crime, there are generally more attempted than completed crimes.

Although most of the actions involved in these crimes are clearly violent (e.g., the victim was shot or money was forcibly taken), whether or not an act is considered a crime depends on factors defined by the criminal law (e.g., whether the offender had the requisite criminal intent). Whether an act should be called a crime is related to whether or not the target of the violent act should be called a crime victim. Defining who is a crime victim can sometimes be problematic, as we will see in subsequent chapters. For example, in bar fights it may not always be clear who is the victim and who is the offender. More often than not, if there is an arrest after the incident, the person taken into custody is likely to be the winner of the fight regardless of what might have happened initially. Generally, whether victims report an event, police make an arrest, prosecutors file charges, or juries or judges convict can be affected by whether the victim did (or is perceived as having done) something to precipitate the crime. Thus, although persons may suffer because of a violent act, according to the law they may or may not be crime victims.

However they are defined, the reality is that in most cases offenders are not punished. For example, only a small proportion of rape cases result in prison sentences (Frazier & Haney, 1996). First, only about 32% of rapes are reported to the police (U.S. Bureau of Justice Statistics, 1997). Of the cases that are reported, the police make an arrest in only 40%. Of those, only about half result in felony charges. About two thirds of the cases in which there are felony rape charges result in convictions, and 40% of those who are convicted of felony rape are sent to prison. In other words, the offenders are incarcerated in less than 5% of the cases.

Costs of Violent Victimizations

Violent victimizations are costly to individuals, to communities, and to the larger society. For example, recent estimates place the cost of assaultive victimizations at $93 billion (Miller, Cohen, & Wiersema, 1996, p. 24). Some of these costs, like medical care, are obvious. Others, such as mental health expenses associated with counseling, are less obvious and often unanticipated.

A good example of the hidden costs associated with violent victimizations may be seen in the aftermath of the 1993 bombing of the World Trade Center. After the bombing, the Port Authority of New York and New Jersey, owner of the building, was faced with all sorts of costs directly and indirectly related to the bombing (Bleakley, 1997). Some of the costs were anticipated; others were unexpected. For example, the Port Authority spent $15 million on psychological counseling, donations to the Red Cross and Salvation Army, small gifts for returning office workers (e.g., mugs, T-shirts), and subsidies to retail stores to help them attract customers. During the two weeks immediately after the bombing, the Port Authority spent $20 million for approximately 3,000 workers who cleaned soot from every square inch of the building, including specialists who cleaned the marble and the electrical lighting. Because it was impossible to keep track of all of the master keys used during the evacuation immediately after the bombing, the Port Authority had to spend $5 million replacing thousands of locks and tens of thousand of keys. Also, in terms of increased security, the Port Authority installed a $50 million security system and now spends $20 million annually on closed-circuit television and security personnel (compared with $8 million before the bombing). In addition, the Port Authority spent more than $100 million on backup electrical, fire alarm, and air-conditioning systems. The cost of higher insurance premiums and deductibles runs more than $110 million.

Although less dramatic, the costs of violent crime to an individual victim are also likely to involve a number of direct and hidden costs. The most systematic examinations of the costs of violence (Cohen, 1988; Miller et al., 1996) suggest that they consist of three parts: (a) direct monetary costs; (b) pain, suffering, and fear of injury; and (c) risk of death. Direct monetary costs include lost days from work, property losses, medical costs, and psychological counseling expenses. The calculation of pain and suffering is based on the estimate for each type of injury multiplied by the probability that the injury would occur. For example, in the case of a specific rape, the probability of broken bones or teeth is 2% and the cost of such injuries, if they occurred, would be $15,273. Thus, the calculated cost for broken bones or teeth is .02 × $15,273, or $305. When similar calculations are conducted for harms such as internal injuries, severe psychological injuries, and gunshot or knife wounds, the cost of pain and suffering for a rape totals $43,561. Risk of death is computed by multiplying the probability of death (for a given year, the number of deaths for a particular type of crime divided by the number of crimes) multiplied by the estimated value of a statistical life ($2 million). A set of calculations for the costs of crime (Cohen, 1988) are presented in Table 1.1. The numbers represent average costs to victims of different types of crimes. It should be noted that, although these sorts of calculations are commonly used in civil suits and workmen's compensation, many individuals are upset by the idea of attaching dollar figures to a person's death or suffering.

These average costs are important for policy decisions. For example, parole boards make decisions about whether a particular offender should be released from prison. In part, a judgment could depend on the cost of continuing to incarcerate the offender versus the costs of release—based on the likelihood that the offender would commit a

TABLE 1.1   Average Cost of Crime to Victims

Crime	Direct Losses	Pain and Suffering	Risk of Death	Total
Kidnapping	$1,872	$15,797	$92,800	$110,469
Bombing	24,737	7,586	44,800	77,123
Rape	4,617	43,561	2,880	51,058
Arson	14,776	6,393	12,380	33,549
Bank robbery	4,422	10,688	3,700	18,810
Robbery	1,114	7,459	4,021	12,594
Assault	422	4,921	6,685	12,028
Car theft	3,069	—	58	3,127
Burglary	939	317	116	1,372
Larceny				
Personal	179	—	2	181
. Household	173	—	—	173

SOURCE: Cohen (1988).

crime, and the projected cost to the victim and to society if that crime was committed.

In addition to these costs to individual victims, there are costs to businesses and communities. One of them is job flight from areas where crime, or at least the fear of crime, is high. Cultural activities can also be affected. For example, the Watts Summer Festival, which started after the 1965 riots in the Watts section of Los Angeles, was discontinued for 2 years in 1989 because of gang violence and was resumed in neutral territory outside of Watts. Potential benefits to the community from many kinds of cultural activities are lost because of the fear of violent crime.

Another cost of violence to the community is that of emergency medical services. Emergency services are likely to see both penetrating wounds (usually inflicted by guns or knives) and blunt trauma injuries (usually caused by car crashes). Victims of penetrating wounds are statistically unlikely to have insurance, whereas victims of blunt trauma injuries are more likely to be insured. Thus, the ratio of penetrating wounds to blunt trauma injuries may be an indicator of whether an emergency medical center will stay in business (Thompson, 1993). The high cost of penetrating injuries has meant that trauma centers have lost millions of dollars, and dozens have closed in Southern California alone.

Many of the costs of violent victimization discussed in this book are easily quantified, such as hospitalization, continuing medical care, and lost wages. Some, such as long-term emotional stress on the victim, are less easily measured. Others, such as the mental impact of victimization on victims' families, neighbors, and friends, may not even be noticed. And costs of violent crime to communities may be hidden. In the following chapters, we will examine these social and psychological effects.

⁻ MEASURING VIOLENT VICTIMIZATION

Although we have asserted that the United States is more violent than other countries, it is important to understand the empirical basis for that contention, or how violent crime is measured. The two most commonly used sources of information for assessing the incidence of crime are official police reports, as collected by the Federal Bureau of Investigation (FBI), and victimization surveys. Because they are basic sources of information, they will be described in some detail. After discussing their strengths and weaknesses and comparing the results of these two methods, we will briefly describe less commonly used methods.

Uniform Crime Reports

The most commonly used source for crime statistics in the United States is *Uniform Crime Reports* (UCR), published by the FBI. When it was first compiled in 1930, fewer than 1,000 police agencies reported. Today, about 10,000 police agencies are included, covering about 97% of the country's population. In the *UCR*, crimes are divided into two categories: the eight serious crimes that make up the category of *index crimes* (homicide, rape, robbery, aggravated assault, burglary, larceny-theft, motor vehicle theft, and arson), and *nonindex crimes,* which include all remaining crimes. One of the limitations of the UCR is that it undercounts the total number of crimes because it uses a hierarchical counting method. Under this procedure, only the most serious part of a crime incident is counted. For example, if an offender hits a driver in the face (an assault), takes the money in her purse (robbery), commits rape, and then steals the car (theft), only the rape would be counted under the *UCR*.

Other limitations of the *UCR* stem from the fact that it relies on crimes reported to the police. In the United States, this is primarily a problem with studies that use *UCR* comparisons across jurisdictions. Such reliance may be problematic because different jurisdictions often have different legal definitions of criminal acts; jurisdictions sometimes change reporting techniques, which means that year-to-year comparisons may not be valid; some types of crime are not fully reported; and police and other reporting agencies may misclassify crimes. Moreover, jurisdictional boundaries (e.g., city limits) are often arbitrary, and cities that have high proportions of middle- and upper-class neighborhoods often have lower crime rates than cities where such neighborhoods are in the adjacent suburbs.

Even within a jurisdiction, crime figures may not be valid because the *UCR* numbers represent only those crimes that are discovered, reported, and recorded (Hindelang, 1974). In other words, if there are differential discovery, reporting, and recording rates within a jurisdiction, the resulting numbers may not be representative of actual crime rates. For example, there might be differences in the rates at which victims call the police to report crimes and the rates at which the police record crimes. If victims are more likely to report crimes committed by groups with low social and economic power (e.g., minority youths), then *UCR* figures may disproportionately represent crimes committed by this group compared to other groups.

Every year, newspapers carry headlines about the "crime capitals" and the "murder capitals" of the country. Should readers believe these rankings? For example, based on the *UCR,* the crime rate for Tallahassee, Florida, is 80% higher than the crime rate for New York City. New York has higher rates of murder and robbery, but Tallahassee has significantly higher rates for burglary, theft, assault, and rape. Is Tallahassee really one of the most dangerous cities in the country?

It is probably misleading to use these figures to conclude that Tallahassee is one of the most crime-ridden cities in the United States (Bennett, 1995). First, the FBI figures are based on crimes reported to the police, and many residents of New York City believe that the local police discourage the reporting of all but the most serious crimes. In Tallahassee, it is easier to report crimes, and citizens show little hesitation in doing so. Second, even when the crime rates are identical, the crimes themselves may not be. For example, both Tallahassee and New York City have rates of about 15 stolen cars per 1,000 residents. However, in Tallahassee, about 60% of the cars are recovered, but only about 25% of stolen cars are recovered in New York City. The difference is that "joy riders" are largely responsible for car theft in Tallahassee, whereas professional "chop shop" thieves predominantly steal cars for parts in New York City.

Although Tallahassee is probably safer than New York, there are reasons why Tallahassee has a high crime rate. First, there are differences among people in terms of their likelihood of becoming victims.

Individuals under the age of 25 are more likely to become victims, especially of larceny, but also of assault and rape. Individuals of college age are also more likely to be the perpetrators of these crimes. Second, the weather in Tallahassee is mild in winter, meaning that criminals spend more time outside. In New York, where the winters are cold, the weather acts as "God's policeman," and keeps crime down. Third, New Yorkers probably take many more precautions to prevent crime, such as locking their cars.

National Crime Victimization Survey

Victimization surveys are the second way in which violent crime is measured. Since 1973, the U.S. Department of Justice has published an annual report first known as the National Crime Survey (NCS) and now called the National Crime Victimization Survey (NCVS). It was intended to provide information about the "dark figure of crime"—the crime that never appeared in the criminal justice system because it was never reported to the police. The NCVS (conducted by the U.S. Bureau of the Census for the Bureau of Justice Statistics) chooses a sample of about 60,000 households using a stratified, multistage cluster-sampling technique. Every 6 months for a period of 3 years, roughly 120,000 residents 12 years of age or older are asked about their experiences with criminal victimization. In any given month, 10,000 households are interviewed, and response rates are generally greater than 90%. Victimization data from the first interview are not analyzed because individuals who are asked to recall victimizations during the prior 6 months may be "telescoping" by including crimes that were actually committed in the period before the survey began. The first interview serves as a boundary point so that only incidents occurring after the first interview are included in the study. Individuals in the sample are asked about victimizations they suffered during the prior 6-month period. They provide information about the crime (e.g., when and where it occurred and details about the offender).

To what extent does the NCVS accurately measure the amount of criminal victimization? Like the *UCR,* the NCVS undercounts the level of crime. First, the NCVS does not include crimes against children under the age of 12. Thus, physical and sexual abuse of children is not included in the national crime statistics. Second, because the NCVS samples households, individuals at high risk of victimization (e.g., prostitutes, panhandlers, and battered women) who may be in jails, public hospitals, women's shelters, or homeless shelters are not included.

Third, there is a problem with repeat victimizations such as break-ins at a home or assaults against a partner. Even when there are as many as six or more events, but the respondent cannot recall them in enough detail, these events are counted once. Another problem arises if the victim cannot distinctly remember the number of events.

A fourth problem with the NCVS concerns victims' unwillingness to say they have been victimized if there is some stigma attached to being called a victim. Although the NCVS is probably a valid indicator of the number of some crimes, such as auto theft, for crimes with more stigma attached to the victim, the NCVS is arguably much less valid. For example, Koss (1993) argued that the NCVS underdetected the amount of rape in the country because the initial "screener questions" used to determine whether a sexual assault had taken place were vague and ambiguous. That is, information about incidents would have been obtained only if respondents had first said they had been the victims of actual, attempted, or threatened attacks. Furthermore, according to Koss, incidents of rape were likely to be missed because the interview was conducted over the telephone rather than in person and, in general, did a poor job of establishing the rapport and guarantee of confidentiality that are essential to the reporting of such incidents. Finally, the phrasing of questions pertinent to rape was likely to lead women to believe that only violent attacks by strangers were "real crimes" and therefore worthy of being mentioned to the interviewer.

To overcome these problems, the NCVS was redesigned over a 10-year period to provide better estimates of the incidence of rape and family violence (Bachman & Saltzman, 1995; Bachman & Taylor, 1994). One major improvement was the addition of an explicit screener question regarding rape:

> Incidents involving forced or unwanted sexual acts are often difficult to talk about. (Other than any incidents already mentioned), have you been forced or coerced to engage in unwanted sexual activity by (a) someone you didn't know before, (b) a casual acquaintance, or (c) someone you know well?

If the victim answers "yes" to this question, the interviewer then asks another question to clarify the exact nature of the sexual activity that occurred. In response to Koss's criticism about victims' possible unwillingness to report a crime because interviewers lacked sensitivity, all NCVS interviewers now receive special training in establishing rapport and asking sensitive questions associated with sexual assault.

These changes in the NCVS produced substantial changes in the estimated number of sexual assaults nationally each year. The new estimate was 310,000 per year (170,000 rapes and 140,000 attempted rapes), up substantially from the prior estimate of 133,000 rapes and attempted rapes per year (Greenfeld, 1997).

Comparing the *UCR* With the NCVS

The *UCR* and the NCVS are the two most important measures of criminal activity. However, although they both indicate the level of crime in the United States, studies have found little relationship between the two. The divergence could be because they measure somewhat different populations. The NCVS samples households and would miss crimes against the homeless and undercount crimes against those who have moved. Moreover, the NCVS does not include crimes against victims who are aged 12 or younger. Another reason for the divergence was suggested by a recent examination of why crime rates appear to be declining based on the NCVS data but increasing based on *UCR* data (O'Brien, 1996). One possible explanation for the rising crime rates, according to the *UCR,* is that police departments are becoming more effective in learning about criminal incidents and recording them as crimes. This explanation makes sense given that during the past two decades, police departments have increased the number of officers and have begun spending more money on record keeping, particularly on computerized records.

An example of the differences between the *UCR* and the NCVS appears in Figure 1.1, which plots the rates for rape from the *UCR* and the NCS/NCVS for the years 1973 to 1998. As indicated, over the 26-year period, there has been both convergence (e.g., 1976-1979 and 1993-1998) and divergence in the rates (e.g., 1973-1976 and 1984-1990). Aside from differences in the population sampled, the two sources differ in their definitions of sexual assault. The *UCR* defines rape as "carnal knowledge of a female forcibly and against her will" (Federal Bureau of Investigation, 1999, p. 23). Thus, the *UCR* excludes other forms of sexual penetration, incapacitation by means other than force, and male and spousal victims. The *UCR* makes these exclusions despite the fact that most state laws include these other offenses in their crime codes (Searles & Berger, 1987). Another possible reason for the divergence in rates may be that the *UCR* numbers reflect general organizational factors of police departments and specific ways in which they manage rape victimizations (Jensen & Karpos,

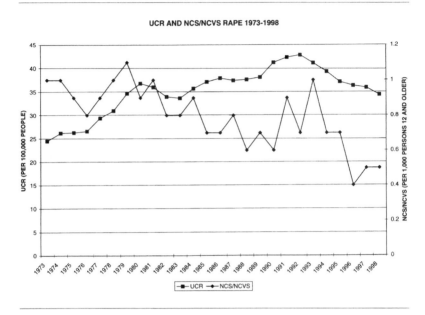

Figure 1.1. *UCR* and NCS/NCVS Rape, 1973 to 1998

SOURCE: Material for the chart comes from the 1994 and 1999 issues of the U.S. Bureau of Justice Statistics' *Sourcebook of Criminal Justice Statistics* (Table 3.2 in both issues), edited by Maguire and Pastore. The *UCR* crime rates are from the 1999 *Sourcebook of Criminal Justice Statistics* (Table 3.114) and the 1999 *UCR* (Federal Bureau of Investigation, 1999).

NOTE: NCS = National Crime Survey; NCVS = National Crime Victimization Survey; *UCR* = *Uniform Crime Reports*.

1993). The *UCR* relies on citizens (primarily victims) to report crimes to the police, and according to the NCVS, only 53% of rape victims do so (Bachman, 1994). Other data sources indicate reporting rates as low as 16% (National Victims Center, 1992). If there are changes over time in reporting to the police but not in the NCVS, there could be divergences between the *UCR* and the NCVS. The fact that there are sometimes inconsistencies between the two measures suggests a need for additional measures of victimization (see Ruback & Ménard, 2001).

The debate about the relative validity of the *UCR* and the NCVS continues. Some scholars believe that the NCVS is the most appropriate measure because, by surveying victims who did not report being victimized, the survey taps into crime that is not known to the police, both less serious crimes and crimes to which stigma may be attached to the victim. Others believe that *UCR* reports are more valid indicators of index crimes than victimization surveys. They argue that serious crimes (e.g., involving bodily injury or stolen valuable property) are likely to be reported to the police, whereas more trivial events (e.g., where there was no injury, or the crime was not completed) are less likely to be reported (Gove, Hughes, & Geerken, 1985).

A summary of the strengths and weaknesses of both the *UCR* and the NCVS appears in Table 1.2.

Other Sources of Information About Crime

Different measures of crime may lead to vastly different conclusions about the amount of crime in a population and about the factors that are associated with criminal behavior. The FBI is currently testing a more detailed information system about reported crimes called the National Incident-Based Reporting System (NIBRS) (Federal Bureau of Investigation, 2000). Under the NIBRS, agencies collect information on each occurrence of 22 offense categories (called Group A offenses), including such information as when and where the crime occurred, the characteristics of the victim, and the characteristics of the perpetrator. Arrest data are collected for the Group A offenses and for an additional 11 offense categories (called Group B offenses). Although the NIBRS will eventually allow for more complete analyses of crimes, the system is not yet widely available to the research community, and only a few published studies have used it. Currently, to understand violence, researchers must look at other sources.

In addition to the *UCR* and the NCVS, three other measures are sometimes used to indicate the level of victimization: (a) specialized victimization surveys, such as the National Violence Against Women Survey (NVAWS); (b) telephone calls to the police, especially 911 calls; and (c) surveys of admissions to hospitals, especially emergency rooms.

National Violence Against Women Survey. Although the NCVS can collect information about a large number of vicitmizations, it cannot gather detailed information about specific types of crime. Specialized surveys have been needed to address particular types of victimizations. One of these was the NVAWS, a national telephone survey jointly sponsored by the National Institute of Justice and the Centers for Disease Control and Prevention. It was conducted by the Center for Policy Research (Tjaden & Thoennes, 1998). The NVAWS asked respondents about their experiences with different forms of violence, including physical assault, rape, and stalking. Respondents were asked about the circumstances of the incidents (victim-perpetrator relationship, location, or recency) as well as the consequences (e.g., physical injuries, psychological problems, or medical care). Data were collected from

TABLE 1.2   Strengths and Weaknesses of the *Unified Crime Reports (UCR)* and the National Crime Victimization Survey (NCVS)

UCR Strengths	*UCR Weaknesses*
1. Uniform across jurisdictions FBI has specified rules and procedures for classifying and scoring offenses. 2. Detailed data regarding homicide – Age, sex, race, and ethnic origin of the victim – Age, sex, race, and ethnic origin of the offender (when known) – Type of weapon involved – Relationship between victim and offender 3. Some detail for other crimes – Weapon used in robberies and aggravated assaults – Residential vs. nonresidential burglary – Different types of larceny (e.g., shoplifting, pickpocketing, purse snatching) 4. Data cover most of the country Police reporting agencies for 97% of the population	1. Not all crimes are included a. Only crimes that are discovered b. Only crimes that are reported • Reporting seems to be primarily the product of the type and seriousness of the crime c. Only crimes that are recorded by the police; recording is influenced by • The seriousness of the crime • The complainant's preference (Black, 1970) • The dispatcher calling the report a crime (Pepinsky, 1976) • The total demand for police services (Maxfield, Lewis, & Szoc, 1980) • The ethnic makeup of the neighborhood 2. When there are multiple crimes, only the most serious is counted based on a hierarchical counting method 3. Problems with comparing crimes across jurisdictions and across time a. Different jurisdictions have different legal definitions of legal acts b. Jurisdictions sometimes change reporting techniques, meaning that year-to-year comparisons may not be valid 4. Little detailed information for crimes other than homicide

NCVS Strengths	*NCVS Weaknesses*
1. Capture the "dark figure of crime" (crimes not reported to the police) 2. Relatively detailed information about crime victims (sex, race, age, urban/rural location, victim-offender relationship)	1. People have difficulty remembering victimizations – When they occurred – Details about the crimes – Sometimes even whether they occurred

3. Data at different levels
   - Individual level data for individual crimes
   - Household level data for household crimes

4. Large samples of households provide relatively stable estimates of victimizations
   - 60,000 households are included at any one time
   - 135,000 individuals

2. Reports of victimizations are linked to social class
   - Better-educated individuals report more victimizations, possibly because they are more cooperative and feel more at ease in the interview or because they have a lower threshold for violence

3. Not clear whether the events are really crimes
   - Not clear how the police would respond

4. Some individuals are not included
   - Crimes against children under 12 years old are not included
   - Individuals who are away from the household during the interview are not included

5. Bias by sampling households
   - Individuals in jails, public hospitals, or shelters are excluded
   - Homeless individuals are likely to be excluded
   - Individuals who move frequently are likely to be excluded

6. Panel bias
   - Those who have been in the panel longer tend to report fewer victimizations (because they know the interview will be longer)

7. Mover-stayer problem
   - Because the sampling unit is the dwelling, sampling will be treated as if it were bounded
   - Movers may be different than stayers

8. Lower reporting rates for victimizations against other members of households than for respondents themselves

9. Limited contextual information about the victimizations
   - Restrictions on release of location identifiers because of confidentiality requirements
   - Cannot determine how factors from census files (e.g., income, percent minority, housing type) affect victimizations

8,000 adult women and 8,000 adult men between November 1995 and May 1996. The sample was derived using random-digit dialing of households and included all 50 states and the District of Columbia. In households with more than one eligible adult, the adult with the most recent birthday was selected to participate in the survey. The participation rate was 72% for females and 69% for males. Computer-assisted telephone interviewing was used, and only females interviewed female respondents. A Spanish language version also was provided.

Unlike the NCVS, the NVAWS was not presented as a crime survey. Rather, respondents were told that the survey concerned personal safety. Probably for this reason, estimates of violent incidents tended to be somewhat higher in the NVAWS than those reported in the NCVS. A comparison of the number of victimizations reported by women in the two surveys suggests that the NCVS may underestimate victimizations for some crimes, whereas for other crimes it may be accurate (Bachman, 2000). Data from the NVAWS indicated that during the past 12 months, approximately 876,064 adult women had been raped, and 5,931,053 had been physically assaulted. In contrast, data from the NCVS indicated that within the past year, approximately 268,640 adult women had been raped, and 6,248,433 had been physically assaulted. The difference in estimates for rape was significant, but the difference in estimates for physical assaults was not.

Telephone Calls to the Police. Some researchers have argued that telephone calls to the police, especially 911 calls, are better indicators of underlying crime than either victimization surveys or the *UCR.* Calls for service may be more valid because they do not involve the memory problems and response biases that limit the validity of surveys. Calls for service may also be more valid than police reports represented in the *UCR* because they do not reflect any of the biases that could be introduced by police decisions to record the incident as one type of crime rather than another, or to record it at all.

Despite these potential advantages, however, there are several problems with using 911 calls as indicators of crime rates in a community (Klinger & Bridges, 1997). One problem is that some crimes come to the attention of the police through means other than phone calls (e.g., people tell officers on patrol or at station houses, or police officers themselves observe the criminal activity on their beats). A second problem is that citizens' descriptions of events may not correctly describe their legal nature (an individual may not know or understand the legal definition of a crime, may not be able to describe the crime, or may purposely mislead the police about the seriousness of the crime). Third, the nature of the event may have changed between the time the citizen called and the time the police arrived. Finally, police telephone operators must translate citizens' reports into categories that convey information to responding officers and that also meet the requirements of departmental record keeping. There is likely to be some discrepancy between the descriptions of callers and the categories used by operators at the police department. Observational data from 60 neighborhoods in 24 cities across the United States suggests that calls-for-service data may undercount total crimes in neighborhoods with high rates of victimization (Klinger & Bridges, 1997). There is also some evidence to suggest that when they respond to 911 calls, the police are less likely to record incidents in neighborhoods with high percentages of poor or minority populations (Warner, 1997).

Emergency Room Admissions. Another way to track victims is to focus on samples of known victims, such as individuals who visited an emergency department at a hospital with gun or knife wounds. Buss and Abdu (1995) examined the records of 378 adult victims of urban violence who were admitted as patients to a major hospital in Youngstown, Ohio, during a 4-year period. In general, the victims were likely to be young, male, minority (African American or Hispanic), poor, single, unemployed, and poorly educated (dropouts with low grade point averages). They were also accustomed to violence: a third of them carried a knife or gun, and about two fifths had witnessed assaults within the prior year. More than half of them knew their attackers. About half of the victims said they had recently used drugs or alcohol at the time of the assault, and 60% said their attackers were under the influence of drugs or alcohol at the time of the assault. This general characterization was even more common in the case of repeat victims. Compared to onetime victims, repeat victims were more likely to be poor, minority, to have witnessed violent attacks, and to carry weapons. Repeat victims were also more likely to have been threatened during the prior year and to have histories of drug or psychiatric treatment.

Emergency room admissions have also been used to investigate victims of violence, particularly victims of intimate partner violence. This research indicates that an estimated 1.4 million people were treated for nonfatal violence-related injuries in 1994 alone (Rand & Strom, 1997). Most of these injuries occurred within the context of assaults. Many of the victims were injured by strangers (23%) or friends/acquaintances (23%), 8% were injured by parents, children, siblings, or relatives, 7% were injured by spouses or ex-spouses, and 10% were injured by current or former boyfriends or girlfriends. Unfortunately, the relationship of the perpetrator to the victim was unknown in about 30% of the cases, a problem that illuminates one of the limitations of using emergency room data to study victims of violence. Oftentimes, this information is not recorded because patients are not asked to provide it. Even if they are, patients may be reluctant to disclose the information due to fear, shame, or embarrassment. For these reasons, emergency room data are likely to underestimate the proportion of injuries caused by partners or family members. This underreporting was demonstrated in a study where the training of health care professionals in the detection and documentation of partner violence was found to increase the identification of such cases five-fold (McLeer & Anwar, 1989). To the extent that violence-related injuries are underrecognized by health care providers, any research system that relies on medical records likely generates an underestimate of these incidents.

It is important to note that emergency medical care varies in quality depending on the hospital. Thus, individuals who are taken to hospitals that provide better-quality care might be expected to suffer less from injuries than those taken to hospitals with lower standards. That argument has been raised as one possible explanation for why underprivileged blacks are more likely than other groups to suffer more severe complications from violent attacks.

Determining the Extent of Crime in Unique Locations

Measuring the nature and extent of crime is not a straightforward process, particularly in places where residents are more likely to report incidents to the supervising authorities within the location rather than go outside to the police. Such locations include hotels, shopping malls, and apartment buildings. College campuses are particularly good examples. Residents, if they report victimizations at all, are more likely to tell resident assistants than the police. Furthermore, crimes committed off campus are not included in the school's crime rate. There is undoubtedly underreporting of crimes; some, such as underage drinking, are often handled administratively within the university. Others, such as sexual assault, are not reported because of confidentiality concerns. Because about 80% of crime on campus is student perpetrated, at least one college has begun asking applicants for statements about criminal records from their hometown police (Graham, 1993).

GENERAL THEORIES
OF VICTIMIZATION

General theories of victimization have focused on situations as well as individuals (Meier & Miethe, 1993). According to the best-known situational explanation, the *social disorganization theory* (Shaw & McKay, 1942), areas that are ethnically heterogeneous, have unstable residential populations, and contain low-income households are likely to have high rates of crime because of weakened formal and informal social control.

More recent theories have incorporated explanations from both individual and situational levels. According to the *lifestyle-exposure* approach (Hindelang, Gottfredson, & Garofalo, 1978), some situations (places and times) are more dangerous than others, and individuals whose activities, through work, school, or leisure, put them in these situations are more likely to be crime victims. In most cases, individuals who spend more time in public places run higher risks of victimization than those who spend more time at home (Felson, 1998, p. 72). Similarly, certain lifestyles are associated with certain roles, and demographic characteristics associated with these roles relate strongly to different risks of victimization. For example, gender is associated with different victimization risks. Women are likely to spend more time in their homes and with friends and relatives rather than alone. Men are likely to spend more time away from home, to frequent high-risk places, and to be active and aggressive in social situations. Thus, because of lifestyle differences, individuals have higher risks if they are younger rather than older, single rather than married, and poor rather than middle or high income.

Overall, men are much more likely than women to be the victims of violent crime. There are also differences in the perpetrators of crimes against men and women (Bachman, 1994). Men are more likely to be victimized by acquaintances (friends, or individuals known only by sight) or by strangers than by intimates (spouses, ex-spouses, or girlfriends). Of all violent victimizations against men, approximately 50% are committed by acquaintances, and 44% by strangers. Only about 5% are committed by intimates or other relatives. In contrast, women are about equally likely to be victimized by intimates (28%), acquaintances (35%), and strangers (31%), with other relatives accounting for the remaining incidents.

Routine activities theory is another theoretical approach to victimization (Cohen & Felson, 1979). It was developed to relate changes in society, particularly those that concern family-based households and activities, to changes in the crime rate. One of the fundamental propositions of the theory is that fewer family-based households and activities result in increased crime rates because there are more targets for crime, and fewer guardians to prevent it. Specifically, increased numbers of single-person households and of households made up of unrelated individuals mean that more consumer goods and merchandise are purchased, which in turn means that there are more attractive items to steal. An increase in such households also means fewer people around the house (spouses, children, or other relatives), whose mere presence protects the property. In addition, an increase in nonfamily households means that individuals are likely to spend more time outside the house, leaving their homes less protected and increasing their exposure to risky situations.

Both lifestyle-exposure theory and routine activities theory explain victimization in terms of contextual- and individual-level variables. Victimization is more likely in high-crime areas because they contain repeat offenders who commit both violent and nonviolent crimes. In the framework of routine activities theory, crime occurs because there is a convergence of motivated offenders, attractive targets, and the absence of guardians. When there is an increase in these factors, the percentage of victims within a given population increases in a linear fashion, but the average number of crimes per capita and crimes per victim are likely to increase at a greater rate because victimizations are not evenly distributed in the population (Farrell, 1995).

Rather than focusing only on factors at the individual or situational levels, some of the more recent theoretical approaches have suggested that a fuller understanding of victimization requires an understanding of how individual factors are conditioned by situational factors (Miethe & McDowall, 1993). That is, rather than consider only the straightforward effects of these factors, it is necessary to determine how aspects of crime opportunity might operate differently in the context of a particular neighborhood (Rountree, Land, & Miethe, 1994).

There are four core concepts in victimization theories: proximity, exposure to crime, target attractiveness, and capable guardianship (Miethe & Meier, 1993). *Proximity* refers to the physical distance between the areas where potential offenders live and the areas where potential targets live. Generally, the closer the proximity, the higher the victimization rate. For example, in some Los Angeles neighborhoods where proximity is high, violence is the leading cause of death and the major cause of spinal cord injuries in black men aged 16 to 29 (Thompson, 1993). *Exposure to crime* refers to factors that increase the degree of risk. For example, the risk of theft and assault increases if people spend more time in public places, in high-risk public places (e.g., bars and convenience stores), and outside at night. *Target attractiveness* initially referred only to the symbolic or economic value of goods, but some statements of the theory also refer to characteristics of persons. *Capable guardianship* refers to both social guardianship (people who are present in a household) and physical guardianship (physical factors that inhibit crime). Social guardianship includes the number of individuals in a household, the number of friends in the neighborhood, and reliance on neighbors to watch property when the owner is out. Physical guardianship refers to "target-hardening" actions (e.g., door locks, window bars, or burglar alarms) and physical impediments to crime (e.g., streetlights).

Miethe and Meier (1994) have suggested a *structural-choice theory* of victimization: there are structural factors that place people at different levels of risk, but within a particular level of risk, some people are still more likely to be targeted as victims. According to Miethe and Meier (1994), proximity and exposure to crime are structural factors that determine the overall level of risk. Target attractiveness and capable guardianship are components that determine which specific targets an offender will choose.

Research of juveniles has been consistent with the idea that people who engage in risky behavior are most at risk for victimization. Engaging in delinquent activities, such as assault, theft, and robbery, is the best predictor of victimization among juveniles. Delinquents are more than twice as likely as nondelinquents to be victims of assault or robbery (Lauritsen, Laub, & Sampson, 1992). Offenders are likely to be crime victims themselves because they are likely to associate with individuals who commit crimes. Offenders may be especially attractive targets because they are unlikely to report their victimizations to the police (Kennedy & Baron, 1993) and have their own behavior called into question.

Repeat Victimization

A small percentage of people account for a disproportionately large number of criminal victimizations. In one study, the 3% of individuals who were the most victimized accounted for about 30% of all criminal victimizations (Farrell, 1995). Given this high rate, it is not surprising that the best predictors of future victimization are past incidents. Studies of burglaries from the United Kingdom and Canada indicate a high risk of revictimization within 4 months of the first crime

(Pease & Laycock, 1996). Repeat burglaries make sense from the criminal's perspective because the factors that made the house an attractive target initially are still present. The burglar is familiar with getting into and out of the house and knows what personal property remains (Pease & Laycock, 1996).

Consistent with the pattern for burglaries, past violent victimization is also a strong predictor of future violent victimization. As mentioned earlier, a study of emergency room admissions (Buss & Abdu, 1995) found that repeat victims of violence were likely to be young, male, minority (African American or Hispanic), poor, single, unemployed, poorly educated (dropouts with low grade point averages), and accustomed to violence (e.g., have witnessed assaults or been threatened). There is also evidence that some victims of sexual assault are repeat victims. For example, data from a nationally representative sample of 8,000 women indicated that 18% of the women who had been raped before the age of 18 were also raped after the age of 18 (Tjaden & Thoennes, 1998).

Repeat victimization is most pronounced in partner violence. A recent government report estimated that in 1998, intimate partners committed about 1 million violent crimes (Rennison & Welchans, 2000). Of these, about 85% were against female victims. In the period between 1993 and 1998, almost half of the women who were victims of intimate partner violence were physically injured. About 40% of those who were physically injured sought medical treatment for their injuries (Rennison & Welchans, 2000). Women victimized by partners are more likely than women victimized by nonpartners to experience ongoing violence at the hands of the same perpetrator. This has been supported by data from both the NVAWS (Tjaden & Thoennes, 2000) and the NCVS (Mahoney, 1999) and will be discussed in more detail in Chapter 4.

Several methodological problems make it difficult to study repeat victimizations. Since the beginning of the NCS (now the NCVS), critics have noted the weaknesses in the measurement of multiple and repeat victimizations. Repetition of violent victimization may be underestimated because the NCVS uses a 6-month reporting period. Some crimes that are repeats of incidents occurring prior to the 6-month period are not counted as repeats; and incidents that occurred after the 6-month period are also omitted from the category (Farrell, 1995). Official statistics are also likely to underestimate repeat victimizations because many victims do not report incidents to the police, and not all reported crimes are officially recorded (Farrell, 1995). The probability that all multiple victimizations will be officially recorded is even lower—sometimes much lower—than the probability for any one of them.

SUMMARY

In this chapter, we described how interest in crime victims has grown over the past 30 years. The federal government and all state governments have given victims more rights in the legal system and provided more money for victim assistance. There is some disagreement about how the extent of violent crime should be measured. Discrepancies exist between findings of the NCVS, which involves a large nationally representative random sample of individuals aged 12 and older, and those of the UCR, which involves crimes reported to the police.

Although the rate of violence has declined in recent years according to national victimization surveys, the United States is still among the most violent of all industrialized countries, particularly with regard to homicide. These victimizations are costly to individuals, to businesses, to communities, and to governments. One estimate places the cost of assaultive victimizations at almost $100 billion per year.

Individuals are at risk of violent crime if they live close to violent offenders, are more exposed to dangerous places, are attractive targets, and are not well protected. The best predictor of future victimization is past victimization; individuals who have been victims of violence in the past are more at risk than those who have never been victimized.

In the following chapters, we discuss the social and psychological costs of violent crime. In Chapter 2, we discuss how the effects of violent victimization are measured. We establish a framework for discussing the consequences for individual victims (Chapters 3 and 4), for victims' families and friends (Chapter 5), and for victims' communities (Chapter 6). In Chapter 7, we discuss the policy implications of and potential interventions to reduce these social and psychological costs.

■■ DISCUSSION QUESTIONS

1. Individuals who are repeatedly victimized are vulnerable to continuing harm and yet their victimizations are probably those about which there is the least information. What are the implications of the fact that much of this information is missing?

2. How important is neighborhood context in understanding victimization? How should neighborhood context be operationalized?

3. What are the policy implications of the different theoretical approaches to victimization?

4. Consistent with other research, Miller, Cohen, and Wiersema (1996) attempt to determine the cost to victims of criminal victimizations. Should ambiguous measures like "quality of life" be included in calculations of the cost of victimization?

5. The measurement of crime is important because it can affect the allocation of resources in the criminal justice system. Because of the weaknesses of traditional measures of crime (the UCR and the NCVS), should there be more targeted surveys like the NVAWS?

NOTE

1. From Koss and Harvey, 1991. *The Rape Victim: Clinical and Community Interventions, Second Edition* (pp. 60-61, 193). Copyright © 1991, reprinted by permission of Sage Publications.

2

Studying the Effects of Victimization

Because the criminal justice system is primarily concerned with preventing and responding to crime, police need to know both the incidence and prevalence of criminal victimizations. Incidence refers to the rate of crime incidents (e.g., the number of crimes per 100,000 people), and prevalence refers to the rate of victims (e.g., the number of individuals victimized per 100,000 people). Estimates of incidence and prevalence come from the *Uniform Crime Reports* (*UCR*) and the National Crime Victimization Survey (NCVS), each of which, as we discussed in Chapter 1, has strengths and weaknesses. Because these measures are widely known and generally accepted, researchers and practitioners use them to gauge the extent of criminal victimization, especially in terms of how the incidence and prevalence of crime change over time.

Although measuring the extent of crime can be problematic, determining the effects of crime on victims, their families, friends, and communities is even less clear-cut. Few indicators are universally accepted, and there are no useful measures for assessing impact at both the individual and community level. In this chapter, we describe the kinds of data and crime-related factors that can be used to assess the social and psychological impact of criminal victimization. We also establish a framework for discussing these effects that we will use in remaining chapters.

DATA SOURCES FOR MEASURING
THE EFFECTS OF VIOLENT VICTIMIZATION

Within the criminal justice system, police collect only the information about victimization that is directly or potentially relevant to subsequent decisions regarding arrest, charges, and conviction. For example, an investigating police officer is likely to record whether or not the offender had or used a weapon or caused physical injury, the extent of the injury, and the occurrence of property loss or damage.

This information is useful and important for processing the offender from arrest through sentencing. It is less useful for understanding victims' reactions to crimes. Generally, there is little information about victims in typical criminal justice files. To discover the effects of crimes on victims, their families, friends, and neighborhoods, researchers must rely on secondary sources and on specially conducted surveys.

Necessary Characteristics of Data Sources

To be useful scientifically, these data sources must be both reliable and valid. *Reliability* refers to the extent to which a particular measure would give the same result if it was used several times (Babbie, 2000). For example, using a stick a yard long would be reliable if a person found after repeated measurements that the length of a room was always the same number of lengths of the yardstick. In the context of measuring the extent of victimization, reliability refers to the degree to which the same results are obtained from measuring the number of incidents and the number of individuals who have been victimized. When measuring the psychological impact of victimization with a multi-item scale, there are two important types of reliability: internal and test-retest. *Internal reliability* refers to the extent to which the items in the scale all measure the same construct. *Test-retest reliability* refers to the extent to which using a scale (e.g., to measure depression or anxiety) at different times leads to the same assessment of impact.

Although a measure must be reliable if it is to be useful, reliability alone is not sufficient; the measure must also be valid. *Validity* refers to the extent to which the measure corresponds with what it is intended to measure. When measuring the length of a room, if the stick intended to be a yard long was actually only 2.5 feet long, repeated measurements would be reliable (consistent) but not valid because they would not reflect the standard length of a yard. When measuring criminal victimization, validity refers to the extent to which a reported criminal incident actually occurred and was actually a crime. When measuring the psychological impact of victimization, validity refers to the extent to which, for example, a score on a scale that measures depression indicates the respondent's actual level of depression.

Measures of victimization must be reliable and valid. The most useful victimization measures are longitudinal and are assessed using multiple methods. *Longitudinal measures* are collected across time. We would expect the impact of a traumatic event such as a crime to change over time, being most severe soon after the incident but becoming less severe as time passed (see Chapter 4). Testing that hypothesis requires multiple observations across time.

Ideally, in addition to longitudinal measures, the observations should involve multiple methods. Each type of research method has both strengths and weaknesses, which is why researchers should be careful when interpreting studies on the effects of violent victimization that use only one method. Results from such studies could be affected by problems associated with the type of method used. However, if consistent results are obtained with multiple methods, the results are less likely to reflect the research method and more likely to reflect some true effect. Thus, researchers are most confident of results produced by multiple research methods.

Similarly, research results that reflect only one type of study population or one location are subject to alternative explanations based on possible unique characteristics of those individuals or places. To discount these alternative explanations, researchers must look across studies to see whether results are consistent regardless of the demographic characteristics of the individuals (e.g., race, sex, or age) and the location (e.g., rural, suburban, or urban). It is important to be sure that research findings are not the result of the particular measure used (e.g., a specific fear-of-crime scale) or the particular way the data were analyzed. In sum, researchers are most confident of findings that are consistent across methods, populations, locations, outcome measures (generally referred to as *dependent measures* by social scientists), and statistical analyses.

Studying the social and psychological impact of violent victimization involves a series of decisions. First, researchers must decide how to obtain a sample of victims—that is, whether to use a representative sample of the general population or samples of known victims. Second, they must decide how to obtain information about victims. The information can come from analyses of existing archives or from surveys of victims. Third, if researchers decide to survey victims, they have the choice of mailing the questions to them, interviewing them in person, or interviewing them over the telephone. Fourth, a decision must be made about what kind of survey questions to ask: open-ended questions, to which respondents are free to respond as they like, or closed-ended questions, to which respondents must respond using categories chosen by the researchers.

Obtaining Samples of Victims

Researchers have used two general approaches to obtaining samples of violent-crime victims. One approach uses a sample that is representative of the larger population in terms of characteristics such as race, age, sex, income, and education. The advantage of this approach is that it permits researchers to draw conclusions about the larger population. For example, such studies allow for comparisons between victims and nonvictims, between victims who reported and those who did not report, and between property victims and violent-crime victims. The primary disadvantage of this approach is that violence is relatively rare, and if researchers are to draw valid conclusions, the sample must be very large. For example, every month, the NCVS interviews individuals in 10,000 households. Because of the enormous expense of such studies, there are not many large-scale representative samples of violent-crime victims.

The second approach to the study of violent-crime victims is to use samples of known victims, such as those who called the police or who visited crisis centers. These samples are relatively convenient and certainly more economical than large random samples from the general population. Their primary disadvantage is that they are not representative of the population, and therefore findings based on them cannot be generalized to other groups. For instance, people who call the police are different from people who do not (e.g., they are more likely to have suffered serious injury), and findings based on "reporters" may not be generalizable to "nonreporters." Women who visit battered-women's shelters are different from victims of partner violence who do not. They are likely to have suffered more severe abuse and to have a history of abuse. In large random-sample surveys of the population, severely abused women are likely to constitute only a tiny percentage, meaning that researchers would not be able to report much about them (Johnson, 1995).

In keeping with our general approach toward the study of victimization, we believe that these two approaches to obtaining samples of victims are complementary. That is, the strongest conclusions about the effects of victimization are supported by studies that use both ran-

TABLE 2.1 Strengths and Weaknesses of Research Methods

Methods	Strengths	Weaknesses
Archival data	Economical (data already collected) Data are important to the decision maker	Data may not operationalize variables correctly High amounts of missing data Limited generalizability Data are limited to the information available in the records No cause-and-effect relationship
Open-ended interviews	Intensive, detailed Excellent way to gain the perspective of the respondent	Expensive to conduct Difficult to code Respondents may not give accurate answers No cause-and-effect relationship
Closed-ended interviews	Typically use scales with good psychometrics Easy to code	None of the options may accurately reflect the person's true thoughts or feelings Respondents may not understand Respondents may not give accurate answers No cause-and-effect relationship
Experiment	Evidence of causation Empirical, objective Replication	Artificial Knowledge of being in an experiment Demand characteristics Ethical issues

dom and selected samples. However, obtaining a sample of violent-crime victims is only the first step. The next issue is how to obtain information about these victims.

There are two primary methods for obtaining such information: archives and surveys. The strengths and weaknesses of these methods are summarized in Table 2.1. Although these methods can provide useful information, generally they cannot provide the evidence of causation that can be gathered from true experiments. But experiments regarding crime victims are rare. They are mentioned here merely for comparison with the other methods. In Chapter 3, there will be more discussion of experiments in connection with research on victims' decisions to report crimes or not.

Archival Analyses

Archival data are records kept by organizations. In the context of determining the impact of criminal victimization, records would most likely be found, for example, in reports to the police and the case files of organizations that serve crime victims, such as rape crisis centers and battered-women's shelters. The primary advantage of archival data is that because the data are already collected and may already be computerized, the research can be conducted relatively economically. In addition, because the data were collected for the purposes of an agency, they are likely to be important and to have been coded correctly. Thus, archives are likely to have both high reliability and high validity.

Archives are not without problems, however. In many cases, the data that most interests researchers are not present or are not operationalized in ways that are most useful to them. For example, police reports do not generally contain any information about the psychological consequences of violent victimizations. Archives are also likely to be missing large amounts of data. In the case of crime victims, data may be missing because the individuals recording the data did not ask for or write down the information, or because the victims did not answer the questions. Data files kept over time may lack follow-up information because victims oftentimes do not return, may have moved, or may have given incorrect addresses and telephone numbers. Archives are also problematic because the sample members are generally self-selected (e.g., the victims themselves chose to call the police or decided to visit a rape crisis center) and are likely to differ in substantively important ways from individuals not included in the sample. This bias limits the generalizability of the research findings. Finally, analyses of data archives can indicate associated variables but not causality.

Surveying Victims

Victims can be surveyed through the mail, in person, or over the telephone. The choice of survey method is determined by the approach that minimizes "total survey error" (Fowler, 1993) within the constraints of realistic costs (Groves, 1989). Total survey error consists of four types (Lavrakas, 1993): sampling error, coverage error, nonresponse error, and measurement error. *Sampling error* refers to the imprecision of a survey that measures only a sample of the population. The amount of sampling error in a study depends on the heterogeneity of what is being measured, the size of the sample, and the size of the population (Lavrakas, 1993). The most direct way of minimizing sampling error is to increase the size of the sample. *Coverage error* refers to the limitations on generalizability of findings based on the probability that certain members of the population will not be included in the sample. For example, coverage error in telephone surveys includes the homeless and households without phones (which have lower incomes and are more transient than the general population). *Nonresponse error* refers to the effect of failing to obtain data from individuals who were sampled but could not be reached or did not agree to participate if they were to differ systematically from those who did provide data. For example, individuals who are not at home to respond to a telephone survey may differ in age and gender from those who are at home. Telephone surveys may be biased by including a disproportionate number of older women because they are more likely than other demographic groups to be at home.

Measurement error refers to inaccurate assessments of the phenomenon of interest. Measurement error in surveys is typically the product of poorly worded questions, but it may also be the result of interviewer bias, inability or unwillingness on the part of the respondent to answer questions, or bias due to the method of survey administration (e.g., in-person vs. telephone). In surveys about violent crime, estimates of prevalence and incidence can vary depending on the way surveys are framed for the respondent. For example, Straus (1999) argued that the more surveys are framed in terms of *violence* or *crime,* the less likely violence is to be reported, but the violence that is reported is likely to be more severe. Especially in the case of partner violence, this type of measurement error is likely to lead to widely varying estimates of incidence and prevalence (see Chapter 3).

Mailed Questionnaires. One means of contacting victims is to send written questionnaires through the mail. Mail questionnaires do not involve the costs of locating respondents and of employing and training interviewers (as do in-person and telephone procedures), but they have several disadvantages. Random mail surveys can be difficult to conduct because of the difficulty of obtaining valid addresses. There is always some uncertainty about who completed the questionnaire, and this poses a serious problem if it is important that respondents be representative of the population. Mail surveys can also be expensive. Obtaining an adequate response rate requires at least three mailings (Dillman, 1978). First, there is an initial letter, in which the purpose of the survey is described, and respondents are informed that they will shortly be receiving a questionnaire. Second, the survey is sent with a postage-paid return envelope. Third, following the survey, one or two reminders are sent (sometimes with another copy of the questionnaire).

In-Person Interviews. Interviews can be conducted in person or over the telephone. In-person interviews have the advantage over other methods of enabling interviewers to better establish rapport with respondents and can generally be more lengthy than other methods. However, in-person interviews are costly, time-consuming, and have limited geographical reach because interviewers must be highly trained and must travel to each of the interview sites.

Telephone Surveys. For several reasons, telephone surveys employing random-digit dialing may be the most cost-effective way to collect quality data (Lavrakas, 1993). Telephone surveys are more cost-efficient than in-person interviews. There are no travel expenses, and items take 10% to 20% less time to administer via the phone (Lavrakas, 1993, p. 6). Moreover, response rates are generally much better when respondents are contacted by telephone than in person, especially when the questions are personal. Telephone surveys also provide better quality control than other methods over the data-collection process (Lavrakas, 1993, p. 5). Telephone interviews have the disadvantage of being limited in the number of questions that can be reasonably asked before respondents become tired (no more than 20-30 minutes compared with 30-40 minutes for in-person interviews). The presentation of questions is also limited (they cannot be too complex). However, because telephone interviews are more cost-efficient and generally produce higher response rates and results comparable to other methods (Vasu, Moriarty, & Pelfrey, 1995), they are the most common means of interviewing crime victims.

Results from telephone surveys can, with limited exceptions, be generalized to the entire population because the universe of telephone owners (including unlisted numbers) encompasses almost all households. Telephone surveys must use random-digit dialing because about one third of household telephone numbers are unlisted. To rely only on listed numbers would result in a biased sample (unlisted numbers are more common in urban than in suburban areas and least common in rural areas; women and single adults are more likely than men and married adults to have unlisted numbers). People without telephones are more likely than those with telephones to live in single-adult households, to be less educated, poorer, minorities, and employed in nonprofessional and nonmanagerial occupations (Groves & Kahn, 1979). These individuals are also more likely to be victims of crime, a bias that causes telephone surveys to underestimate the true number of victimizations.

After choosing a method to obtain a sample of victims and a method of surveying them, researchers must decide what measures of the impact of victimization to collect. The most commonly used methods of study involve self-report measures, in which victims themselves provide information about the crime and what occurred subsequently.

Self-Report Measures

Self-report information can be obtained through open-ended questions, in which respondents are free to respond in any way they choose, or through closed-ended questions, in which respondents must choose from specific answers prechosen by the researchers. For example, an open-ended question would be, "How did the victimization make you feel?" A closed-ended question would be, "How fearful did the victimization make you feel? (a) not at all (b) somewhat (c) very much." Open-ended questions are generally used during in-person interviews, whereas closed-ended questions are most commonly used in telephone interviews and written questionnaires. The primary advantage of open-ended questions is that they allow respondents to answer in ways they believe are appropriate. Researchers are also free to follow up answers, which allows them to obtain detailed information. Because open-ended interviews place few constraints on interviewers and respondents, they are often best used in the initial stages of a study when researchers must identify important research questions and possible dependent variables. The primary disadvantage of open-ended questions is the difficulty of developing a coding system that permits some understanding of the answers from all of the respondents. Much of the initial research on the psychological impact of victimization used open-ended questions and unstructured interviews, which made sense given how little was known about crime victims. In recent years, however, most of the published research on the impact of victimization has used closed-ended questions, particularly published scales assessing attitudes, emotions, and psychological health. Scales are sets of homogeneous items that measure some underlying construct (Robinson, Shaver, & Wrightsman, 1991). Published scales are important to research on victimization because they generally have high reliability and validity. In addition, when the same scales are used by many investigators, it is easier to compare, contrast, and integrate research findings.

Scales Measuring Psychological Distress. Several scales have been used to assess psychological distress following criminal victimization. Post-

TABLE 2.2   Criteria for Posttraumatic Stress Disorder

A. Individual has experienced or witnessed a traumatic event that involved actual or threatened death or serious injury, or a threat to the physical integrity of self or others

B. Symptoms of reexperiencing a traumatic event
   - Recurrent and intrusive distressing recollections of the event
   - Recurrent distressing dreams of the event
   - Feeling as if the traumatic event were recurring
   - Intense psychological distress when exposed to reminders of the event
   - Physiological reactivity when exposed to reminders of the event

C. Avoidance symptoms
   - Efforts to avoid thoughts or feelings associated with the event
   - Efforts to avoid activities, places, or people that remind one of the event
   - Unable to recall an important aspect of the event
   - Diminished interest or participation in significant activities
   - Feeling detached or estranged from others
   - Restricted range of affect
   - Sense of a foreshortened future

D. Arousal symptoms
   - Difficulty falling or staying asleep
   - Irritability or anger outbursts
   - Difficulty concentrating
   - Hypervigilance
   - Exaggerated startle response

---

traumatic stress disorder (PTSD) refers to a common set of symptoms often experienced by trauma victims, including victims of crime. According to the fourth edition of the *Diagnostic and Statistical Manual of Mental Disorders* (*DSM-IV*), by the American Psychiatric Association (APA, 1994), PTSD is an anxiety disorder precipitated by exposure to a traumatic life event entailing life threat or serious injury to one's self or physical integrity, learning of an unexpected or violent death or serious harm to a significant other, or witnessing a violent or threatening event (Criterion A). Three clusters of symptoms are collectively used to assess PTSD: (a) cognitive symptoms, such as intrusive thoughts and nightmares (Criterion B); (b) interpersonal and affective symptoms, such as estrangement from others, numbness of feelings, and avoidance of activities (Criterion C); and (c) arousal symptoms, such as hypervigilance and irritability (Criterion D). Table 2.2 lists the symptoms of PTSD.

There is often no external standard of accuracy for Criterion A (traumatic events), making it generally impossible to establish validity.

Rather, researchers have relied on checklists of events that seem reasonable (Norris & Riad, 1997). In the revised third edition of the *Diagnostic and Statistical Manual of Mental Disorders* (*DSM-III-R*), by the APA (1987), the definition of Criterion A emphasizes the event itself: "an event that is outside the range of usual human experience and that would be markedly distressing to almost anyone" (p. 250). In contrast, the *DSM-IV* emphasizes the subjective appraisal of the event:

> the personal experience of an event that involves actual or threatened death or serious injury, or other threat to one's physical integrity; or witnessing an event that involves death, injury, or a threat to the physical integrity of another person; or learning about unexpected or violent death, serious harm, or threat of death or injury experienced by a family member or other close associate. . . . The person's response to the event must involve intense fear, helplessness, or horror. (p. 424)

One scale used to measure Criterion A is the Traumatic Stress Schedule (Norris, 1990), which assesses violent events caused by individuals (e.g., crime), nature (e.g., hurricanes), or technology (e.g., chemical spills). This scale incorporates two assumptions: (a) that it is important to assess rates of impairment within specific event-defined populations (crime victims) as well as assessing those rates within the population at large and (b) that it is important to quantify stressful experiences generically, using descriptors such as life threat, loss, and scope, which are not unique to any one event.

Criteria B, C, and D of PTSD concern symptom histories, and their rules for establishing reliability and validity for symptom measures are much better developed than those for Criterion A. All three symptom measures must establish both internal consistency and stability over time. Criterion B involves the victim's reexperiencing of the trauma (intrusive symptoms) and includes items such as thinking about the event when the individual does not intend to, having nightmares or flashbacks, and being suddenly reminded of the event by environmental stimuli. Criterion C involves the victim's feelings of avoidance and hopelessness and a numbing of his or her responsiveness to the external world. Criterion D involves symptoms indicative of increased arousal, including being jumpy, easily startled, or hyperalert; having trouble sleeping or concentrating; and feeling easily angered or irritated.

To satisfy *DSM-IV* criteria for PTSD, a person must meet Criterion A and must show one of the intrusion symptoms from Criterion B, three of the avoidance symptoms from Criterion C, and two of the arousal symptoms from Criterion D. Most victims of traumatic events will show some of these symptoms, but only a small number (less than 10%) develop chronic PTSD.

As discussed by Norris and Riad (1997), there are four broad types of measurement strategies for assessing PTSD. First, many scales follow precisely the symptom criteria listed in the *DSM-IV*: A respondent can be classified as having PTSD based on reporting at least 1 symptom in Criterion B, 3 symptoms in Criterion C, and 2 symptoms in Criterion D. These scales tend to include 17 items because there are 17 symptoms outlined in the *DSM-IV*. Second, some scales assess symptoms of PTSD on a continuous scale. Rather than classifying an individual as having or not having PTSD, they provide a PTSD score that ranges in severity. Although these scales assess all three PTSD criteria (reexperiencing, avoidance, and arousal), they are less likely to probe for the exact items listed in the *DSM-IV*. Third, some PTSD scales are derived from longer scales that assess psychological symptomatology. Fourth, some PTSD scales focus specifically on certain types of people, such as refugees or veterans. Examples of the first type include the National Women's Study PTSD Module (Kilpatrick, Resnick, Saunders, & Best, 1989), the PTSD Symptom Scale (Foa, Riggs, Dancu, & Rothbaum, 1993), and the Los Angeles Symptom Checklist (Foy, Sipprelle, Rueger, & Carroll, 1984). Examples of the second type scale include the Civilian Mississippi Scale (Keane, Caddell, & Taylor, 1988), the Penn Inventory for PTSD (Hammarberg, 1992), and the Impact of Event Scale (Weiss & Marmar, 1997). Examples of the third type include the Minnesota Multiphasic Personality Inventory PTSD scale (Keane, Malloy, & Fairbank, 1984) and the Symptom Checklist–90 PTSD scale (Saunders, Arata, & Kilpatrick, 1990). Examples of the fourth type of PTSD scale include the Harvard Trauma Questionnaire (Mollica et al., 1992) and the Mississippi Scale for Combat-Related PTSD (Keane, Caddell, & Taylor, 1988).

Scales Measuring Physical Health. Criminal victimizations affect physical as well as mental health. Women with histories of victimization report more physical symptoms, perceive their health less favorably, and seek medical care twice as often as nonvictims (Koss, Koss, & Woodruff, 1991). Moreover, individuals who have experienced traumatic events are likely to suffer alcohol-related problems, more severe trauma being associated with more severe alcohol-related problems (Stewart, 1996). Both epidemiological and clinical studies have found a link between criminal victimization and substance abuse. Women with a history of sexual assault are over twice as likely as demographically matched nonvictims to have alcohol, drug abuse, or drug dependence disorders (Burnam et al., 1988; Sorenson, Stein, Siegel, Golding, & Burnam, 1987).

Fear of Crime. One important effect of victimization on victims, their families, friends, and neighbors is the fear of crime. Fear also affects communities (see Chapter 6).

Citizens' fear of crime has been high in the past but has become an even greater concern in recent years. For example, a 1997 ABC News poll found that 51% of respondents were more afraid of crime than they were 5 years ago, and only 7% were less worried by crime (Shuster, 1998, pp. A1, A32, A33). The fear of crime is higher now for several reasons: First, it is higher among older individuals than it is among younger ones (even though the risk of crime is higher among the young), and the aging of the population makes it reasonable to expect an overall increase in the fear of crime. Second, it may be replacing other past fears that are now no longer relevant, such as a fear of nuclear war with the Soviet Union. Third, citizens may not yet have realized that crime rates have been declining for the past several years. Fourth, even though crime is less common now than it was previously, it has become more random. For example, although the number of homicides has declined, a larger proportion of homicides are committed by strangers, and people may feel that there is nothing they can do to prevent such actions. Without any sense that they can reduce their risk, people are likely to be afraid.

Fifth, politicians and police may to some extent capitalize on the public's fear of crime. Politicians often use the issue to their advantage when campaigning for office. In 1993, Richard Riordan won the mayor's race in Los Angeles with the slogan, "Tough enough to turn L.A. around." In 1999, Mayor Rudolph Giuliani of New York emphasized his success as a crime fighter while running for a second term. Police agencies may also benefit from fearful citizens because they are likely to respond to police departments' calls for more resources (money, employees, and better equipment) to combat crime.

Sixth, several types of businesses are involved in fighting crime. Expenditures on security against crime amount to almost $15 billion annually on electronic security products and services for homes and cars (Fletcher, 1999). Today, more than one fifth of all homes in the United States and Canada have electronic alarm systems. Citizens spend billions more on self-defense courses, guns, and guard dogs.

Finally, the media benefit from increased visibility and ad revenues because of crime stories, which have increased greatly over recent years. During the period 1990 through 1995, network news coverage of murder increased 336% (not including the O. J. Simpson case) even though the *UCR* homicide rate dropped 13%. Crime was also the leading television news topic in the 1990s, ahead of international and national news and presidential campaign coverage. This reliance on crime stories is even more common in local news, where the motto is, "If it bleeds, it leads."

Measuring Fear of Crime. There are several problems with the way fear of crime is usually measured (LaGrange & Ferraro, 1989). First, many studies do not actually measure *fear.* They examine citizens' general concerns about crime or their beliefs about their risks of being victimized rather than their fear of these things. Also, one of the problems with attempting to measure fear is that the only feasible and ethical method is to use items on a questionnaire (rather than physiological measures) at a time when the person is not likely to be afraid (e.g., several months after a crime rather than immediately or even soon after a crime occurred).

A second problem with fear-of-crime measures is that they do not actually measure fear of *crime* (LaGrange & Ferraro, 1989). The most commonly used indicator of fear of crime is the one used in the NCVS: "How safe do you feel or would you feel being out alone in your neighborhood at night?" A similar question is used in the General Social Survey, a national survey conducted by the National Opinion Research Corporation: "Is there any place right around here—that is, within a mile—where you would be afraid to walk alone at night?" Rather than explicitly asking about crime, both of these questions refer to crime implicitly. The type of activity that the questions refer to, walking alone at night, is something that individuals might not do for reasons unrelated to fear of crime (e.g., they do not walk anywhere, day or night). And because the reference is to crime in general, it is impossible to know whether people might respond differently to different types of crime. Finally, because these are single-item measures, they are more likely than multiple-item measures to lead to erroneous conclusions.

In general, studies of fear of crime suggest that women are more afraid than men. In part, this difference may be due to sex role socialization as a result of which men are more likely to believe in a sense of personal control, to value excitement, adventure, and power, and to understate their fears (Walklate, 1997). Women may be more likely than men to acknowledge that they have fears. The difference in fear of crime might also be attributable to women having greater risks of some types of violent crime, such as rape and partner violence (Walklate, 1997). Some scholars have suggested that for women, fear of crime is really the fear of rape (Warr, 1994).

Although it would seem natural to want to reduce the fear of crime, there may actually be some benefits to moderate levels of fear. Garofalo (1981) suggested an inverted-U relationship between general fear of crime and functional behavior. According to this model, individuals who have very low levels of fear are not motivated to take precautions at all and might take foolish risks. At the other extreme, individuals who have very high levels of fear might avoid interactions that would be rewarding. Only at moderate levels of fear are individuals likely to take reasonable precautions while not completely eliminating all outside activities and all interpersonal interactions.

One of the possible effects of victimization is greater fear of crime. Generally, studies suggest that victims are more afraid of crime than are nonvictims. However, comparisons of fear levels between victims and nonvictims are confounded by demographic differences relating to the likelihood of victimization. For example, women and the elderly are more afraid of crime compared to men and young people, but they are less likely to be victimized. Typically, even when these demographic differences are controlled statistically, crime victims, particularly victims of violent crimes that resulted in injury, are still more afraid of crime than nonvictims (Skogan & Maxfield, 1981).

A second possible effect of victimization is an increase in the likelihood of revictimization. Most of the research on repeat victimization comes from the United Kingdom and suggests that the rates of repeat victimization are higher there than in the United States. However, this difference is almost certainly due to methodological differences between the victimization surveys in the two countries (Farrell, 1995). Specifically, the British Crime Survey (BCS) uses a recall period of 12 months rather than the 6-month period in the NCVS (which means there is more opportunity for repeat crimes to be included in the BCS), and the BCS includes series victimizations, whereas the NCVS does not.

Even so, using U.S. data only, crime victims have much higher odds than nonvictims of being victimized again, a phenomenon that Farrell and Pease (1993) refer to as "Once bitten, twice bitten." Revictimization is likely for three reasons (Davis, Taylor, & Titus, 1997). First, prior victims may be more attractive targets than nonvictims because of some specific characteristics, and these characteristics might be attractive to all future offenders. That is, prior victims may have more wealth, or some characteristic (e.g., age or handicap) that makes it more likely an offender will be able to avoid capture. Second, criminal victimization might cause changes in victims that make them more likely to become victims again, such as feeling more helpless and becoming less careful. For example, they might choose to take routes to and from work that increase their risk of victimization. A third way that prior victimization might increase the chances of future victimization relates to the effects of psychological harm. For example, a victim might start abusing drugs after suffering a violent victimization, and because drug use increases the likelihood of future victimization, these individuals are more likely to suffer a second victimization.

Because researchers have found a link between past and subsequent victimizations, it is important to know what processes may be occurring—in particular, to know the answer to two questions: (a) whether victimization causes victims to use precautions more often and (b) whether those precautions are effective in preventing crime. Research suggests that the answer to both questions is "no."

Before the first question can be answered—whether individuals who have been victimized are more likely than nonvictims to take precautions to prevent future victimizations—it is necessary to understand several measurement problems involved in assessing precautionary behaviors (Weinstein, 1989). First, there are often preexisting differences between victimized and nonvictimized groups, such as burglary victims being less likely than nonvictims to use locks or victims of street crime being more likely than nonvictims to go out. Thus, if the results show that victims were no more likely than nonvictims to use locks, the conclusion that victimization had no effect on victims would be incorrect if the researchers did not take into account the initial differences between the two groups. Second, because most data collection efforts are cross-sectional, it is difficult to know whether individuals started practicing precautionary behavior before or after the crime. Third, many crime prevention questions are vague and ambiguous: "Have you limited or changed your activities in the past few years because of crime?" Fourth, there are often measurement problems associated with the time frame of the measurement. For example, oftentimes changes in precautions must be measured soon after the event because the effects of the victimization may be brief. On the other hand, researchers cannot make the time period too short. For example, they may ask about events during the past year when the assault occurred 14 months earlier. Fifth, variables are often confounded with victimization and precautions, making it difficult to identify causal factors. For example, young men are more likely than others to be victims of violent crime and less likely than others to use precautions. The resulting connection between victimization and failure to use precautions may be simply because both variables are confounded with the age and sex of victims. Finally, it is important that the measures of precautionary behavior coincide with the type of victimization. For example, if a woman was attacked by her boyfriend at his home, we would not necessarily expect her to change her behavior related to going to her workplace. It is especially important to measure the precautionary behaviors relevant to the particular crime; knowing that people practice one type of precautionary behavior does not reveal much about whether or not they do or do not practice some other kind (Weinstein, 1989).

Being victimized can affect individuals' judgments in several ways (Weinstein, 1989). First, it can affect victims' perceived vulnerability, or their notion of the likelihood that they will be harmed if they do not change their behavior. Second, it can affect their assessments of perceived severity, or the amount of harm they experienced in the past or will experience if they are victimized again. Third, it can affect the perceived effectiveness of precautionary measures. Thus, victimizations might cause individuals to believe that particular precautions are more effective or less effective than they were prior to the incidents. Finally, victimizations might cause individuals to be more aware of certain preventive measures and might also affect their perceptions of the availability and costs of those measures.

Personal experience with victimization does not seem to create a general feeling of vulnerability, but it does seem to increase victims' beliefs about their risks specific to the type and degree of harm they experienced. Depending on the event and the victims' prior expectations, victimizations can lead to strong feelings of helplessness, especially if victims had taken precautions and the crime still occurred. In contrast, if a victim had not taken precautions, and the crime was less severe than it could have been (e.g., attempted rather than completed robbery), he or she is not likely to feel completely helpless regarding future victimizations.

In general, victimization seems to have only small effects on increasing victims' use of precautions to prevent future victimizations, probably because most harms are relatively minor, victims are not confident that the suggested precautions will actually reduce their risk of harm, or they are inclined to act only for a short period after the victimization (Weinstein, 1989). Thus, with regard to the first question (whether victims are more likely than nonvictims to take precautions), victimization does not always seem to be linked to increased use of precautionary behaviors.

With regard to the second question (whether increased precaution reduces victimization), the evidence suggests that precautions do not generally reduce crime (Lindsay & McGillis, 1986; Norris & Johnson, 1988; Rosenbaum, Lewis, & Grant, 1986). In fact, there is some evidence that the use of precautions at the neighborhood level (e.g., through block watch programs) and at the individual level increases fear of crime (Rosenbaum et al., 1986).

In their survey of a representative sample of Kentucky residents, Norris and Kaniasty (1992) found that different types of precautionary behaviors were practiced by different groups of people. Women, minorities, and the elderly, the groups that have the highest levels of fear of crime, were the most likely to use precautions related to vigilance (e.g., being more alert and aware of the possibility of victimization, avoiding potentially dangerous places). Locks were most likely to be used by individuals who had been victims of larceny, burglary, or violence and by short-term residents of apartment buildings. Relying on neighbors for surveillance (e.g., for reporting suspicious behavior) was most commonly used by long-term residents of single-family dwellings. Overall, Norris and Kaniasty found that precautionary behaviors did not reduce the probability of subsequent victimization.

However, respondents' fear of crime was found to be predictive of their subsequent victimizations (Norris & Kaniasty, 1992). One possible reason is that potential victims with more fear have different nonverbal behaviors than individuals who are less fearful. Offenders may be able to detect potential victims' vulnerabilities to crime through these nonverbal behaviors (see cartoon in Figure 2.1).

FRAMEWORK FOR CONSIDERING THE EFFECTS OF VIOLENT VICTIMIZATION

Violent victimization affects individual victims, their families and friends, their communities, and the larger society. In our consideration of the social and psychological effects of violent victimization in the remainder of this book, we discuss how violent victimizations affect each of these individuals and groups. The best single predictor of these effects is the severity of the crime, which depends on factors such as whether or not there was a weapon or injury.

Figure 2.1. Fear of Crime May Be Communicated Nonverbally

In the case of individual victims, we discuss violent victimization at four different stages: the victimization itself, the immediate aftermath, the short-term effects over the first few weeks after the crime, and the long-term effects over subsequent months and years. At each of these stages, we focus on the victim's emotions, beliefs, and actions—that is, what the victim is feeling (e.g., psychological distress), thinking (e.g., beliefs about the criminal justice system), and doing (e.g., precautionary behaviors).

For families and friends, we discuss (a) their interactions with the victim immediately after the crime and over the following weeks and months and (b) the effects of the victimization on their own emotions (especially fear), beliefs, and behaviors. For communities, we discuss how victimizations affect residents' emotions (especially fear), their beliefs (e.g., about the criminal justice system), and behaviors (e.g., the precautions they take to prevent crime).

In the next chapter, we examine the violent victimization and its immediate aftermath. In particular, we focus on factors concerning the offender, the victim, and the situations that relate to the amount of violence involved in the crime. We also examine the way violent-crime victims cope immediately after the crime, including their decisions about calling the police.

■■ DISCUSSION QUESTIONS

1. Under federal law, colleges and universities are required to publish official crime statistics. How much weight should be attached

to these figures? Why? How do these reasons relate to beliefs about the validity of the *UCR* generally? Assuming there is a need to find out the true rate of crime on campus, how could this be done? If there is to be a campus victimization survey, what methodological and ethical considerations should be addressed?

2. A disproportionate amount of crime involves children and teenagers. Do either the *UCR* or the NCVS adequately address these problems? Can these problems be overcome?

3. There is error in all retrospective accounts. How could the type of questioning be improved to reduce this error?

4. What is the relationship between fear and precautions? That is, are people who use more precautions less afraid of crime? Are precautions instrumental or emotion-based? Are precautions effective?

5. How should fear of crime be measured? Why aren't young men more afraid of crime? Would you expect there to be racial/ethnic differences in the fear of crime?

3 ▪▪

Violent Victimization and the Immediate Aftermath

Violent crimes generally occur quickly and without warning. Because victims of these crimes are likely to be highly aroused, emotionally upset, and physically injured, perhaps seriously, it is not surprising that victims are often uncertain about what to do during and after the crime. Nor is it surprising that at some later point, their actions might appear to themselves and to others to have been irrational and ineffective. Those later judgments have important implications for a victim's emotional and physical recovery during the weeks and months following the victimization.

This chapter consists of three parts. First, we give general characterizations of the participants in violent victimizations, including characteristics of offenders, victims, and the relationships between them. Second, we discuss what happens during violent victimizations. This interaction depends on the offender's characteristics and actions, the victim's actions before and during the crime, and situational factors, including the behavior of bystanders. Third, we discuss what happens immediately after a violent crime. These postcrime actions depend in part on the same factors that influence what happens during the crime, but they also depend on the level of violence during the crime, the degree of injury the victim suffered, and the behavior of others. One of the most important decisions a victim makes after the crime is whether or not to report the victimization to the police, a decision that is often influenced by friends, relatives, and even strangers.

CHARACTERISTICS OF
THE PARTICIPANTS IN
VIOLENT VICTIMIZATIONS

There are five primary crimes of violence: homicide, robbery, sexual assault, aggravated assault, and simple assault. Although these crimes differ in several dimensions, some characteristics about offenders and victims seem to be common across crime types.

Offender Characteristics

Most violent offenders, particularly in crimes involving strangers, are young males. Of those arrested for violent crimes, 89% are males, and they are disproportionately members of racial and ethnic minority groups (Reiss & Roth, 1993). Individuals who commit any type of violence have a relatively high probability of committing other types of violence—although this is least true for homicide because many of these are onetime acts committed in the heat of anger (Reiss & Roth, 1993, Appendix A, p. 362). Offenders do not appear to specialize in violent crimes. Rather, what differentiates violent offenders from other offenders is that they commit crimes more frequently (Reiss & Roth, 1993), and individuals who commit more crimes are also more likely to have committed violent crimes. Although most juvenile violent offenders become adult violent offenders, only a small percentage (less than 15%) of all adult violent offenders had been juvenile violent offenders. In sum, most offenders are not violent offenders. But those who do commit violence are likely to be young males who do not specialize in any particular type of violence.

Victim Characteristics

Victims of violence are stereotyped as weak, inexperienced, and easy targets (von Hentig, 1948), such as the very young, the elderly, females, the mentally retarded, the mentally ill, and the disabled. In fact, the most likely victims of violence have the same characteristics as the perpetrators of violence. That is, the typical victim of violence is a young male, most often minority. According to a report from the National Academy of Sciences, blacks are 41% and Hispanics 32% more likely than whites to be victims of violent crime (Reiss & Roth, 1993). Blacks are 5 times more likely than whites to be victims of homicide.

The Victim-Offender Overlap

Offenders and victims have traditionally been considered to be distinct groups, and offending and victimization have traditionally been considered distinct problems (Fagan, Piper, & Cheng, 1987; Singer, 1981). Despite these views, there is considerable evidence that many of the same individual, situational, and community factors that predict offending also predict victimization. For example, in New York City during the period 1850 to 1870, Irish and German men between the ages of 20 and 30 were both killers and victims in numbers disproportionate to their numbers amongst the general population (Monkkonen, 1989). Similarly, most studies over the past two decades indicate that both offenders and victims are typically young black males residing in socially disorganized urban areas (Gottfredson, 1986; Hindelang, Gottfredson, & Garofalo 1978).

Several explanations have been offered as to why individuals who are victims are also likely to be offenders. One possibility, based on life-style-exposure and routine activity theories (Cohen & Felson, 1979; Hindelang et al., 1978) discussed in Chapter 1, is that victimization risk is a function of exposure or proximity to offender populations, and exposure, in turn, is a function of individuals' lifestyle and routine activities. Because individuals are most likely to come into contact with people who are similar to themselves, if those people are offenders, individuals should be at greater risk for victimization. Hindelang et al. (1978) suggest that the more characteristics an individual shares with an offender, the greater his or her risk of victimization. Thus, young nonwhite males are more likely than older white females to be victimized because they share a greater number of characteristics with offenders. Generally, offenders are more likely than nonoffenders to become victims because their lifestyle-routine activities frequently bring them into contact with other offenders, particularly if offending itself is seen as a type of lifestyle-routine activity (Jensen & Brownfield, 1986). Offenders are also more likely to use alcohol or illegal drugs (which lowers their ability to protect themselves and their belongings) and to live in socially disorganized neighborhoods (which increases their exposure) (Sampson & Lauritsen, 1994).

In addition to exposure and proximity, offenders can be attractive targets for two reasons. First, they are likely to have property worth taking. For example, drug traffickers may have a high "potential yield" (Hough, 1987) as victims because they possess a valuable and easily disposed-of commodity. Second, offenders may be attractive targets because they can be victimized with little chance of legal consequences (Sparks, 1982). Offenders are less likely than nonoffenders to report victimizations to the police because calling the police could draw attention to their own illegal behavior (e.g., they started the altercation, the property was stolen, or they are carrying illegal drugs). And if they do report, they will probably be seen as less credible than nonoffenders.

A second reason for a substantial overlap between victims and offenders relates to the existence of a group of people who alternate between offending and victimization (Wolfgang & Singer, 1978). Such individuals are particularly likely to come from groups that encourage retaliation for perceived wrongs, and individuals within this "subculture of violence" (Wolfgang & Ferracuti, 1967) tend to be involved in events in which violence between individuals escalates during the interaction. Victims who have favorable attitudes toward the use of violence and who value courage, honor, and retribution are likely to respond to an offender with force and subsequently become an offender in the incident (Kennedy & Baron, 1993; Luckenbill & Doyle, 1989; Markowitz & Felson, 1998; Singer, 1986). Thus, in incidents such as bar fights, it is often difficult to determine who is the offender and who is the victim.

A third reason that victims and offenders are likely to be the same individuals relates to the psychological costs of being victimized, which may be both directly and indirectly linked to offending. Directly, the distress of victimization might lead to offending because some individuals respond with anger, deviant outcomes, and criminal behavior. According to *general strain theory* (Agnew, 1992), whether or not a person responds antisocially is determined by conventional social supports, intelligence, self-esteem, and temperament. Indirectly, the distress of victimization might lead to offending because of the connection between victimization and substance abuse. In general, individuals who have experienced traumatic events are more likely to suffer alcohol problems, and the greater the trauma, the more severe the problems (Kilpatrick & Resnick, 1993; Stewart, 1996). Moreover, individuals who use alcohol—and particularly those who use drugs—may commit crimes because of a need for money to purchase these substances. There is also a greater likelihood that individuals will commit crimes while under the influence.

Finally, victims and offenders may be the same individuals because criminal victimization is generally associated with tangible losses. Clearly, property victimization causes material losses which, depending on the severity of the crime, can be substantial. But even minor property crimes can be problematic for individuals who have few material possessions and no hope for compensation. Violent crimes may result in tangible losses such as medical expenses, lost income from being unable to work, and, over time, lost child support. To reduce these losses, victims of crime may engage in crime themselves. For example, they may feel the need to steal money if their own money had been stolen and they perceive no way (e.g., insurance) of making up the loss.

Consistent with this idea that victims and offenders are often the same individuals, recent research with probationers suggests a reciprocal relationship between offending and victimization (Shaffer, 2000). That is, offending seems to be predictive of victimization, and victimization seems to be predictive of offending.

Victim-Offender Relationship

The relationship between the victim and the offender is an important predictor of what happens during a crime as well as afterward. A high percentage of violent crimes are committed by relatives, friends, and acquaintances. Unfortunately, because many of these crimes committed by someone known to the victim are not reported to the police or to victimization survey interviewers, it is impossible to tell the exact percentage of victims who knew their offenders.

What is known from the National Crime Victimization Survey (NCVS), however, is that across all violent crimes, 57% are committed by strangers, 31% by acquaintances, and 8% by relatives of the victims (in the remaining cases, the relationship is unknown) (Laub, 1997). The percentage committed by strangers varies considerably, though, depending on the type of crime: 81% of robberies, 56% of assaults, 48% of rapes, and 14% of homicides (Laub, 1997).

Partner Violence

Partner violence does not fit many of the generalizations about interpersonal violence between strangers. For example, victims of partner violence are generally female. Moreover, many of the theories that have been developed to explain violence by strangers, such as routine activities theory, are problematic when applied to partner situations. For instance, being away from home at night is generally considered a risk factor for stranger crime because it exposes potential victims to potential offenders. However, if the violence is committed by a woman's spouse, staying at home is no longer a protective factor and is in fact putting her at risk. Although some attempts have been made to correct these theoretical limitations, no single theory adequately explains both stranger and partner violence.

Violence between intimates is also different from violence between strangers because it is more likely to result in both nonfatal and fatal physical injuries. In the case of nonfatal injuries, data indicate that approximately 20% of emergency department visits made by women involve partner violence (Rand & Strom, 1997). In the case of fatal injuries, data indicate that about one third of all females killed in the United States are killed by their male partners (Federal Bureau of Investigation, 1999), and women are approximately 4 times more likely to be killed by their male partners than by strangers (Kellermann & Mercy, 1992). This increased risk of injuries and death among women victimized by intimate partners compared with women victimized by strangers probably occurs because women assaulted by partners are more likely to suffer ongoing violence (Finkelhor & Yllö, 1985; Mahoney, 1999; Russell, 1990; Tjaden & Thoennes, 2000).

Women victimized by intimates also differ from women victimized by nonintimates in their increased safety concerns, which can in large part be attributed to their realistic appraisals of their risk for injury and death. This increased fear can also be attributed to the threats often endured by women with abusive partners. Data from a nationally representative survey (Tjaden & Thoennes, 2000) indicate that 33% of females physically assaulted by male partners reported that their partners had threatened to harm or kill them, and 45% reported fearing bodily injury or death. Although it might seem that women could escape these fears and risks of death by leaving the relationship, this is not always the case. For example, one study found that women who had ended relationships within the past year were 7 times more likely to have experienced recent partner abuse than women who had not recently ended a relationship (Dearwater et al., 1998).

The type of partner violence determines both the extent of abuse and the actions women are likely to take subsequently. Johnson (1995) suggested that there are two types of male violence against female partners: (a) "patriarchal terrorism," which refers to the use of violence to exert control over the female partner, and (b) "common couple violence," which refers to violence that arises in the context of specific arguments. Compared with relationships characterized by common couple violence, relationships characterized by patriarchal terrorism are likely to have more incidents of violence, the violence is more likely to escalate than to de-escalate over time, and women are more likely to be injured (Johnson, 2000). Moreover, in an analysis of responses from

4,967 married women who were interviewed as part of the National Violence Against Women Survey (NVAWS) (Tjaden & Thoennes, 1999), Johnson and Leone (2000) found that victims of patriarchal terrorism were significantly more likely than victims of common couple violence to be severely injured, to score higher on a measure of posttraumatic stress disorder (PTSD), to be depressed, to use tranquilizers, to have missed work as a result of the most recent incident of violence, and to have left their husbands, at any time and more than once.

Victim Precipitation

Several scholars have suggested that victims may sometimes precipitate their own victimization. What constitutes precipitation varies depending on the type of violent crime involved. In his analysis of police homicide records in Philadelphia, Wolfgang (1958) found that in 26% of the cases, the "victim was the first to show and use a deadly weapon, to strike a blow in an altercation—in short, the first to commence the interplay of resort to physical force" (p. 252). This percentage may be overinclusive, however, because 44% of the cases were missing information about victim precipitation. On the other hand, that number could be low if the victim had attacked or threatened the offender in the past, but the precipitation was not recorded in the homicide report.

The definition of victim precipitation that Wolfgang used for homicide was used by other researchers to investigate the role of victim precipitation in other types of crimes. Mulvihill and Tumin (1969) found that victim precipitation occurred in 14% of aggravated assaults, 4% of rapes, and 8% of robberies. However, there are problems with these data because the definitions of victim precipitation for rape and robbery are not clear.

Amir (1971) examined police reports of rape in Philadelphia and found high rates of victim precipitation. However, his definition of precipitation is especially problematic: "the victim agreed to sexual relations but retracted before the actual act, or where she clearly invited sexual relations through language, gestures, or the like." In this definition, Amir included potentially risky activities such as hitchhiking but also included factors such as sexual "misconduct" (e.g., prostitution or juvenile intercourse) and "bad reputations." Amir's work generated much criticism, primarily because his definition of precipitation was overly inclusive and victim blaming. Although he was incorrect in including such behavior in the category of precipitating sexual assault, it is probably true that the victim's behavior does affect the processing of sexual assault cases by the criminal justice system. For example, victims are less likely to be taken seriously if they had engaged in behavior, such as hitchhiking or drinking, that had put them at risk. Normandeau (1968, cited in Meier & Miethe, 1993) defined victim precipitation in connection with robbery as not engaging in reasonable self-protective behavior in the handling of money or valuable goods. Similar to Amir's analysis of victim precipitation in rape, Normandeau's definition mistakenly confuses victims' vulnerability with the motivation for criminal behavior.

Rather than arguing that victims precipitate their victimization, Finkelhor and Asdigian (1996) asserted that three types of victim characteristics, vulnerability, gratifiability, and antagonism, increase individuals' likelihood of victimization because these personal characteristics are congruent with the needs or motives of offenders. Vulnerability refers to characteristics that increase risk because they reduce the potential victim's ability to resist or deter victimization. These characteristics include small size, physical weakness, and psychological problems. Gratifiability refers to characteristics that increase risk because they are qualities, possessions, skills, or attributes that the offender wants to take, use, or manipulate. These characteristics include valuable possessions or, in the case of sexual assault, a potential victim's gender. Antagonism refers to characteristics that increase risk because they provoke anger, jealousy, or destructive impulses. These characteristics include ethnic features, religious attributes, and indications regarding sexual orientation. The last category, antagonism, is generally referred to as a *hate crime* (see Box 3.1 at the end of this chapter).

A good example of a factor that increases an individual's chances of being victimized is intoxication. Research on sexual assault indicates that alcohol consumption increases the likelihood that an individual will become an offender (Scully & Marolla, 1984), and alcohol consumption by victims increases their risk of being raped (Harrington & Leitenberg, 1994). One reason for an increase in offending risk is that drinking may activate stereotypes and myths held by certain men about perceived provocative behavior on the part of women (e.g., they're "asking for it"). Victimization risk increases for women who drink alcohol because drinking decreases resistance. Women who are drinking seem less likely to quickly and clearly state that they do not consent to the sexual activity. They may also be less aware that men are interpreting their behavior as indicating consent.

In a survey of female undergraduates who, since the age of 16, had been victims of sexual aggression involving force or the threat of force by acquaintances (25% of the sample), Harrington and Leitenberg (1994) found that 55% of the victims were at least partially intoxicated at the time of the sexual assault. When the assault was committed by a nonromantic acquaintance, 71% of the women were at least partially intoxicated. These women were likely to use lower levels of resistance than women who were not at all intoxicated.

ACTIONS DURING
VIOLENT VICTIMIZATIONS

What happens during a violent crime can be thought of as a sequence of behaviors, beginning with the offender's threat or act of violence. The victim may resist the offender, which may lead to the offender's committing further violence, which may lead to further resistance, and so on. In other cases, the victim's resistance may cause the offender to leave the situation.

How this sequence of behaviors plays out is important for four reasons. First, the victim's initial resistance may cause the offender to desist from further criminal behavior, meaning that the criminal behavior may be only an attempted rather than a completed crime. This difference between an attempted and a completed crime has implications for the victim's willingness to report the crime to the police and the willingness of the police to investigate and make an arrest. Second, resistance can affect the amount of physical injury the victim suffers because the action might end the attack or provoke the offender to further violence. Third, the effect of the resistance on the seriousness of the crime greatly influences the psychological consequences of the crime; generally in less serious crimes, the victim suffers not only less physical injury but also less psychological injury. For example, victims of completed rape experience more psychological problems than victims of attempted rape (Kilpatrick, Veronen, & Best, 1985). Finally, whether and how much victims resist can determine how victims' families and friends, police and prosecutors in the criminal justice system, and the victims themselves determine responsibility for the crime. They—and society in general—are probably less likely to blame the victim for the crime if he or she had resisted.

Before discussing this sequence of behaviors in a violent interaction, it is important to consider the difficulty of characterizing what occurs during a violent crime. One set of problems concerns the sequencing of particular actions. That is, there are likely to be problems in determining the order of events. Individuals involved in the episode and even bystanders may recall the sequence of events differently because they had different perspectives of the event, and because their views and subsequent recall could be affected by their biases.

A second set of potential problems concerns what types of violent acts occurred. The research on partner violence is a good example of the difficulty of trying to characterize what occurs during violent crimes. There are many problems with official records, especially police reports, in trying to characterize violent crimes. The most notable problem is that only a small percentage of partner assaults (perhaps only 20%) are included in police records. Because of these problems, Straus and his colleagues developed the Conflict Tactics Scale (CTS), which has become the most common method of measuring household violence (Straus, 1979). This scale is a self-report measure of how respondents used various violent and nonviolent means to deal with conflict. For example, in the CTS, serious violence includes kicking, biting, hitting with a fist or object, beating up, or using a weapon on the victim.

Despite its use in dozens of studies of household violence, there have been several criticisms of the CTS. It does not have information about the force behind an action, the relative size and strength of the offender and victim, the victim's ability to resist or escape the offender, or the point of impact of the action (Browne & Williams, 1992). Because the scale does not do a very good job of distinguishing between minor and severe assaults, it probably underestimates the amount of violence by males and overestimates the amount of violence by females. There is also a question about the level of the aggressive acts; men's and women's aggressive acts are equated in the scale even though men tend to be bigger and stronger. Furthermore, because there are no data in the scale about the antecedents of the violence, it might be, as Walker (1989) contends, that women's violence is a reaction to men's violence. There is also some evidence that men understate the severity of their actions and the harm inflicted (Stets & Straus, 1990), whereas women tend to overreport their aggressive acts (Walker, 1989). In addition, the CTS has been criticized because it does not measure the intention behind an action (how much harm was intended). And because the CTS score is based on the responses of one individual per couple, there is always a question about the validity of the responses (Browne, 1993). Finally, some kinds of violence, such as marital rape, are not included in the scale.

The most recent review of the research on gender differences in physical aggression toward partners suggests that different results are obtained depending on whether the measures are based on acts or consequences (Archer, 2000a). When specific acts are considered, results indicate that women are significantly more likely than men to have used physical aggression. But when physical consequences of aggression are considered, results indicate that men are significantly more likely than women to have injured their partners. For both conclusions, the effects, although not due to chance, are small. Also, the samples for the act-based measures were biased toward young dating samples, which means that the findings may not generalize to cohabiting and married relationships, especially those involving physically abusive men (O'Leary, 2000; White, Smith, Koss, & Figueredo, 2000).

Researchers of violence other than partner violence confront many of the same problems inherent in the CTS, including the relative sizes of victims and offenders and the level of harm intended. Moreover, because with few exceptions most studies use only victims' characterizations of the violent incidents; there may be a systematic bias toward reporting the crime as more serious (or in some cases, less serious) than what an observer might report about the same incidents.

The Effects of Resistance on
Crime Completion and Injury

Understanding the level of violence in a crime and the sequencing of actions between offenders and victims is especially important for understanding the role of victim resistance in avoiding crimes and in sustaining injury. Overall, about three fourths of violent crime victims resist their assailant in some way (U.S. Bureau of Justice Statistics, 1997). These resistance measures range from verbal strategies (such as reasoning, pleading, and yelling for help) to physical strategies (such as fighting and using a weapon). In general, research from the NCVS indicates that (a) victims of assault and rape are more likely to resist than victims of robbery, (b) victims are more likely to resist offenders they know than offenders who are strangers, and (c) victims are more likely to resist unarmed than armed offenders.

The most important question regarding resistance, especially physical resistance, is whether it enables the victim to avoid both the crime and the injury. The answer is not straightforward because of the weaknesses of the data that can be used to address the issue. Relying on crimes reported to the police or on records of crisis centers will probably result in an underestimate of the extent to which resistance is successful because individuals who have avoided injury and financial loss are less likely than those who have not to call the police (Block & Skogan, 1986).

There have been several studies of resistance to violent crimes, most of which have found that success depends on multiple factors, including the type of crime and the type of resistance. For example, in their analysis of NCVS data from 1973 through 1979, Block and Skogan (1986) found that in the case of stranger robbery, forceful resistance (physically fighting with or without a weapon) reduced the likelihood of robbery completion but increased the risk of physical injury. Nonforceful resistance (talking, yelling, or trying to leave) reduced the likelihood of both robbery completion and physical injury.

Most of the research on resistance to violent crimes has focused on sexual assault, specifically on whether victims who resist a sexual assault are more or less likely to suffer a completed sexual assault and to suffer additional physical injury. The potential benefits of fighting back include avoiding the rape, outside intervention, a more positive reaction from friends and relatives, a more positive response from the criminal justice system (police and prosecutors), and greater psychological recovery. The potential costs of fighting back include additional injury and perhaps even death. Those who advocate resistance argue that the probability of avoiding rape is high, and the risk of serious injury is low, even if the risk of physical injury is increased by physical resistance. In contrast, those who oppose resistance place primary emphasis on avoiding serious injury, even if its probability is low, and less emphasis on avoiding rape.

Studies on the effects of resistance in sexual assault offenses suggest that resistance can be effective in reducing the likelihood of rape completion or of additional injury but generally not both. This effectiveness also depends on the type of resistance, as shown in Table 3.1, which is based on a review by Ullman (1997). According to Ullman's framework, physical and verbal resistance can be forceful or nonforceful, and these different strategies can have different effects on rape avoidance and physical injury. In addition, sexual assault victims may rely on physiological resistance or psychological deception, although the results of these strategies are unclear.

Although there is a link between resistance and injury (Prentky, Burgess, & Carter, 1986; Ruback & Ivie, 1988), it is not clear whether victim resistance precedes or follows offender aggression. That is, because the data are correlational, it is not clear whether the attacker's physical violence causes the victim's resistance or whether the victim's

TABLE 3.1 Summary of the Effects of Rape Resistance, by Type of Strategy

	Forceful Physical Resistance	Nonforceful Physical Resistance	Forceful Verbal Resistance	Nonforceful Verbal Resistance	Physiological Resistance	Psychological Deception
Examples of the strategy	Wrestling, punching, scratching, kicking, using a weapon	Pulling away, shielding with hands, fleeing	Screaming, yelling, threatening the offender	Pleading, talking, reasoning, crying	Vomiting, urinating, defecating	Lying about STD or being pregnant, promising to return later
Effect on rape avoidance or completion	Increases likelihood of rape avoidance	Increases likelihood of rape avoidance	Increases likelihood of rape avoidance	Increases likelihood of rape completion	Results are unclear	Results are unclear
Effect on additional injury	Increases likelihood of additional injury	Does not increase the risk of physical injury	Results are unclear	Does not increase the risk of physical injury	Results are unclear	Results are unclear

SOURCE: Ullman (1997).

resistance provokes the attacker to be more violent, thereby causing more injury. To answer this question requires some information about the temporal sequence of events, but very little information exists. In the context of rape, two studies that have analyzed the sequence of offender violence and victim resistance suggest that physical resistance is related to a lower likelihood of completed rape and no increase in physical injury (Quinsey & Upfold, 1985; Ullman & Knight, 1992).

To overcome the problem of determining whether the resistance occurred before or after the injury, the U.S. Bureau of Justice Statistics redesigned the NCVS to ask questions about when the resistance occurred, and the data for the years 1992 through 1995 have recently become available. In an analysis of 3,206 incidents from those years, in which females were physically assaulted by a lone male offender, Thompson, Simon, Saltzman, and Mercy (1999) found that 68% of the women used self-protective measures before or during the assault, an additional 6% used self-protective measures after the assault, and 26% did not use self-protective measures at all. The researchers found that women who used self-protective measures before or during the assault were significantly less likely to be injured than women who did not use self-protective measures at all or who used self-protective measures after being injured. This relationship held after controlling for other potential risk factors, including the relationship between the victim and the offender.

There is some suggestion that the relationship between resistance and injury is affected by other variables, such as the relationship between the victim and the offender. For example, Ruback and Ivie (1988) found, using a sample of 2,526 adult females, that physical resistance was less common when the offender was a stranger than when the offender was known to the victim, probably because strangers were more likely than nonstrangers to use weapons. Although less common against strangers, physical resistance was more strongly related to injury when the offender was a stranger rather than a nonstranger.

More recent research suggests that the level of offender violence explains both the level of the woman's resistance and the amount of injury she suffers, and that the level of her resistance explains little in terms of injury once offender violence is taken into account (Ullman & Knight, 1991, 1992). Ullman and Knight (1995) concluded that it is not necessary for women to try to determine what type of rapist has attacked them in order to determine what strategy they should use. Rather, their research suggests that, regardless of the type of rapist, women who used forceful strategies (fighting or screaming) were more successful at avoiding both severe sexual abuse and physical injury than women who used nonforceful strategies, such as attempting to flee.

A second factor that affects the relationship between resistance and injury is the use of alcohol. In the case of the offender, it seems that more alcohol use leads to higher levels of aggression because of lowered inhibitions. In the case of the victim, alcohol use seems to lead to greater injury because of a lowered ability to resist the attack (Ullman & Knight, 1993).

Bystander Behavior

Although in many violent crimes, the victim and the offender are the only individuals present, in some cases, bystanders witness the violence. At one extreme, these bystanders may increase the violence by encouraging the offender and perhaps instigating the violence (Felson & Tedeschi, 1995). For example, the 1983 rape incident in a barroom in New Bedford, Massachusetts, which served as the basis for the movie *The Accused,* involved four rapists who were cheered on by several onlookers. In less extreme instances, bystanders may have an effect on violence by serving as an audience; for example, bullies and violent men concerned with building a reputation for violence need witnesses who can spread information about their fierceness. Bystanders may also mediate between antagonists to prevent escalation to violence (Felson & Tedeschi, 1995).

At the other extreme, bystanders may not become involved at all, refusing even to call the police. Although instances of bystander nonintervention are reported in the media every so often, the best-known case involved the rape and murder of Kitty Genovese, in 1964, under the eyes of 38 witnesses. One person eventually called the police but only after talking with others and after almost 30 minutes had passed from the time Genovese screamed as she was first stabbed (Seedman & Hellman, 1975).

Part of the reason bystanders are reluctant to become involved in violent crimes is that individuals in groups often behave differently than they do when they are alone. Specifically, research indicates that the more bystanders who are present, the less likely any one of them is to intervene (Darley & Latané, 1968). Although the mere presence of other bystanders reduces the likelihood of intervention, it is reduced even further by three factors (Latané & Darley, 1970). First, through a process of social influence, individuals are less likely to become involved in helping if other bystanders appear to be unconcerned—given the others' lack of alarm, individuals might conclude that the situation is not an emergency. Second, through a process of audience inhibition, individuals might not help if they think they will be seen as foolish for intervening when, in fact, there is no emergency. Third, through a process of diffusion of responsibility, individuals may decide not to intervene even though they know the situation is an emergency if they also know that the blame for not acting will be divided among the whole group.

These conditions might explain why bystanders are reluctant to intervene when they believe that a violent situation involving a man hitting a woman is an argument between partners rather than an attack by a stranger (Shotland & Straw, 1976). When the two are assumed to know one another, bystanders are likely to define the situation as not serious for the victim because they assume that the woman is not going to suffer serious injury. However, bystanders are likely to believe that intervention would have quite serious consequences for themselves because they assume that they might incur injury if they attempt to intervene. In contrast, when the two are assumed to be strangers, bystanders are likely to believe that the woman will be injured seriously, but that if they intervene, the attacker would probably flee rather than fight.

Another reason that bystanders might be reluctant to intervene concerns their tendency to blame victims for their own suffering. In large part, this tendency reflects a belief in a just world (Lerner, Miller, & Holmes, 1976), a world where good things happen to good people, and bad things happen to bad people. When bad things happen to good people, individuals are likely to feel uncomfortable because that result is inconsistent with the notion that the world is fair. This inconsistency is upsetting because it suggests that bad things could randomly and arbitrarily happen to them. Such a possibility is disturbing, and they are more likely to believe that the victim must have deserved to be victimized. That being the case, bystanders to crimes might not intervene because of their belief in a just world as well as a fear that intervening might be too costly.

Aside from their roles in encouraging or discouraging violence and in reporting or not reporting the violence to the police, bystanders are also important because they affect how others react. For example, police are more likely to make arrests when bystanders are present (23%) than when they are not present (10%) (Smith & Visher, 1981).

VICTIMS' ACTIONS AFTER
VIOLENT VICTIMIZATIONS

After a crime, victims are likely to be distressed, angry, and in disbelief. These emotional and cognitive reactions can make victims confused and can affect their ability to make decisions and to recall what happened in a coherent way (Lurigio & Mechanic, 2000). Thus, victims' actions may not always appear to be rational.

After violent crimes occur, victims have several options about what actions to take. They can do nothing, they can tell a friend or family member, they can report the crime to a stranger who by virtue of some position of authority (e.g., security personnel at a shopping mall) is in a position to handle the problem, or they can call the police. Which of these options victims choose depends on whether they define the event as a crime and how they weigh the costs and benefits associated with each of these options. Although some victims might make these determinations by themselves, in many cases, victims make these judgments with information and advice from others (Greenberg & Ruback, 1992).

Defining an Event as a Crime

Whether an event is a crime is a determination made by a criminal jury or judge that all of the elements of a statutory offense have been proven beyond a reasonable doubt. Prior to a trial or a guilty plea, if the defendant chooses not to go to trial, police and prosecutors make judgments about the sufficiency of the evidence in the case and the likelihood that the defendant would be found guilty if he or she went to trial.

Like police, prosecutors, judges, and juries, victims make judgments about whether a crime occurred and how likely it is that the offender would be found guilty. Victims might differ from criminal justice system personnel, however, in their definitions of what constitutes a crime. For example, a wife might believe regardless of what the law says that it is not a crime for her husband to beat her. In such a case, she would not call the police and perhaps would not even tell anyone about the incident. Whether or not victims define an act as criminal is based on the law and on their own beliefs. Moreover, as in the reporting of crime, defining an act as criminal is subject to social influence from others.

Reporting of Crime

Although on television and in the movies, crimes are almost always in progress when the police arrive at a scene, in actuality, the police rarely see crimes as they occur. Instead, police initiate 97% of their crime investigations after being notified by citizens, most of whom (60%) are victims (U.S. Bureau of Justice Statistics, 1985). Thus, the traditional view that the police are the "gatekeepers of the criminal justice system," because their decisions to arrest or not arrest individuals initiate the criminal justice process, is not really correct. Citizens, particularly victims, are the true gatekeepers of the criminal justice system (Hindelang & Gottfredson, 1976).

An understanding of the decision to report or not report a crime to the police must begin with the NCVS, which is the largest and longest continuing study of victimization. After considering the NCVS, we turn to the importance of social influence on the reporting decision as indicated by research from experimental, archival, and survey studies. Finally, we examine how the advice victims are given may vary as a function of characteristics of the victim and of larger cultural factors.

National Crime Victimization Survey. Beginning in the 1970s, researchers using the National Crime Surveys (NCS) found that less than half of all crimes, including violent crimes, were reported to the police. For reasons related to decisions such as the deployment of police and the expenditure of criminal justice resources, it was important for policymakers to know the true extent of crime and what factors predicted the reporting or nonreporting of a criminal victimization. In addition, for reasons relating to theories about decision making and social influence, researchers were interested in knowing how factors about the crime, the criminal, and the victim related to reporting. Thus, for reasons relating to both policy and theory, researchers have tried to describe and explain the "dark figure of crime" (the crime that never appeared in the criminal justice system because it was never reported to police).

According to victimization survey data (U.S. Bureau of Justice Statistics, 1997), most crimes are not reported to the police (only 37% of all crimes and 42% of all violent crimes are reported). These figures are not too different from comparable statistics in late 16th-century England; one justice in 1596 estimated that only 20% of crimes were reported (Greenberg & Greenberg, 1982). The same reasons that explained nonreporting in late 16th-century England still exist today (Greenberg & Greenberg, 1982): (a) Reporting and prosecuting a case can be very time-consuming, (b) the larger community might reject a victim who used formal social control mechanisms rather than more informal methods of resolving disputes, (c) the offender might retaliate against the victim, and (d) often, little could be done because suspects were not apprehended or fled before trial, and stolen property had been quickly disposed of.

As briefly discussed in Chapter 1, the best single predictor of whether or not a crime will be reported is the seriousness of the crime. Thus, according to the NCVS (U.S. Bureau of Justice Statistics, 1997, Table 91), 55% of robberies, 50% of household burglaries, 40% of assaults, and 27% of personal thefts were reported to the police. Generally, reporting is more likely if (a) the crime involved interpersonal violence rather than theft, (b) it was completed rather than only attempted, (c) the property taken was of greater rather than lesser value, (d) a weapon was involved, and (e) the victim was more seriously injured. But the seriousness of the crime is not the only factor that affects whether or not a crime will be reported. For example, 92% of completed motor vehicle thefts are reported to the police (U.S. Bureau of Justice Statistics, 1997, Table 91), almost certainly because victims must report the crime if they are to collect from their insurance companies.

Based on responses to the NCVS (U.S. Bureau of Justice Statistics, 1997, Table 101), these were the most common reasons victims gave for reporting their violent victimizations to the police: (a) The simple fact that it was a crime required them to call the police, and (b) they were trying to prevent the offender from committing crimes in the future. A list of the most common reasons for reporting appears in Table 3.2.

Based on responses to the NCVS (U.S. Bureau of Justice Statistics, 1997, Table 102), the most common reasons victims gave for not reporting their violent victimizations to the police were (a) that they viewed the crime as a private matter rather than a concern of the police, (b) the offender did not complete the crime, and (c) they told some other official about the crime. A list of the most common reasons for not reporting appears in Table 3.3.

Factors Related to Reporting. Results from victimization surveys indicate that the best predictor of reporting is the seriousness of the incident. In a survey of more than 3,900 Oregon residents, Schneider, Burcart, and Wilson (1976) found that 24% of less serious, 49% of moderately serious, and 80% of highly serious crimes were reported to the police. Attitudes toward the police (e.g., trust in police, po-

TABLE 3.2   Most Common Reasons for Reporting

Reason for Reporting	Percentage of Victims Giving That Reason
Because it was a crime	23.2
To prevent further crimes by offender against victim	17.8
To stop or prevent this incident	14.9
To prevent crime by offender against anyone	9.0
To punish offender	7.4
To catch or find offender	5.7
Duty to notify police	5.1
To recover property	3.9
Needed help due to injury	2.2
To improve police surveillance	2.1
Some other reason or reason not available	8.7

SOURCE: National Crime Victims' Survey (NCVS) (U.S. Bureau of Justice Statistics, 1997, Table 101).

TABLE 3.3   Most Common Reasons for Not Reporting

Reason for Not Reporting	Percentage of Victims Giving That Reason
Private or personal matter	20.4
Offender unsuccessful	19.1
Reported to another official	11.5
Police would not want to be bothered	5.9
Not important enough	5.2
Police inefficient, ineffective, or biased	4.2
Fear of reprisal	3.9
Too inconvenient or time-consuming	3.9
Lack of proof	3.2
Other reasons	22.7

SOURCE: National Crime Victims' Survey (NCVS) (U.S. Bureau of Justice Statistics, 1997, Table 102).

lice-community relations, or belief that police can catch the person) showed statistically significant but much weaker relationships to reporting. Similarly, Skogan (1984) found that attitudes toward the police were not important predictors of reporting. Garofalo (1977) found that in the case of serious crimes, attitudes toward the police had no effect on reporting, but in the case of less serious crimes, more favorable attitudes were associated with more reporting.

One of victims' fears of reporting a crime to the police, often as great or greater than the dread of having to relive their victimizations in court, is the fear of media attention (Hetter, 1993). Even when the possibility of such attention is negligible, however, victims may still be afraid of being asked questions such as, "How did you feel when this happened to you?" and "Do you think you could have prevented it from happening?" Victims' fears are grounded not only in the anxiety of having to answer such questions but also in the fact that reporters often reveal private matters about their lives that may not be at all relevant, or only tangentially relevant, to the crime. For example, in a case from Methuen, Massachusetts, a woman was attacked by two men who punched her in the face, beat her with a metal rod, and kicked her (Hetter, 1993). The woman, who was a reserve police officer, wanted her assailants to be prosecuted but was afraid that the fact that she was a lesbian would become public.

To help victims cope with the media, the National Victims Center has published a guide that gives victims basic information such as their rights to refuse interviews, to set the time and conditions for the interviews if they do decide to give them, and to have a spokesperson deal with the media instead of talking to the media themselves. In addition, the American Press Institute and the National Press Photographers Association have held seminars and published handbooks addressing issues such as treating crime victims with respect and showing more concern for their feelings.

Aside from wanting to avoid the embarrassment and other costs that might follow if they become involved with the criminal justice system, victims may also be reluctant to call the police if they believe they could be implicated in the crime. For example, victims in barroom fights are very unlikely to call the police, because they might be perceived as having done something to precipitate the assault. As another example, several men who had been beaten and sexually attacked by John Gacy, the convicted murderer of 33 boys and young men, did not report their victimizations. Some had not reported the attacks because they were prostitutes or had gone to Gacy's home for drugs (Hermann, Morrison, Sor, Norman, & Neff, 1984). Even if victims do go to the police, their reports may be ignored if the police do not believe they are completely innocent or if they had committed other crimes. One of Gacy's victims who had reported being attacked believed that the police disregarded his complaint when they learned he was a homosexual and had previously been arrested for possession of marijuana (Hermann et al., 1984).

Because many victims fear a "second injury" from being involved with the system, they often seek alternatives to the criminal justice system, as is illustrated by crimes that occur on college campuses. At many colleges, administrators prefer to handle criminal matters within the college rather than to bring in police and prosecutors. For the most part, administrators are concerned with resolving issues quickly and sensitively because the criminal justice system is often slow and ineffective (Bernstein, 1996b). In addition, by relying on internal disciplinary boards, colleges can resolve the matter while still protecting the victim's privacy, thereby protecting the victim from harassment and embarrassment. But the internal resolution of crimes also protects the college from having to report criminal incidents as required by federal law, particularly those that occur off campus at recognized student organizations (Bernstein, 1996a). Some colleges have actively dissuaded victims from pursuing matters in the criminal justice system (Bernstein, 1996b). Moreover, most campus police departments have the power to arrest suspects for criminal activity and have the choice to turn the matter over to the criminal justice system or to handle matters within the institution (Bernstein, 1996a). Thus, campus police can ensure that crimes will be handled internally.

But do the police always want victims to report crimes? More reported crimes mean more paperwork and also increased crime statistics, making the city and the police look less reputable. And one way to reduce reporting would be to make it inconvenient to report. For example, consider this account by an assistant editor at a newspaper in New York City who had her wallet stolen:

> Sunday, after I reported my wallet's disappearance to mall security and sat in my apartment for over an hour canceling credit cards, I called the police precinct for the mall where the theft took place. A weary voice answered, and I stated my business. "I can't take that information over the phone. You have to come in and file a report," the officer said. I was surprised. Surely, by now, I thought they'd have this down to a science—for pickpocketings, press 1. For muggings, press 2. . . .
>
> I still haven't gone down to the precinct and feel a little guilty. But then, I don't really want to take a day off from work to do it, or take a 5-mile cab ride at night to a neighborhood I don't know very well. If by some miracle, they recover my things and catch the thief, then they can call me, and I will press charges. As the situation stands, it doesn't seem worth the trip.

TABLE 3.4   Summary of Arguments for Reporting or Not Reporting, by the Effects on the Victim, the Criminal Justice System, and Society

	Arguments for Reporting	*Arguments for Not Reporting*
Victim	Right thing to do, especially if crime is serious Insurance/compensation Punish the offender	Costs of system hostile to victim Relive trauma Fear of retaliation Private matter Police can't do anything
Criminal justice system	Catch offenders More accurate records	Police can't do anything anyway Limited resources should be directed at those cases where the police can do something
Society	Prevent future crimes Reallocate resources more efficiently	Increased media coverage and fear

But perhaps there is method to this madness. Making reporting crimes a hassle is one way to keep the statistics down. (Phillips, 1994, p. A18)[1]

This example suggests that the question of whether or not crimes should be reported is not necessarily straightforward; for example, the police may not believe it is worth their time to investigate. In addition to the reasons that victims choose to report or not to report (see Tables 3.2 and 3.3), reasons relevant to the operation of the criminal justice system and to the larger goals of society could also lead to conclusions about whether a crime should or should not be reported (see Table 3.4). In the case of the criminal justice system, reporting can lead to more accurate records and perhaps less crime, although it can also lead to the police devoting resources to crimes that are unlikely to be solved. At the societal level, reporting might mean better allocation of resources but also increased media coverage and fear.

Social Influence and the Reporting Decision. A victim's decision to call the police or not is often made after talking with others (Greenberg & Ruback, 1992). Friends, relatives, or sometimes even strangers can influence victims' decisions in three ways (Ruback, Greenberg, & Westcott, 1984): giving information and advice, exerting normative pressure, and providing social support or nonsupport. First, others can provide victims with information about the police (e.g., whether they can do anything) and about the costs of reporting a crime (e.g., how much time it will take for the police to take a statement). Victims are also likely to rely on others' perceptions of the crimes (e.g., the intent of the offenders), because this information can give them some perspective about how the police are likely to react to the crimes.

Victims' needs for information are likely to vary depending on how serious the crimes are and how aroused they are by the crimes (Ruback et al., 1984). When the crimes are very serious, and victims are very aroused and upset, they may not be able to think rationally and to carefully weigh the costs and benefits of calling the police. Under such conditions, they might be especially influenced by specific advice to call or not to call the police. On the other hand, even when the crime is not very serious, victims still may not be able to determine whether it would be worthwhile to call the police. Information from others in the form of specific costs (e.g., amount of time involved in reporting) and specific benefits (e.g., the likelihood that the offenders will be punished) might help victims make informed decisions.

Although victims are likely to rely on the advice they receive from others, it is important for them to recognize that, for several reasons, this advice may not be best for them (Ruback et al., 1984). It might be the product of others' self-interests rather than victims' best interests. For example, in the 1999 movie *The General's Daughter,* a general advises his daughter, a cadet at West Point, not to tell authorities about being raped because of his concern that the report would harm the U.S. Military Academy, the Army, and his own career. The advice of others may also be the product of their own biases (e.g., of blaming victims) rather than of more neutral and disinterested decision making. Finally, others may sincerely want to help victims and believe that their advice will further that end. However, if they incorrectly identify the source of the victim's distress, their advice may increase rather than decrease the distress.

In addition to giving information, other people can influence victims' decisions by exerting normative pressure on them. Norms are rules or standards for behavior that group members are expected to follow (Levine & Moreland, 1998). People can apply normative pressure by, for example, threatening victims with harm if they decide to report. Short of actual threats, others may remind victims of the group norms and of the negative reactions that are likely to follow the decision to report or not. Thus, within a gang, it would be understood with little need for reminder that injuries caused by other gang members are not the province of the police.

Finally, aside from providing information and exerting pressure, others may provide victims with social support or nonsupport. Several lines of research indicate that individuals who have suffered harm often seek social support in the form of tangible items (e.g., money or food) and emotional support (e.g., expressions of interest and concern). Individuals who receive emotional support are likely to experience less distress than those who do not. And with less distress, they will probably consider more factors (Easterbrook, 1959) and make better-quality decisions about what to do. However, it is also possible that other people can cause victims to experience even more distress by, for example, blaming the victims for being victimized.

The investigation of the role of social influence on victims' decisions about reporting their victimizations has involved multiple methods. As described in Chapter 2, the results from any one research method may reflect problems with that particular research method. The only way to avoid this potential bias is to attempt to find similar results across research methods. If researchers obtain consistent findings across research methods, it is more likely that the findings are due to an underlying cause rather than to the biases of the research method.

Experimental Research. One series of studies on the role of social influence in victim decision making used an experimental methodology (Greenberg & Ruback, 1992). This research was conducted in a field-laboratory paradigm: a bogus business consulting firm in which paid volunteers, recruited via newspaper advertisements, participated in an ostensible study of clerical efficiency. Actually, the research was a study of social influence on crime victims. During the study, participants learned that an experimental confederate had taken $11 from them. Across the six studies, a second confederate, a bystander to the crime, attempted to influence their decisions to call or not to call the police by variously providing information, advice, and social support.

This research (Greenberg & Ruback, 1992) indicated that social influence strongly influenced victims' decisions to call or not to call the police. Victims who were advised to call the police were more likely to do so than those who were advised not to call or who were not given any advice. Bystanders were particularly likely to influence victims to report the crime if (a) their advice was specific ("Call the police" rather than "Do something"), (b) they remained with the victim after giving the advice, and (c) they offered the victim support in future dealings with the police and the criminal justice system. These last two conditions suggest that some victims may need to believe they have both present and future social support before they become involved with the criminal justice system. Multivariate analyses across the six studies indicated that the bystander's advice was the single strongest predictor of the victim's reporting decision.

This research is limited by weaknesses of all laboratory research and of this paradigm in particular: Participants were volunteers, participants knew they were in a research study even though they did not know that the research involved reactions to theft, the staged crime was minor, and participants were exposed to a social influence agent. The research did not address the role of social influence in more serious crimes and, specifically, whether victims seek, receive, and follow advice from others. Those questions require additional methodologies.

One alternative methodology is to analyze archival data. For example, Ruback and Ivie (1988) used the records of 2,526 rape victims (over the age of 14, with a median age of 23) who visited the Rape Crisis Center (RCC) at Grady Memorial Hospital in Atlanta, Georgia, during a 3-year period. To investigate the role of social influence, the researchers examined the first action the women took following the rape. Of the sample, 28% called the police, 19% went home, and 12% took some other action (e.g., took a shower). The remaining 41% spoke with someone else (15% spoke with a friend, 11% spoke with a family member, and 15% spoke with a stranger). This 41% figure is conservative because it describes only those who first spoke with someone. Other victims, after going home or taking some other action, probably consulted with someone before deciding whether or not to call the police. This reasoning is supported by the fact that in 45% of those cases in which the police were notified, someone other than the victim notified the police. Younger victims who were raped by a stranger were most likely to talk with others immediately after the crime.

Although archival studies have the advantage of large sample sizes with real victims, they also have the disadvantage of sample bias (only those who went or were taken to the RCC are included). In addition, the records oftentimes do not contain information that can be used to address mediating processes (e.g., whether those who first did something else talked to someone eventually). To address this problem, Ruback and Ivie (1988) used a three-stage panel design of women 18 years of age and older who had visited the RCC during the months December 1984 through May 1985. In addition to using the information available from the initial intake interview, the researchers spoke to the women approximately 2 months after their visit to the RCC and again 6 to 9 months after the second interview (8-11 months after the attack). Of the 150 women, 55 (37%) said they had received advice about reporting: 51 had been advised to report and 4 had been advised not to report. Of those 55 women who had received advice, 12 (22%) said they had asked for advice and 42 (78%) said the advice had been volunteered to them.

Six to 9 months after the second interview, 79 of the 150 respondents were again contacted, and 77 agreed to be reinterviewed. The number of negative long-term effects the women reported was positively related to the following: (a) the number of people they stated they would tell about the crime when they first visited the RCC, (b) the number of people they actually talked to, (c) the number of people they sought help from, and (d) the number of people who advised them not to notify the police. The number of preventive changes in behavior (e.g., adding home security devices or obtaining a weapon) was positively related to talking to more people and to reporting more negative effects, but it was not related to the level of fear or anger the women reported when they had initially visited the RCC. The researchers learned about the subsequent outcome of 78 of the cases by questioning the victims or their relatives and by consulting the RCC and police records. The case was likely to have gone further in the system if more people had reacted positively to the victims within 2 months of the attack and if others had not pressured them to drop the charges.

In addition to the questions of whether victims seek, receive, or follow advice from others, there is the issue of how others decide what advice to give. In a series of studies (Greenberg & Ruback, 1992; Ruback, Gupta, & Kohli, 1988), researchers asked subjects (college students and adults from different ethnic groups) to judge on a continuum whether the appropriate action for each of 49 crimes would be to call the police or to handle the matter privately. The research indicated that social norms for reporting depend on the seriousness of the crime, the gender of the victim, the victim-offender relationship, and the gender of the adviser. There was also evidence of cultural and ethnic differences in norms.

This work, which showed that crime victims' reporting decisions are influenced by others, was extended in two statewide stratified random-digit telephone surveys in Georgia (ns = 817 and 832). Respondents were asked about the appropriateness of reporting specific crimes to the police (Ruback, 1994). Based on between-crime comparisons (e.g., robbery vs. assault vs. sexual assault) and within-crime comparisons (e.g., sexual assault by a stranger vs. sexual assault by a boyfriend), respondents are more likely to advise reporting if the crime is more serious, if the victim is female, if the victim and offender are strangers, and if the adviser is female. More recent work with college students suggests that advisers to victims also take into account the victim's age and whether the victim has been drinking. Students are generally less likely to advise reporting if the victim had been drinking, especially if the victim is below the legal drinking age (Ruback, Ménard, Outlaw, & Shaffer, 1999).

That men and women are likely to give different advice is especially evident in cases of sexual assault, based on differences in judgments of victim blameworthiness. For instance, a review of 60 studies assessing how much blame observers attribute to victims indicated that males are more likely than females to attribute victim blame (Whatley, 1996). A meta-analytic review of 72 studies of individual-difference variables related to attitudes about rape found that the strongest demographic predictor was the gender of the respondent, with men being more likely to find rape acceptable; and black men were much more likely than white men to have accepting attitudes about rape. There was also evidence that individuals from lower socioeconomic backgrounds were more likely to have accepting attitudes about rape than individuals with higher socioeconomic status. In addition, the study found that both men and women who had traditional gender role beliefs were more likely to buy into rape myths, although the effect was even stronger for women.

Table 3.5 summarizes the role of others in influencing victims' decisions to call the police or not.

Mental Health Consequences of Reporting

Reporting a crime to the police may have several important mental health consequences, both immediate and long-term (Frieze, Hymer, & Greenberg, 1987). If the report results in the offender's being apprehended, the victim is likely to feel better knowing that the offender will be punished and that the offender and others may be deterred from committing similar crimes in the future (Greenberg & Ruback, 1992). The victim might also gain comfort from the return of stolen property and from restitution payments by the offender. Finally, the victim may feel good about having morally done the right thing by calling the police.

In contrast to these possible positive effects of reporting, possible negative effects may make the victim feel worse, a result that Symonds (1980) called the "second injury." These negative effects include treatment by police officers and prosecutors who seem unsympathetic and,

TABLE 3.5   Summary of the Role of Social Influence on
Crime Victims

1. **Crime victims often consult with others.** They seek and receive both social support and advice about whether or not to report the crime to the police. With regard to rape, research suggests that younger and more fearful rape victims are more likely to consult with others.

2. **Crime victims are influenced by their interactions with others.** The strongest evidence of this influence comes from experimental research, in which the bystander's advice was the strongest single predictor of the victim's reporting decision. However, interviews with rape victims also indicate that these others can influence victims' initial reporting decision and subsequent interactions with the criminal justice system.

3. **The advice given to victims depends on the seriousness of the crime, the gender of the victim, and the gender of the adviser.** Crime seriousness is an important factor in determining the importance of reporting, although there are some cultural differences in the perceived seriousness of crimes. In general, crimes against women are seen as more appropriate for police involvement, and women are more likely to think reporting to the police is the appropriate action.

because they handle so many cases, may fail to keep victims informed about the status of the case. Moreover, if the case goes to trial, the victim may be humiliated by the defense attorney's cross-examination. Even if the offender is caught, prosecuted, and punished, the punishment may not be severe, thus violating the victim's sense of justice. In addition, after undergoing the punishment, the offender may be motivated to retaliate against the victim for reporting, leading to further fear of crime.

INFLUENCE OF OTHERS
ON THE VICTIM'S RECOVERY

How others respond to a violent victimization can have important effects on a victim's psychological recovery. In addition to the responses of friends and families, victims are affected by the responses of organizations, such as crisis centers, and their treatment by criminal justice system personnel.

Organizations

Rape victims are often taken to large city hospitals, because these hospitals generally are the best at emergency room medicine, and their staffs are usually more knowledgeable about rape exams. That is not to say that rape victims who are taken to these hospitals are necessarily treated with sensitivity. In many emergency rooms, there are often long lines of people, and rape victims who are not in immediate need of care might have to wait hours for an examination. During the examination, the doctor, who is likely to be a resident doing a rotation in the emergency room and may not be very experienced in conducting the procedure, takes semen and saliva samples and combs the victim's pubic hair for evidence.

The procedure is made less onerous in many locations that have rape crisis centers, where volunteers stay with the victim during the entire time she is in the emergency room, providing both information and informal counseling. For example, in Tulsa, the victim is taken to a separate room and met by a volunteer and a specially trained nurse (a sexual assault nurse examiner) who conducts the exam (Quindlen, 1994).

Criminal Justice System

How police respond to victims can affect the quality of the information victims give as well as their immediate coping and long-term recovery (Lurigio & Mechanic, 2000). When police are sensitive and courteous to victims, victims are better able to give higher-quality information about the crime and are more willing to participate in the criminal justice process. Not surprisingly, if victims feel that police are not supportive, they are less likely to cooperate. For example, the first-known victim of a serial rapist wanted for five sexual assaults and the 1998 murder of a college student in Philadelphia refused to cooperate with police because they had not believed her almost three years earlier, when she had initially reported the rape ("Rape Victim Refuses," 2000). DNA tests conducted on hair the victim had collected from her bedsheets after the attack confirmed that the same rapist had committed all of the crimes.

We would expect any victim to be reluctant to report a crime if he or she expected to be treated badly. Indeed, prior research has indicated that at least part of the reason for rape victims' general unwillingness to report their rapes was the skepticism with which their claims were viewed, and the poor way in which they were treated by agents of the criminal justice system.

One of the outcomes of pressure from women's groups, based partly on research findings, was a nationwide reform of rape laws and procedures. These rape reforms included (a) broadening the definition of rape, (b) eliminating the requirement that the woman must resist, (c) eliminating the requirement that the victim's testimony be corroborated by some independent evidence, and (d) restricting information about the woman's prior sexual behavior. It was expected that these reforms would result in higher levels of reporting, because rape victims could expect to be treated better, and in higher rates of arrest and conviction, because it would be easier to collect evidence against defendants.

In an analysis of the effects of law reform on reporting, arrests, and convictions in six cities (Atlanta, Chicago, Detroit, Houston, Philadelphia, and Washington), Horney and Spohn (1991) found no evidence that these laws had any effect in five of the jurisdictions and evidence of only slight effects in the sixth city, Detroit. Why didn't the laws produce stronger effects? For one thing, these laws can really affect only those cases in which the defendant and the victim knew each other, the issue was consent, and the defendant asked for a jury trial (Horney & Spohn, 1991). In addition, legal rules alone do not determine behavior. Without incentives to change their usual way of dealing with a problem, agents in the criminal justice system continue to use their discretion as they have in the past (Horney & Spohn, 1991). For example, the rape law reforms that eliminated the requirement of corroboration assumed that prosecutors would act in accordance with the law. What Horney and Spohn found, however, was that prosecutors generally did not file charges unless there was corroborating evidence, despite the fact that corroboration was not required. Prosecutors were behaving consistently with how they expected jurors to act, and "jurors are still looking for corroborating evidence—physical injury, a weapon, a hysterical call to the police. Old habits and attitudes die hard, and we can change the law, but we can't necessarily change attitudes" (Horney & Spohn, 1991, p. 140).

Agents in the criminal justice system have a great deal of discretion with regard to dropping a case, such as not arresting a suspect, not charging a suspect, or not going to trial. They are particularly likely to drop a case if the evidence is not very strong. Thus, victims must be aware that their actions can make a big difference in whether or not a suspected offender is arrested and prosecuted. In cases of rape, the chances of arrest and prosecution are greater when victims attend to the advice shown in Table 3.6 (McIntosh, 1993).

Although most criminal complaints are initiated by the police, in most jurisdictions, citizens can initiate complaints in cases (usually against family members or neighbors) in which there was no arrest. One study of 294 complaints in a county in western Massachusetts

TABLE 3.6   Increasing the Likelihood of Prosecuting a Rapist

---

1. **Never give consent** to the attack, even if overpowered. Giving consent in any form can be misconstrued by police, prosecutors, and juries.

2. **Take several photographs** of your injuries. People respond to visible injuries.

3. **Try to remember identifying features of the attacker,** such as scars, tattoos, moles, or an accent.

4. **Try to remember where the rape occurred.** Being able to tell the police where the crime occurred can help them in their search for evidence.

5. **Call the police as soon as possible.** Not only will the police be better able to find evidence, but juries will be more persuaded if the report was made quickly.

6. **Do not wash or change clothing.** With new tests for DNA, sperm and pubic hair is strong evidence against the rapist.

SOURCE: S. McIntosh (1993). Copyright © 1993 by the *Atlanta Journal and Constitution*. Reprinted with permission *Atlanta Journal and Constitution* via Copyright Clearance Center.

(Yngvesson, 1988) found that most court workers referred to these complaints as "garbage" cases. In the view of most court staff members, these everyday conflicts—a "shoving match in which somebody threw the first punch," "kids pushing kids," a "lovers' quarrel"—are private matters that require a third party to act as a referee or an adviser, but they do not require intervention by the court. In the words of one court worker, the individuals filing these complaints need "to be heard" so that they "don't take it into their own hands if they can't resolve them" (Yngvesson, 1988, p. 414). In other words, these cases primarily involve people who want to be heard rather than to go through the criminal process. Thus, it is not surprising that two thirds of these citizen complaints are either withdrawn by the complainant or dismissed by the clerk.

The clerks in the Massachusetts courts that Yngvesson (1988) studied did not have legal training, but their role as lay magistrates provides a clear example of how the law and society at large intersect so that justice can be done. Yngvesson suggests that these clerks do more than simply dismiss, and sometimes resolve, the private conflicts that constitute the bulk of the informal complaints filed by citizens. She argues that their role maintains moral order by defining certain types of "normal trouble" (e.g., disputes between neighbors or fights between children) as either criminal or not. The clerks she observed in her study relied on their knowledge of the community and what was customary to define, for example, a good versus a bad neighbor, a responsible versus an irresponsible parent, and dangerous versus normal behavior.

SUMMARY

In this chapter, we examined the circumstances and immediate after-math of violent victimizations. Although the offender's actions are the strongest determinant of what happens during and after a violent crime, the victim's behavior and the behavior of others can sometimes also affect the level of violence in the interaction and the degree of in-jury that the victim suffers. After the crime is over, the victim must de-cide whether or not to report the crime to the police. When victims are making these decisions, they often seek out and rely on the advice of others, advice that is based on the seriousness of the crime, the gender of the victim, and the nature of the victim-offender relationship. Vic-tims who become involved with the criminal justice system, because they or someone else reported the crime, are likely to find that whether and how police and prosecutors pursue their cases depend on judg-ments made by these individuals about the strength of the case as well as about the credibility of the victim.

Chapter 4 examines the long-term impact of violent crimes on crime victims. This impact depends on events that occurred immedi-ately after the crime as well as on what happened during the crime. Chapter 5 examines the long-term impact of violent crimes on the fam-ilies and friends of victims, individuals who, as we saw in this chapter, tend to have influenced victims immediately after the crime.

Box 3.1

HATE CRIMES

The 1998 murders of Matthew Shepard, a gay college student at the University of Wyoming who was beaten and tied to a fence, and James Byrd Jr., a black man beaten and dragged for 3 miles along a logging road near Jasper, Texas, focused national attention on hate crimes. All states and the federal government have some type of law against hate crimes, those incidents motivated by prejudice based on race, color, religion, or national origin. Some states also include prejudice based on gender or sexual orientation (Jacobs & Potter, 1997). Typically, hate crime statutes make an offense more serious or increase the maximum penalty.

The rationale for having hate crime statutes is that because these crimes are based on the victim's membership or perceived membership in a demographic group, they arguably "are more likely to provoke retaliatory crimes, inflict distinct emotional harms on their victims, and incite community unrest" (*Wisconsin v. Mitchell*, 1993, p. 488). Individuals who are members of these targeted groups often have very high levels of fear, because every incident of hate crime reminds them that they are potential targets and "could be next" (Craig & Waldo, 1996). Because hate crimes affect the entire community differently than ordinary crimes, some argue that they must be addressed in a more forceful way.

Three arguments have been raised against these statutes, however (Jacobs & Potter, 1997). Some critics believe the laws are unnecessary because the criminal law already punishes injurious behavior. Second, some argue that the additional punishment from hate crime statutes amounts to a punishment for people's thoughts and ideas, which is counter to the First Amendment. Third, critics of these laws suggest that they amount to punishing individuals differently depending on who the victim is.

The federal Hate Crime Statistics Act requires law enforcement agencies to report hate crime incidents to the FBI. However, as seen in the *Uniform Crime Reports* (*UCR*) discussed in Chapter 1, incidents are known to the police only if citizens report them, and victims may be even less inclined to report hate incidents than to report more typical crimes if they believe their actions are likely to lead to retaliation or cause them embarrassment. Victims may also be reluctant to report if they do not believe that the police will take their complaints seriously, as illustrated by the editorial cartoon on the next page (Martin, 1996).

6/8/00 8A GIL

LETTERS TO THE EDITOR

MIKE RITTER

Law Enforcement May Not Always Take Hate Crimes Seriously

SOURCE: Reprinted with special permission of King Features Syndicate.

Given the caveat that hate crime victimizations may be under-counted, particularly those against gay and lesbian victims, racial hatred appears to be the most common motivation, and religious hatred is the second most common motivation (Garofalo, 1997). Crimes motivated by hatred of race, ethnicity, or sexual orientation tend to be crimes of violence (e.g., assault or intimidation), whereas crimes motivated by hatred of religion tend to be property crimes, especially vandalism (Garofalo, 1997).

The law enforcement agency that has probably been the most active in countering hate crimes is the New York City Police Department, which created a Bias Incident Investigating Unit (BIU) in 1980. If the first officer on the scene believes that the incident was motivated by bias, the officer's superiors and an investigator from the BIU go to the scene (Martin, 1996). Compared with similar crimes, the arrest rates for bias crimes in New York are more than twice as high, primarily because police officers devote more time and resources to solving bias crimes (e.g., conducting interviews, taking photos, or looking for witnesses).

■ DISCUSSION QUESTIONS

1. Should all crimes be reported to the police? Consider matters of policy, resource constraints, and victim impact. Should there be campaigns to increase reporting? What would these campaigns look like?

2. How important is it to police and prosecutors, to rape victims' friends and families, and to rape victims themselves that the victims physically resisted the attack? Aside from these postcrime effects, is physical resistance effective?

3. Rape victims' fear of media attention prompted victims' rights groups to push for shield laws that kept victims' identities out of the public eye. Should there be similar laws for victims of other kinds of violence?

4. The review article by Archer (2000a) was referred to in the discussion of physical aggression to partners as it relates to specific acts or physical consequences. This raises several issues in addition to the question of how interpersonal violence can and should be measured. For example, what are the implications of including sexual aggression and stalking in the definition of heterosexual violence (Frieze, 2000)? How important is it to compare violence in homosexual relationships with violence in heterosexual relationships? What are the policy implications of research on violence in close relationships? Because police might change their behavior as a result of research showing women are more violent than men, should researchers be concerned with the way they present their findings to the public (Archer, 2000b; White et al., 2000)?

5. Should there be a separate classification for hate crimes? Should there be a classification for substantive hate crimes as well as sentence enhancements for crimes motivated by prejudice? Should the federal Hate Crimes Sentencing Enhancement Act be extended to cover crimes motivated by prejudice based on disability, sex, and sexual orientation?

6. The notion of victim precipitation is currently out of favor. Is this because victim precipitation has been overstated or because it is politically incorrect? In what ways is victim precipitation different from the lifestyle-routine activities approach to victimization?

7. Given the overlap between offending and victimization, do we need theories of victimization, or are theories of offending sufficient?

NOTE

1. Reprinted with permission of the *Wall Street Journal*. Copyright © 1994, Dow Jones & Company, Inc. All rights reserved.

4 ∷

Affective, Behavioral, and Cognitive Consequences of Violent Victimization on Direct Crime Victims

Although we generally think of violent crime in terms of specific types of crime (e.g., rape, physical assault, or partner violence), research suggests that the psychological consequences of crime are fairly consistent regardless of the type of crime. Thus, this chapter describes the general affective, behavioral, and cognitive effects of violent victimization and presents the contextual factors that may affect the severity and duration of these effects.

AFFECTIVE CONSEQUENCES
OF VIOLENT CRIME

Victims of violent crime suffer numerous emotional consequences, including posttraumatic stress disorder (PTSD), depression, anxiety, and suicidal ideations. We discuss each of these affective consequences in some detail. For a brief explanation of why burglary victims are also likely to be distressed, see Box 4.1 (at the end of this chapter).

Posttraumatic Stress Disorder

The similarities in postcrime consequences across types of crimes were reflected by the American Psychiatric Association's (APA) introduction of PTSD into the revised third edition of the *Diagnostic and Statistical Manual of Mental Disorders* (*DSM-III-R*) (APA, 1987). Although the diagnosis of PTSD in the *DSM-III-R* was originally developed to describe reactions to traumatic events "outside the range of usual human experience," such as heavy combat and natural disaster, more recently it has been used to characterize the experience of victimized women, especially rape victims, who are the largest group of individuals diagnosed with PTSD (Goodman, Koss, Fitzgerald, Russo, & Keita, 1993). According to the fourth edition of the *DSM* (APA, 1994), PTSD is an anxiety disorder precipitated by exposure to a traumatic life event that entails a life threat or serious injury to one's self or one's integrity, learning of an unexpected or violent death or serious harm to a significant other, or witnessing a violent or threatening event (APA, 1994). PTSD encompasses three clusters of symptoms: cognitive, affective, and physiological. Cognitive symptoms include intrusive thoughts and nightmares; affective symptoms include feelings of estrangement from others, numbness of feelings, and avoidance of activities; and physiological symptoms include hypervigilance and irritability (see Chapter 2).

Goodman et al. (1993) suggest four reasons that a diagnosis of PTSD is advantageous for victimized women. First, the diagnosis makes it clear that victims' responses are the normal psychological consequences of abnormal events such as crimes. Thus, given that these responses are normal, victims should not be seen as pathological. Second, the availability of a PTSD diagnosis means that clinicians can use the more general research findings on psychological trauma to help victimized women. Third, a PTSD diagnosis integrates the various symptoms while also differentiating these psychological consequences from other disorders. Finally, the PTSD diagnosis encourages broad theoretical models for explaining the wide variety of symptoms women experience in reaction to violent victimizations.

Research consistently indicates that PTSD is associated with criminal victimization. In a sample of 1,000 adults, victims of physical and sexual assault reported higher current (within the past month) PTSD rates (13% and 14%, respectively) than victims of nonviolent crimes such as robbery (6%) and victims of noncriminal traumatic events such as injury or property damage from fire (6%), natural or man-made disaster (5%), and combat (2%) (Norris, 1992). These differential

TABLE 4.1   Current and Lifetime Posttraumatic Stress Disorder
(PTSD) Rates for Crime and Noncrime Victims

Type of Event	Current PTSD	Lifetime PTSD
Physical assault	18%	39%
Completed rape	12%	32%
Other sexual assault	13%	31%
Indirect victimization via homicide of family member or close friend	9%	22%
Disaster, accident, or other noncrime event	3%	9%

SOURCE: Resnick, Kilpatrick, Dansky, Saunders, and Best (1993). Copyright © 1993 by the American Psychological Association, reprinted with permission of the APA and the author.

rates of PTSD across crime types have also been noted in a sample of more than 4,000 adult women in the United States (Resnick, Kilpatrick, Dansky, Saunders, & Best, 1993). In this study, researchers divided the country into 12 groupings and then used random-digit dialing to select households within each of the 12 groupings. The number of households from each of the 12 groupings was proportional to the population of that grouping. This procedure produces a population-based random sample, meaning that the results can be used to give estimates of the frequency of events within the entire population. Within each of the households contacted, an adult woman was randomly chosen and interviewed. Both current (in the past 6 months) and lifetime PTSD rates were significantly higher for criminal than for noncriminal traumatic events (26% vs. 9%). The highest rates of PTSD (see Table 4.1) were found among victims of physical assault, followed by rape and other sexual assaults (Resnick et al., 1993).

Rape victims in this study were 6 times as likely to develop PTSD as women who had never been victims of crime. Translating these percentages into population estimates, 3.8 million women have had rape-related PTSD, 1.3 million women currently have rape-related PTSD, and 211,000 women can be expected to develop rape-related PTSD each year. Unfortunately, a survey like this one cannot tell us whether the rape incident actually caused the PTSD. As with all correlational studies, some other factor may be at work. For example, women who are likely to become rape victims may already be likely to experience PTSD.

Data from several Epidemiological Catchment Area (ECA) study sites also indicate that victims of sexual assault are at risk for developing PTSD. The purpose of the ECA study, a 5-site collaboration funded by the National Institute of Mental Health (NIMH), was to assess the prevalence and incidence of various psychiatric disorders and the extent to which people seek health services for these disorders. Participants were diagnosed for psychiatric disorders using the Diagnostic Interview Schedule, a clinically administered and highly structured interview instrument. The sample included over 18,000 respondents, aged 18 and older, who were randomly selected from five communities: St. Louis, Missouri; Durham, North Carolina; Los Angeles, California; New Haven, Connecticut; and Baltimore, Maryland.

Among the approximately 3,000 people surveyed in the North Carolina ECA study, 45% of individuals with a history of sexual assault reported PTSD symptoms compared with only 14% of respondents with no history of sexual assault (Davidson, Hughes, George, & Blazer, 1996). In the St. Louis ECA study, approximately 13% of the females and 5% of the males were diagnosed with PTSD. Whereas for males, the highest proportion of PTSD cases were related to combat experiences, for females the highest proportion of PTSD cases were related to physical assaults (Helzer, Robins, & McEvoy, 1987). These rates compare with a 1% prevalence rate of PTSD in the general population.

PTSD rates are even higher when victims are interviewed soon after the crime. In a study of rape victims, 94% met PTSD diagnostic criteria 12 days postassault, and 46% still met the criteria 3 months later (Rothbaum, Foa, Murdock, Riggs, & Walsh, 1992). Researchers found similar high rates in a study with nonsexual assault victims; more than 71% of women and 50% of men were diagnosed with PTSD at 18 days postcrime (Riggs, Rothbaum, & Foa, 1995).

Depression

Generally, victims of violent crime do not experience just one type of psychological distress such as PTSD. Rather, they show elevated symptoms of other indicators of distress such as depression, anxiety, somatization, and hostility. For example, crime victims who developed PTSD were 32 times more likely than nonvictims to meet criteria for major depression, and 7 times more likely than crime victims without PTSD to meet diagnostic criteria for major depression (Kilpatrick & Resnick, 1993).

Depression can include symptoms of depressed or sad mood, a decreased interest in daily activities, insomnia or hypersomnia (increased sleep), fatigue or loss of energy, feelings of worthlessness and guilt, feelings of hopelessness, low self-esteem, and decreased concentration (APA, 1994). Crime victims are at increased risk for experiencing significant depressive symptoms (Burnam et al., 1988; Ellis, Atkeson, & Calhoun, 1981; Sorenson, Stein, Siegel, Golding, & Burnam, 1987). This finding has been reported for both physical and sexual assault victims. In the National Women's Study, which included a national household probability sample of approximately 4,000 adult women, 55% of aggravated assault victims met diagnostic criteria for major depression (Hanson, Kilpatrick, Falsetti, & Resnick, 1995). Regarding sexual assault, in a study of 34 rape victims interviewed within a month following the rape, 44% scored in the moderate to severe depression range (Frank, Turner, & Duffy, 1979).

Sexual assault victims have reported relatively high depression scores in a study conducted at one of the five ECA survey sites. The Los Angeles ECA study site received supplemental funding from the NIMH to include more detailed questions regarding sexual assault. This sample consisted of over 3,000 adults residing in households located in one of two mental health catchment areas in metropolitan Los Angeles. Over half of the sample was female (53%), and the sample was ethnically diverse (40% Mexican American, 6% Hispanics of other cultural origins, 42% non-Hispanic whites, and 12% other). Of the sample, 13% reported having experienced a sexual assault defined as forced or pressured sexual contact. Of these sexual assault victims, 18% reported experiencing a major depressive disorder compared with only 5% of nonvictims (Burnam et al., 1988). However, sexual assault was not associated with depression in the North Carolina ECA study site, although it was associated with PTSD and suicide attempts (Davidson et al., 1996).

Anxiety

Anxiety is another common consequence of violent victimization. It can take the form of generalized anxiety, PTSD, panic disorder, obsessive-compulsive anxiety, or phobias. *Generalized anxiety* includes symptoms of unrealistic or excessive worry, restlessness, feeling shaky, shortness of breath, accelerated heart rate, nausea, difficulty concentrating, irritability, and trouble falling or staying asleep (APA, 1994). A *panic disorder* or panic attack is a discrete period of unexpected, intense discomfort. Attacks typically begin with apprehension and fear coupled with symptoms of shortness of breath, dizziness, accelerated heart beat, trembling, sweating, tingling sensations, or fear of dying (APA, 1994). *Obsessive-compulsive disorder* involves recurrent

TABLE 4.2   Victimization and Suicide

	Suicidal Ideations	Suicide Attempts
Completed rape	44%	19%
Attempted rape	30%	9%
Completed molestation	22%	4%
Attempted molestation	32%	8%
Aggravated assault	15%	4%
Completed robbery	11%	3%
Attempted robbery	9%	12%
Nonvictims	7%	2%

SOURCE: Kilpatrick, Best, et al. (1985). Copyright © 1985 by the American Psychological Association, reprinted with permission of the APA and the author.

intrusive, senseless thoughts (obsessions) and purposeful behaviors that neutralize the obsessive thoughts (compulsions). These obsessions and compulsions are experienced as distressing and may interfere with one's daily functioning (APA, 1994). *Phobias* are persistent fears of a situation or object that cause increased anxiety. The person either endures confrontation of the situation with intense anxiety or tries to avoid the situation (APA, 1994).

Data from the Los Angles ECA study site revealed that respondents who had been sexually assaulted were more likely to experience anxiety disorders than respondents who had not (Burnam et al., 1988; Sorenson et al., 1987). Almost one quarter of respondents who had been sexually assaulted had a diagnosis of phobia, almost 5% had a diagnosis of panic disorder, and 5% had a diagnosis of obsessive-compulsive disorder compared with 10%, 1%, and 1%, respectively, of those who had never been sexually assaulted (Burnam et al., 1988). Sexual assault victims have reported higher anxiety than nonvictims in clinical studies as well. In a longitudinal study of 20 rape victims and 20 matched nonvictim controls, victims reported significantly higher anxiety symptoms than nonvictims at 1 month, 6 months, and 1 year after the rape (Kilpatrick, Resick, & Veronen, 1981).

Suicidal Behavior

Unfortunately, the consequences of violent victimization can be so dire that they result in completed or attempted suicide. The association between violent crime and suicidal behavior has been found in victims of partner violence (Kaslow et al., 1998; Stark & Flitcraft, 1988) and sexual assault victims (Davidson et al., 1996).

In the North Carolina ECA study, those reporting histories of sexual assault were 6 times more likely to have attempted suicide than individuals who had not (Davidson et al., 1996). Similarly, in a sample of over 2,000 women, those with histories of victimization were more likely to report having suicidal ideations and to have attempted suicide following the crime compared with women who had never been criminally victimized (Kilpatrick, Best et al., 1985). Table 4.2 presents the percentages of victims experiencing one or more of the listed crimes who also reported suicidal ideations (i.e., thinking about committing suicide) and suicide attempts.

BEHAVIORAL CONSEQUENCES
OF VIOLENT CRIME

Drug and Alcohol Abuse/Dependence

The association between violent victimization and substance abuse has been documented in both epidemiological and clinical studies. Epidemiological studies generally include large sample sizes and are often representative of the population from which they are drawn. However, epidemiological studies are generally lacking in contextual data, such as detailed information about the crime event and the victim's coping efforts. Clinical studies, on the other hand, typically are composed of smaller samples of people seeking clinical services. They provide richer data on the context of the crime and the victim's coping efforts. Thus, epidemiological studies and clinical studies complement one another because their strengths and weaknesses are complementary, and when these two studies produce similar findings, we can be more confident in the results. Women interviewed in the Los Angeles ECA were twice as likely to have alcohol or drug abuse/dependence disorders if they had experienced a sexual assault in their lifetimes (Burnam et al., 1988; Sorenson et al., 1987). Data from the North Carolina ECA study, in which sexual assault victims were compared with respondents who had never experienced a sexual assault, indicated similar results. Approximately 16% of those who had been sexually assaulted reported drug or alcohol abuse/dependence, compared with 10% of the respondents who had never experienced a sexual assault (Davidson et al., 1996).

In another epidemiological study that interviewed 3,000 adult women representing a cross section of the United States, women who had been criminally victimized were at an increased risk for alcohol and drug abuse problems, even after controlling for the effects of a family history of substance abuse (Kilpatrick, Resnick, Saunders, Best, & Epstein, 1994). This result suggests that a history of criminal victimization is related to serious alcohol and/or drug abuse problems. Because the women in the national probability data set were interviewed three times over a 2-year period, the researchers were able to examine whether victimization was causing women to abuse substances or whether substance-abusing women were at greater risk for victimization. Results revealed that drug use, but not alcohol use, increased a woman's risk for a new assault. Reciprocally, women who were victims of a new assault were at increased risk for developing both alcohol and drug use problems. In other words, these results support a cyclical relationship between substance abuse and victimization (Kilpatrick, Acierno, Resnick, Saunders, & Best, 1997).

Victims interviewed in clinical studies also appear to be at risk for substance abuse. In a sample of 2,322 women seeking medical care from a publicly funded treatment center between 1992 and 1996, women with histories of physical or sexual victimization or both were significantly more likely than women who had never been physically or sexually victimized to have histories of substance abuse (Liebschutz, Mulvey, & Samet, 1997). Almost half (48%) of the women who identified alcohol as their preferred substance had experienced a victimization during their lives, 40% of women who identified crack as their primary substance had been victimized, and 40% of those who identified heroin as their primary substance had been victimized.

Avoidance

In addition to substance use, violent crime affects victims' lifestyles in other ways, especially by causing them to avoid particular people and places. For example, one study asked respondents about the extent to which they avoided other people or places because of the threat of crime (e.g., "During the past 4 weeks, how often did you stay away from certain types of people because of the fear of crime?"). Violent-crime victims were significantly more likely than nonvictims to report increased avoidance behavior, even after taking into account levels of crime in the community and the age, race, sex, and social status of the victims (Thompson & Norris, 1992). Similarly, in a nationally representative survey conducted by the National Crime Victims

Research and Treatment Center (Kilpatrick, Seymour, & Boyle, 1991), 60% of those surveyed reported that they limit the places they go by themselves because of their fear of crime. Of the sample, 32% reported restricting the times and places they go shopping, and 22% reported limiting the times or places they will work.

Among victims of completed and attempted rape, avoidance of social contact and of leaving home were commonly reported ways of dealing with the victimization experience (Scheppele & Bart, 1983). Only 12% of victims reported no change in their behavior. Thirty-three percent reported behavior changes only in situations similar to the one in which the attack occurred (e.g., a woman who was raped while walking home from the bus stop late at night reported changing her schedule so that she did not have to walk home at night alone). Thirty-two percent reported changes in a broader range of situations than the one in which the attack occurred (e.g., a women who was raped in the morning while at home would not ride the bus at night anymore; a woman who was attacked while walking from her car to work changed all the locks on her doors at home). And 23% reported being constantly afraid all the time (e.g., "I'm always afraid someone's out for me now"; "I never walk past a bush anymore"). All of these women reported major disruptions in their lives.

Reporting

Surveys of crime victims allow for determining the proportion of crimes reported to the police as well as determining what factors increase the likelihood that a victim will report the crime. Data from the National Crime Victimization Survey (NCVS) in 1994 indicate that only 42% of violent crimes were reported to the police (U.S. Bureau of Justice Statistics, 1997, Table 91). Reporting of the crime to the police depended on the type of crime experienced. For example, 32% of victims of rape or sexual assault reported the crime to the police, 40% of victims of aggravated and simple assaults, and 55% of victims of robbery. Other factors were related to the likelihood of reporting the crime to the police. Victims who were injured during the crime incident were more likely to report than victims not injured. Female victims of violent crime (44%) were more likely than male victims (40%) to report the crime, black victims were more likely than white victims to report a violent crime, and older victims were more likely than younger victims to report to the police (U.S. Bureau of Justice Statistics, 1997). Chapter 3 presents a detailed discussion of the factors related to victims' decisions to report crimes to the police or not.

Researchers have focused not only on the factors related to a victim's decision to report a crime to the police but also on the psychological consequences of reporting. Some research suggests that victims who report their victimization experiences to the police seem to cope better than those who do not report the crime. For example, in one study of rape victims, women who had reported the rape to the police experienced significantly better adjustment and reported less fear than women who did not report the rape (Cohen & Roth, 1987).

Reporting crimes to the police can help victims cope in several ways (Frieze, Hymer, & Greenberg, 1987). First, a crime must come to the attention of the police for a perpetrator to be charged and prosecuted. If the perpetrator is arrested and subsequently convicted, a victim's sense of injustice can be reduced. Second, if a perpetrator is convicted, a victim's sense of personal safety can be increased. Many victims feel threatened by the idea that perpetrators can come after them again because they know where the victims live or work. Third, even if the perpetrator is not caught, a victim must report a crime to the police soon after the crime occurs to be eligible for victim compensation (e.g., money from insurance companies or money to receive counseling). Receipt of victim compensation may help reduce an individual's sense that the justice system is not designed to help victims, thereby gaining an increased sense of trust in the system.

Medical Use

About 1.4 million people were treated for confirmed or suspected violence-related injuries in 1994 (Rand & Strom, 1997). Overall, crime-related injuries constitute a significant proportion of medical care costs. For example, data from the NCVS indicate that violent crime causes 3% of U.S. medical spending and 14% of injury-related medical spending (Miller, Cohen, & Wiersema, 1996). These figures probably underestimate the extent of violence-related injuries because many victims who are injured do not seek medical care. For example, among rape victims who are injured during the crime, only about half seek formal medical care (Koss, Woodruff, & Koss, 1991).

In one study of the association between criminal victimization and women's medical use, 390 women who received medical coverage from a work-site health maintenance organization were interviewed about their criminal victimization histories and perceived health. Data were also obtained regarding health service use, such as the number of physician visits and outpatient costs. The results indicated that severely victimized females made physician visits twice as frequently as nonvictimized women (approximately six visits a year compared with approximately three visits a year) and had outpatient costs that were 2.5 times as great (Koss, Koss, & Woodruff, 1991). Sexually transmitted diseases have been found to occur among 4% to 30% of rape victims (Murphy, 1990). AIDS is mentioned as a concern by about one fourth (26%) of rape victims (Baker, Burgess, Brickman, & Davis, 1990).

Increased medical use is also apparent among victims of partner violence. In a recent study, 1,152 women 18 to 65 years of age were recruited from family practice clinics and screened for intimate-partner violence during a 5- to 10-minute clinic interview. Follow-up interviews by telephone assessed women's health histories and health status (Coker, Smith, Bethea, King, & McKeown, 2000). Women who reported experiencing either psychological or physical abuse by a partner were significantly more likely than women who did not to report poor physical and mental health. Psychological partner abuse was also associated with an increased likelihood of the following medical diagnoses: disabilities preventing work, chronic neck or back pain, arthritis, migraines, urinary tract infections, chronic pelvic pain, stomach ulcers, spastic colon, frequent indigestion, diarrhea, or constipation. Physical partner abuse was associated with the following: increased likelihood of diagnoses of disabilities preventing work, chronic neck or back pain, arthritis, migraines, stammering or stuttering, eyesight problems, hearing loss, angina, other heart or circulatory problems, bladder/kidney infections, sexually transmitted diseases, hysterectomy, chronic pelvic pain, stomach ulcers, gastric reflux, spastic colon, frequent indigestion, diarrhea, or constipation. The increased risk of these health problems was not associated with age, race, or insurance status.

Severity of criminal victimization is related not only to objective indicators of health status but also to subjective perceptions of health. In primary care settings, women with histories of victimization report more negative health symptoms and perceive their health less favorably (Koss, Koss, & Woodruff, 1991). In terms of rape, victims have been found to report more somatization symptoms than nonvictims, and these somatic problems do not significantly decrease over time (Kilpatrick et al., 1981).

A few studies have examined risk factors for injuries among victimized women. In a case control study conducted at three inner-city emergency departments, females who had been intentionally injured were compared with females who sought care for medical problems not related to violent injury (Grisso et al., 1999). The injured women were more likely than noninjured controls to have male partners who used cocaine, to have male partners who had been arrested, to use alcohol and other drugs themselves, and to reside in neighborhoods characterized by low income, low education, and high rates of residential mobility. Several other risk factors for injuries were identified in another case control study conducted at eight university-affiliated emergency departments (Kyriacou et al., 1999). Women injured following physical assaults by current or former male partners were more likely than women seeking medical services for other conditions to have partners who abused alcohol and other drugs, partners with intermittent employment and recent unemployment, and partners with less than a high school education. In a study that selected respondents from the general population rather than among women seeking medical care, researchers used data from the NCVS to examine risk factors for physical injuries. Women who did not use self-protective behaviors, women assaulted by intimate partners, and women with less than a high school education were at increased risk of injury compared with women without these respective risk factors (Thompson, Simon, Saltzman, & Mercy, 1999).

COGNITIVE CONSEQUENCES OF VIOLENT CRIME

In addition to the emotional and behavioral consequences of violent crime, another set of consequences involves the cognitive schemas or assumptions people hold about themselves, the world, and their relationship to it. These assumptions have been referred to in various ways, such as "structures of meaning" (Marris, 1975), "theories of reality" (Epstein, 1980), and "assumptive worlds" (Parkes, 1975). Much research has focused on how an experience with violent crime can challenge a victim's basic assumptions or cognitions about the world. This research indicates that the resiliency of these cognitions against the negative impact of the crime determines which victims will cope most effectively (Janoff-Bulman & Frieze, 1983; Taylor, 1983). Although these assumptions can be challenged by any type of traumatic event, a human-induced traumatic experience, such as a violent crime, is the most likely to call a survivor's worldview into question (Bettleheim, 1979). Below, we discuss several different types of cognitions and review the literature regarding how these cognitions can be affected by a direct experience with violent crime.

Fear of Crime

Most of the research about the effects of violent victimization on cognitions has to do with fear of crime (see Chapters 2 and 6). Empirical research reveals that fear of crime and a heightened sense of vulnerability may be among the most frequent, salient, and durable responses to an experience with violent crime (Bard & Sangrey, 1986; Calhoun, Atkeson, & Resick, 1982; Greenberg & Ruback, 1992; Skogan, 1987). Sometimes, this fear generalizes to virtually all situations. For example, a rape victim testifying in court reported that if she looked behind her while walking down the street and saw someone, she would cross to the other side of the street (McDonald, 1993). Another female rape victim reported that she is always afraid someone is out to get her. In a phenomenological study of 50 crime victims, fear was found to be a central experience reported by many of the victims. They reported that just thinking about the crime caused them to get frightened. Some victims reported changing the locks on their houses and getting burglar alarms (Fischer, 1984).

Interestingly, crime victims' increased fears are in contrast with the tendencies of nonvictims to underestimate their own vulnerabilities to crime (Perloff, 1983), a tendency that has been termed the *illusion of invulnerability*. When this illusion is challenged by experiences with crime, victims are forced to change their perceptions regarding their personal vulnerability. It is not unusual to hear them say that they never thought they would become crime victims. People who had illusions of invulnerability prior to their victimization experiences may be more likely to report greater postcrime distress than victims who did not have those previous perceptions. For example, they may have all the more difficulty coping with unforeseen, unpredictable, or uncontrollable events (Wortman, 1976).

In a longitudinal study comparing rape victims' with nonvictims' fear of crime, victims reported significantly higher levels of fear than nonvictims at 2-weeks postcrime (Calhoun et al., 1982). Although victims' fear levels declined and stabilized at approximately 2-months postassault, they continued to report significantly greater levels of fear than nonvictims a year after the crime.

Self-Blame/Attributions

When a person becomes a crime victim, one of the first things he or she tends to wonder is, "Why me?" This search to explain the reason for a victimization is part of an attributional process of causal explanation. According to attribution theory, people spontaneously search for causes in stressful circumstances, and these attributions are more closely related to their psychological reactions than their global personality traits. Attribution theory posits three dimensions of attributions: (a) internal/external, (b) stable/unstable, and (c) global/specific. The internal/external domain assesses whether people view the cause of a particular event as related to some characteristic about themselves (internal) or about the environment (external). The stable/unstable domain assesses whether people view the cause of some event as being enduring and consistent over time (stable) or variable and inconsistent (unstable). The global/specific domain assesses the extent to which people view the cause of the event as being generalizable across time and all aspects of their lives (global) or particular to this one time and situation (specific). Attribution theory predicts that making internal, stable, and global attributions for bad events and making external, unstable, and specific attributions for good events is likely to be related to the poorest coping abilities (Abramson, Seligman, & Teasdale, 1978).

There are several attributions a crime victim can make, including self-blaming, blaming the perpetrator, blaming society, or blaming God. Attributions are important because they can affect victims' psychological reactions to the crime and in particular because victims often blame themselves for a crime (Coates, Wortman, & Abbey, 1979; Wortman, 1976). For example, victims of sexual assault have been found to be more likely than nonvictims to attribute causes of bad events (e.g., rape) to internal, stable, and global factors and also more likely to attribute causes of good events to external factors (Gold, 1986). Research has also indicated that self-blame results in greater psychological distress than blaming others or the situation, and thus, self-blame can be considered a maladaptive response (Katz & Burt, 1988; Meyer & Taylor, 1986).

Some research, however, suggests that the *type* of self-blame in which a victim engages may have different implications for coping (Janoff-Bulman, 1982). Thus, it is not enough to examine only whether a victim makes an internal or external attribution. We need to know more about the type of internal attribution a victim makes. That is, victims can blame themselves for doing a particular act, *behavioral self-blame,* or they can blame themselves for their personalities and characters, *characterological self-blame.* Work by Janoff-Bulman (1982) suggests that victims who engage in behavioral self-blame (e.g., "I should not have walked home alone that night") may cope more effectively than victims who engage in characterological self-blame (e.g., "I deserved to be victimized because I am an unworthy person") because behavioral self-blame allows them a sense of control over future crime susceptibility. For example, a rape victim who attributes her victimization to her own behavior may feel less vulnerable to future rape because she believes that if she changes the behavior in question, she can prevent a future rape.

Although this distinction between behavioral self-blame and characterological self-blame makes intuitive sense, other studies have found that both behavioral and characterological self-blame are related to poorer coping (Frazier, 1990; Meyer & Taylor, 1986). For example, a study of rape victims found that any kind of self-blame was strongly associated with depression 3-days postrape, and it did not matter whether this self-blame was behavioral or characterological in nature (Frazier, 1990).

Related to the concept of attributions is the concept of *counterfactual thinking*. Counterfactual thinking entails imagining alternative outcomes of the crime event that are different than those that actually occurred (Roese, 1997). For example, victims who were raped may say to themselves, "At least I didn't get AIDS or get pregnant." Conversely, if victims feel that they could have possibly avoided the crime, they are more likely to have more negative psychological consequences. Interestingly, victims are more likely to have counterfactual thoughts about their own behavior than about the perpetrator's behavior (Davis, Lehman, Wortman, Silver, & Thompson, 1995). That is, rather than imagining what the offender could or should have done differently, victims typically imagine things that they could or should have done differently. Victims are more likely to engage in counterfactual thinking when a particular crime event is unusual and when the crime was a result of doing something (e.g., going to a bar alone at night) rather than not doing something (e.g., failing to notice a perpetrator following them home).

Self-Esteem

A victim's self-esteem is likely to be undermined following an experience with violent crime (Bard & Sangrey, 1986; Janoff-Bulman & Frieze, 1983; Norris & Kaniasty, 1991; Taylor, Wood, & Lichtman, 1983). Positive self-perceptions are one of three types of beliefs challenged by an experience with violent crime (Janoff-Bulman & Frieze, 1983; Taylor et al., 1983). The shattering of a basic belief such as "the self as worthy" may explain a victim's increased psychological distress (Janoff-Bulman & Frieze, 1983). Whereas most individuals view themselves as generally good people, experiences with violent crime can activate negative self-images (Horowitz, Wilner, Marmar, & Krupnick, 1980) and lead victims to question their views of themselves as worthy and good (Janoff-Bulman & Frieze, 1983; Norris & Kaniasty, 1991). In trying to understand why a bad event occurred to them, victims may engage in self-stigmatizing thoughts, such as perceiving themselves as weak or having done something to bring about the traumatic event.

Perceptions of self-worth have been found to be the best discriminators between victims and nonvictims among various traumatic events (Janoff-Bulman, 1989). In a sample of rape victims and nonvictims, victims reported significantly less self-esteem than nonvictims for up to a year after the rape (Murphy et al., 1988). In a comparison of rape and robbery victims, victims of both rape and robbery reported less self-esteem than victims of either rape or robbery alone at 1- and 3-months postassault. By 6-months postcrime, victims of both rape and robbery continued to report lower self-esteem than robbery victims (Resick, 1993).

Low self-esteem is an important predictor of the psychological distress that crime victims experience. For example, in a sample of 181 victims of robbery, burglary, and nonsexual assaults, victims with negative self-perceptions reported significantly more distress at 1-month and 4-months postcrime than victims who reported positive self-perceptions (Davis, Taylor, & Lurigio, 1996).

Meaning and Trust of Others

Theorists have proposed that an important, perhaps critical, task of dealing with trauma is finding meaning in the event. This may take one of two forms: finding significance in the event and understanding the event (Davis, Nolen-Hoeksema, & Larson, 1998). Meaning as significance includes realizing benefits of the traumatic event and gaining an ability to develop new goals and a new, perhaps wiser sense of self. Meaning as understanding is similar to making attributions for the crime event. This entails trying to make sense of the traumatic event—that is, trying to accommodate one's view of the world to fit with the victimization experience. This might take the form of attributing the event to God's will, assuming some degree of personal responsibility for the event's occurrence, or attributing the event to a particular lifestyle or behavior that makes it more understandable. In general, people who make sense of the traumatic event adjust better than those who do not, and this is especially true during the first 6 months (Davis et al., 1998).

According to Erikson (1963), the development of trust is one of the earliest tasks for a young child. This includes trust in one's own perceptions or judgments as well as trust in the benevolence of others. An experience with violent crime may lead to an erosion of trust in other people and undermine the victim's beliefs in the world as meaningful, benign, trustworthy, and predictable (Bard & Sangrey, 1986). When one is victimized, the world does not seem controllable, meaningful, or comprehensible.

A related psychological construct that is relevant for understanding reactions to victimization is *anomie,* which refers to the perception of the world as untrustworthy, a lack of attachment to society, and the feeling of psychic isolation. One study of the psychological consequences of crime found that persons who had been victims of violent crime within the past 6 months were significantly more likely than nonvictims to report higher levels of anomie (Norris & Kaniasty, 1991; Thompson & Norris, 1992). Furthermore, low levels of trust (high anomie) were related to increased levels of psychological distress (Norris & Kaniasty, 1991).

SUMMARY OF AFFECTIVE, BEHAVIORAL, AND COGNITIVE CONSEQUENCES OF VICTIMIZATION

Research on the affective, behavioral, and cognitive consequences of violent victimization suggests that an experience with violent crime has negative effects on victims in all three of these domains. Table 4.3 lists the types of outcomes in each area that researchers have found to be negatively affected by an experience with violent crime.

Long- and Short-Term Consequences

For most crime victims, the psychological consequences of victimization gradually lessen within 6 months of the crime (Atkeson, Calhoun, Resick, & Ellis, 1982; Rothbaum et al., 1992). For example, a longitudinal study of 115 female rape victims and 87 matched controls who were seen at a large public health system hospital found that victims were significantly higher in depressive symptoms than their nonvictim counterparts at 2 weeks, 1 month, and 2 months following

TABLE 4.3 Summary of Emotional, Behavioral, and Cognitive Consequences of Victimization

Affective Consequences	Behavioral Consequences	Cognitive Consequences
↑ PTSD	↑ Drug and alcohol abuse	↑ Fear of crime
↑ Depression	↑ Avoidant behavior	↑ Self-blame/attributions
↑ Anxiety	↑ Medical use	↓ Self-esteem
↑ Suicidal behavior		↓ Meaning/trust

NOTE: ↑ = increase; ↓ = decrease.

the assault. At 2-weeks postassault, 75% of victims fell within the mild to moderate depression range, but by 4-months postassault, victims' depressive symptoms had lessened and were not significantly different from the controls (Atkeson et al., 1982). A similar recovery pattern has been observed for victims of nonsexual assault (Riggs et al., 1995), with most victims showing substantial improvement in symptomatology within 4 months following the crime.

Although most victims improve, in some cases, symptoms may persist for many months or even years (Burnam et al., 1988; Ellis et al., 1981; Hanson, 1990). In one sample of rape victims, symptoms diminished during the first 6 months following the crime, but victims did not return to precrime levels of distress at any time within the 3 years in which assessments were made (Sales, Baum, & Shore, 1984). Thus, although symptoms diminish in severity, they do not fully subside to precrime levels.

Studies with rape victims reveal that many victims continue to manifest PTSD more than a year following the assault (Calhoun et al., 1982; Kilpatrick & Resnick, 1992; Kilpatrick et al., 1981). In addition, although these rape victims' negative psychological symptoms decreased over time, victims still had significantly higher distress levels compared to women with no history of rape at the 1-year follow-up (Kilpatrick et al., 1981).

This pattern appears to be true across crimes. For example, among a randomly selected sample of violent-crime victims, property-crime victims, and nonvictims, crime victims reported levels of distress well above norms for nonpatient adults, although these levels were below norms for psychiatric samples (Norris & Kaniasty, 1994). Of violent-crime victims, 25% reported extremely high distress levels (defined as being higher than 98% of the population), and about 25% showed moderate distress levels (defined as being higher than 84% of the population). The most severe symptoms were avoidance, fear of crime, anxiety, depression, hostility, somatization, and phobic anxiety. Victims' distress levels decreased over time, with the largest decrease occurring between 3- and 9-months postcrime. At 15-months postcrime, 16% of violent-crime victims still showed severe depressive symptoms, and violent-crime victims were still more symptomatic than property-crime victims, who in turn were more symptomatic than nonvictims.

CONTEXTUAL FACTORS
AFFECTING OUTCOMES

Although violent crime has negative effects on victims' emotions, behaviors, and beliefs and these effects may be relatively long-lasting, they are not the same for everyone. What effects a particular victim experiences depends on contextual factors, including the victim's pre- crime functioning, characteristics of the crime, and the type and amount of social support that the victim has.

Precrime Functioning

Although research indicates that a history of violent crime victimization is more prevalent among individuals with mental health problems, it is unclear whether these individuals had the problems prior to their first victimization experience. It could be that mental health problems result from a victimization episode or that mental health problems serve as a risk factor for future victimization (Hanson et al., 1995).

Despite this uncertainty, research shows that precrime mental health problems are a risk factor for increased distress after one does become a crime victim. That is, victims with mental health problems prior to a violent crime will likely have more difficulty coping with a crime than victims without prior mental health problems (Atkeson et al., 1982; Krupnick & Horowitz, 1980; Symonds, 1980).

The strongest evidence for the link between precrime mental health functioning and postcrime coping comes from a longitudinal study of rape victims. Among 115 female rape victims and 87 matched controls, precrime mental health functioning (physical health problems, depression, suidical history, sexual adjustment prior to the rape, anxiety attacks, obsessive-compulsive behaviors, and psychiatric treatment history) was more strongly related to postrape depressive symptoms than to demographic variables or variables associated with the rape or its aftermath (Atkeson et al., 1982).

The strong link between precrime distress symptoms and postcrime symptoms has been replicated in other studies of rape victims (Frank, Turner, Stewart, Jacob, & West, 1981; Sales et al., 1984). In one study, clinical interviews conducted with rape victims indicated that victims who had received prior psychiatric diagnoses were more likely than those who had not to meet clinical criteria for a psychiatric problem at 1-month postrape (Frank & Anderson, 1987). Furthermore, a history of suicide attempts and psychiatric medications were related to higher distress levels at 1-month postrape (Frank et al., 1981). Other research, however, has not supported the link between previctimization adjustment and postcrime psychological distress. In a sample of robbery victims, burglary victims, and nonsexual assault victims, precrime adjustment measures were not related to distress levels at 1-month or 3-month postcrime (Davis et al., 1996). Thus, it appears that precrime mental health functioning may be especially important in the case of rape victims.

Crime Characteristics

Crime-related characteristics, such as the relationship of the victim to the perpetrator, the severity of the offense, the presence of weapons during the assault, and whether or not an injury was sustained by the victim have been found to be associated with postcrime distress levels.

Relationship Between Victim and Perpetrator. Studies that have examined how the victim-perpetrator relationship affects the psychological consequences of crime have produced mixed results. Some studies have found that women sexually assaulted by strangers reported greater distress than victims assaulted by known assailants (Bownes, O'Gorman, & Sayers, 1991; Cascardi, Riggs, Hearst-Ikeda, & Foa, 1996; Girelli, Resick, Marhoefer-Dvorak, & Hutter, 1986; Ruch & Chandler, 1983). Other studies, however, have found that women sexually assaulted by acquaintances report greater distress after the crime than women assaulted by strangers (Burgess & Holmstrom, 1979; Scheppele & Bart, 1983). Still other studies have found no differences in postcrime distress among victims who knew their perpetrators and those who did not (Frank, Turner, & Stewart, 1980; Kilpatrick, Saunders, Veronen, Best, & Von, 1987; Riggs, Kilpatrick, & Resnick, 1992).

There are two possible explanations for these contradictory findings. First, women sexually assaulted by partners or acquaintances may be less likely than women sexually assaulted by strangers to define the event as a sexual assault or rape. That is, women may have higher thresholds for defining events as sexual assaults when they know the perpetrator. Consequently, the same event may be interpreted as a sexual assault according to a woman victimized by a stranger but not according to a woman victimized by a partner. Thus, for women to label an attack by a known assailant as a sexual assault, to consider themselves rape victims, and to be included in the sample, they may have to have experienced more severe and brutal assaults. This explanation would account for the finding that women assaulted by known assailants have greater psychological distress than women assaulted by strangers.

Cascardi et al. (1996) proposed a possible explanation for the reverse finding that women assaulted by strangers report more distress after the crime than women assaulted by known assailants. Women assaulted by known assailants are familiar with their attackers before the crime. Thus, they are less likely to generalize their fear to other men following the attack. Conversely, women assaulted by strangers may generalize their fear to other individuals who have similar attributes as the assailant (e.g., same race or hair color). This generalized fear results in greater PTSD symptoms.

Results are clearer when it comes to looking at how the victim-perpetrator relationship affects physical outcomes. Data from several different sources (e.g., victim surveys or hospital emergency departments) have consistently revealed that women victimized by intimates (e.g., spouses or boyfriends) are significantly more likely to be injured than women victimized by nonintimates (e.g., strangers or acquaintances) (Bachman & Saltzman, 1995; Craven, 1996; Rand & Strom, 1997). Data from the NCVS indicate that whereas 52% of women victimized by an intimate partner or ex-partner sustained a physical injury, only 20% of women victimized by strangers sustained an injury (Bachman & Saltzman, 1995; Craven, 1996). Similarly, emergency room data indicate that over one third of women seeking emergency medical care for violence-related injuries had been injured by a current or former spouse (Rand & Strom, 1997). Women who experience violence perpetrated by intimates are probably more likely to incur an injury compared with women who experience violence perpetrated by nonintimates, because violence perpetrated by intimates is more likely to occur on a chronic basis and to occur in the privacy of the home without bystanders or witnesses. That is, women who have been physically assaulted by the same offender more than once, and women who were physically assaulted in the home are more likely to be injured (Thompson, Simon et al., 1999).

Severity of Offense. As the extent of violence experienced during the crime increases, psychological distress symptoms increase proportionately (Bard & Sangrey, 1986). For example, PTSD rates following nonsexual assaults are significantly lower than PTSD rates following sexual assaults. This difference is likely due to the severity typically associated with rape (Riggs et al., 1995).

Another indicator of severity of an assault is whether or not a victim suffered physical injuries as a result of the victimization. Life threat and injury experienced during the crime place a victim at higher risk for developing PTSD. In a sample of robbery, nonsexual assault, and burglary victims who had reported their crimes to the police, life threat and injury incurred during the commission of the crime significantly predicted distress 3-months postcrime (Davis et al., 1996). Another study found that women who had experienced assaults that entailed life threat and resulted in injury were twice as likely as women who had experienced crimes without those factors to meet criteria for PTSD (Resnick et al., 1993). The threat of death during rape has been found to increase symptom severity, although this relation was found immediately after the crime and at short-term follow-up but not at long-term follow-up (Sales et al., 1984). Moreover, the need for medical care following the assault as well as the presence of medical complications secondary to the rape were strongly related to increased distress at long-term follow-up. In addition, in cases of rape, the strongest crime-related predictor of postrape distress was whether or not penetration had occurred, such that victims who were penetrated during the rape reported the highest levels of distress.

Reviews of the literature suggest that the presence of injury and life threat place victims at an increased risk for developing PTSD (Kilpatrick & Resnick, 1993). Victims who experienced neither life threat nor injury had PTSD rates ranging from 9% to 15% across studies, whereas 35% to 39% of victims who experienced threat but no injury met PTSD criteria, as did 43% of victims who were injured but did not report experiencing life threat. Victims who experienced both injury and life threat were most at risk for developing PTSD: 59% to 66% met diagnostic criteria for PTSD. Thus, life threat and injury independently increased a victim's risk for developing PTSD, and the combination of life threat and injury placed a victim at even higher risk for the disorder.

Prior Victimization. Prior victimization is probably the best predictor of subsequent victimization (Davis, Taylor, & Titus, 1997; Koss & Dinero, 1989; Norris & Kaniasty, 1994). The extent of revictimization of crime victims is reflected in the fact that a small proportion of the population experience a large proportion of the crime incidents (Farrell, 1995). Unfortunately, police records and crime surveys, such as the NCVS and the British Crime Survey (BCS), do not collect reliable data on revictimizations. These sources probably underestimate the extent of revictimization due to a limited number of crime incidents the victim is allowed to report and the number of times a particular victim is surveyed (Farrell, 1995). Data from the BCS conducted in 1992 indicate that 24% of property crime and 54% of personal crime is experienced by people who reported five or more offenses during the past year (Ellingworth, Farrell, & Pease, 1995). Certain types of crime are more likely than others to be repeat victimizations. These crimes include partner violence, racially motivated crimes, physical and sexual abuse of children, burglary, robbery, and car theft (Farrell, Phillips, & Pease, 1995). They are more likely to be repeated because the offender has learned, from experiences with previous offenses, the expected risks and rewards of committing a particular crime against the same victim (Farrell et al., 1995).

Data from the NCVS indicate that rates of assault are higher among persons who have been assaulted previously than among first-time assault victims (Zawitz, 1988). Several studies indicate that women who were sexually abused as children are at increased risk for experiencing revictimization (Follette, Polusny, Bechtle, & Naugle, 1996) such as rape, other types of sexual assault, and partner abuse (Briere & Runtz, 1987). For example, one study found that 56% of women abused in childhood had experienced adult sexual assault compared with 21% of women who were not abused in childhood (Wyatt, Guthrie, & Notgrass, 1992). Some studies of victims of partner violence have found that over half of the women had experienced sexual abuse before the age of 17 (Dutton, Burghardt, Perrin, Chrestman, & Halle, 1994). And 66% of battered women in another sample also reported experiencing prior abuse either in childhood or adulthood (Kemp, Rawlings, & Green, 1991).

Not only is prior victimization related to future risk for victimization but the more victimizations one has experienced, the greater the postcrime distress. That is, multiple victimization experiences seem to have a cumulative effect on posttrauma symptomatology (Ruch, Amedeo, Leon, & Gartrell, 1991). In a retrospective study conducted with rape victims, a prior history of sexual assault was related to higher distress symptoms and rape-related fears (Cohen & Roth, 1987). Longitudinal research indicates that first-time victims may report more distress immediately following a sexual assault, but prior victims manifest increased distress over time, ultimately becoming more distressed than first-time victims (Ruch et al., 1991).

Social Support

In addition to their relationships to precrime functioning and characteristics of the crime, crime victims' coping efforts are embedded within the larger context of social relationships (Janoff-Bulman, 1992). Research indicates that crime victims with adequate social support cope better than crime victims without adequate support (Janoff-Bulman & Frieze, 1983; Silver & Wortman, 1980; Symonds, 1980). For example, in a large representative sample of victims and nonvictims of crime, social support helped both violent-crime victims and property-crime victims cope with their experiences (Kaniasty & Norris, 1992). To investigate the protective role of social support, the study investigators measured three kinds of support: *informational support* (e.g., "There are several people that I trust to help solve my problems"), *emotional support* (e.g., "I feel like I am a person of worth"), and *tangible support* (e.g., "If I needed an emergency loan of $100, there is someone I could get it from"). Victims of violent crime who perceived that informational support was available to them reported lower levels of fear and anxiety than victims who did not. Victims of violent crime who perceived that tangible support was available had lower levels of depression and anxiety than victims who did not. And victims of violent crime who had high levels of emotional support reported lower levels of depression and anxiety than victims who had low levels of emotional support. Victims of property crime who perceived that tangible support was available had lower levels of depression than victims of property crime who did not. Property-crime victims who had high levels of emotional support reported lower levels of hostility than property-crime victims who had low levels of emotional support. Overall, it appears that social support seemed to matter more for violent-crime victims' coping than for property-crime victims' coping.

Although it is common for victims to turn to others for emotional help, they may not be as helpful as victims expect. People tend to see victims as responsible for their fate (Lerner, 1980; Ryan, 1971). Thus, individuals who have not been victimized can maintain their beliefs in their own personal invulnerability (Janoff-Bulman, 1982). Other people may ignore victims completely because they are seen as "losers" (Bard & Sangrey, 1986) or because they are often depressed and most people do not want to be around unhappy people (Coates et al., 1979). As a consequence, victims may be socially isolated at a time when social support is especially important (Symonds, 1980).

Certain types of crimes, such as intimate-partner violence, may be more likely to erode perceptions of social support than other types of crimes. Battered women often experience a lack of tangible support resources (e.g., alternative housing, money, or employment) as well as a lack of emotional support from family and friends (Bowker, 1984; Gelles, 1979; Sullivan, Tan, Basta, Rumptz, & Davidson, 1992). Together, the chronicity of the abuse and the stigmatization that many battered women face or anticipate are likely to result in low levels of perceived social support. Because battered women may perceive themselves as stigmatized if others know of their abuse status, many women in violent relationships may become isolated at a time when support is most needed. For example, in a study of 60 women who had sought help from a battered-women's shelter, not discussing battering with friends and not having contact with family and friends were related to increased depression (Mitchell & Hodson, 1983). Battered women may not seek support because they believe that violence in the home is a private matter or because they are afraid, as a result of their partners' coercive threats, to disclose the violence (Mitchell & Hodson, 1983; Sullivan et al., 1992). In addition, even though battered women seek support, they may not receive the support they need because support providers may blame the victim in order to maintain their own feelings of invulnerability or may feel uncomfortable discussing sensitive and emotionally laden topics (Ryan, 1971; Coates et al., 1979). Furthermore, there may be *provider burnout.* That is, the chronicity of the violence may deplete the support provider's emotional and tangible support resources (Kaniasty & Norris, 1993; Lepore, Evans, & Schneider, 1991). After a long period of time, providers may simply be unable to continue helping the victim.

Social support is important to crime victims because it is related to subsequent psychological functioning. For example, a study examined partner violence and social support among 138 African American women seeking medical care at a large urban hospital. Results indicated that women who had experienced partner violence within the past year had lower levels of perceived social support than women who had not experienced partner violence. This low level of perceived social support was directly related to partner-violence victims having relatively higher psychological distress levels than nonvictims (Thompson,

Kaslow, Kingree, Puett, Thompson, & Meadows, 1999). These findings point to the need for service providers to address the role of social support resources in preventive interventions with victims of violent crime.

POSTCRIME INFLUENCES

After a crime, the victim may have contact with the criminal justice system and mental health agencies. Both are likely to have important impacts on the victim's psychological recovery from the crime.

Interaction With the Criminal Justice System

Although a criminal act typically lasts only a few minutes, if the crime is reported, it may require the victim's involvement with the justice system for years. Research suggests that victimization can cause considerable disenchantment with the justice system and the broader society (Campbell, Sefl et al., 1999; Elias, 1984; Freedy, Resnick, Kilpatrick, Dansky, & Tidwell, 1994; Resick, 1984; Shapland, 1984; Thompson & Norris, 1992). This postvictimization period, in which crime victims come to perceive themselves as neglected and blamed by the criminal justice system and society, has been termed the "second injury" to victims (Symonds, 1980). Although the bulk of the research suggests that crime victims are dissatisfied with their treatment by the justice system, other studies have found that victims report high levels of satisfaction with criminal justice officials (Forst & Hernon, 1985; Sales et al., 1984; Skogan, 1989). Other findings indicate that both conclusions—disenchantment and satisfaction—oversimplify a highly variable and dynamic state of affairs.

Satisfaction with the criminal justice system depends on the type of crime experienced as well as a victim's perceptions of treatment by various players in the criminal justice system (e.g., police, prosecutor, or judge) (Kilpatrick et al., 1987). Satisfaction is relatively low among victims of sexual assault but is higher for victims of robbery and aggravated assault. In addition, research has shown that whether or not an arrest is made is generally less important in improving victim satisfaction than victims' perceptions that the police were keeping them involved and informed (Norris & Thompson, 1993).

Victims' perceptions of how they were treated by justice system personnel seem to be of primary importance in understanding victims' overall satisfaction with the criminal justice system. Because longitudinal research indicates that victims' initial satisfaction declines over the course of a case (Shapland, 1983, 1984, 1985), it is important to consider interactions with personnel at various stages of the criminal justice process.

Police. The manner of the police and whether they appear to take the case seriously are important determinants of victim satisfaction (Lurigio & Mechanic, 2000; Maguire, 1980; Shapland, 1985). Studies suggest that victims are very displeased if the police officer did not listen carefully, did not appear to take some action, or treated the case as routine. Other researchers have found that victims are more likely to be satisfied with police performance when they perceive a high degree of investigative effort (Brandl & Horvath, 1991).

Most studies with direct crime victims have found relatively high levels of satisfaction with the police (Forst & Hernon, 1985). For example, the rape victims in Atlanta assessed at 2-months postassault reported that the police had been concerned and courteous (see Chapter 3). In another study of rape victims, their attitudes toward the police were more favorable than their attitudes toward the legal system in general (Frazier & Haney, 1996), and victims who were relatively satisfied with the police handling of their cases were less likely to be further traumatized. Similarly, among a sample of property- and violent-crime victims, victims who were satisfied with the justice system were less likely than victims who were dissatisfied to report symptoms indicative of alienation (Norris & Thompson, 1993).

Prosecutor. Another frequent finding by researchers is that victims want a larger role in the criminal justice system after an arrest is made. They want to do more than merely report the crime. Specifically, they want to be consulted by the prosecutor at significant stages in the process and to be given more information about the progress of their case in exchange for their time and effort.

Victims' desires for larger roles are consistent with procedures used 250 years ago. In the colonial period, victims of felonies had the right to initiate and prosecute criminal cases against the offender. Victims conducted their own investigations, secured warrants, paid witnesses, and hired private prosecutors to handle their cases (Elias, 1986). Victims could gain compensation from offenders and, if they could afford the cost, they could pay the state to incarcerate offenders. Over time, private prosecutions were replaced by public prosecutors who represented the interests of the public, not the victims. Today, because the defendant is the central figure in public prosecutions, victims often do not know about proceedings that affect the defendant, such as bail hearings to release the defendant before trial and plea negotiations in which the defendant can plead guilty to a reduced charge in exchange for dropping more serious charges. At trial, victims are excluded from the courtroom because it is presumed that their testimony as witnesses may be affected by the testimony of others.

One of the main criticisms victims have about the criminal justice system is the lack of information granted to them concerning their cases and the criminal justice process (Shapland, Willmore, & Duff, 1985; Skogan, 1989). They want to know about the progress of the case, for example, about criminal charges, whether the offender is in custody, whether bail has been set, scheduled court appearances, what will be expected of them in court, and sentencing (Shapland, 1985).

Victims are often frustrated with the handling of their cases (Frazier & Haney, 1996). For example, in the study with rape victims in Atlanta (see Chapter 3), 11% of the victims reported being encouraged by the criminal justice system to drop the charges. This result has unfortunate implications in light of another study of rape victims (Cluss, Boughton, Frank, Stewart, & West, 1983) in which those who decided not to prosecute had lower self-esteem a year after the assault compared with victims who decided to press charges.

Judges. In 1991, victims gained more opportunity to play a role in the criminal justice process when the U.S. Supreme Court ruled that allowing victim impact statements during the sentencing phase of capital trials did not violate the defendant's Eighth Amendment rights (*Payne v. Tennessee,* 1991). A victim impact statement allows victims to tell the jury and judge how the crime has affected them. This new trend gives victims more input into the criminal justice system by allowing them the chance to remind those doing the sentencing that they, as victims, have suffered and that their rights as individuals should be respected as much as the rights of accused offenders (see Chapter 7). According to Kelly and Erez (1997), victim impact statements are now allowed in almost every state. Forty states allow victim participation in parole hearings, and approximately half of the states allow victim participation in plea bargaining.

Victims and their families made emotionally charged statements that attracted national attention in the sentencing of Colin Ferguson, who was convicted of killing 6 individuals and injuring 19 others on a Long Island railroad train in 1993. One of the injured, Kevin McCarthy, a 27-year-old who had been shot in the head and left partially paralyzed—and whose father had been killed—spoke as follows: "Your honor, I was sentenced to a life of pain and suffering because of this one man's actions. I did not have the luxury of a trial or appeal. I was convicted and sentenced by a depraved mad man with an assault gun") ("Put Gunman Away," 1995, p. A8). Ferguson was ordered to serve six consecutive sentences of 25 years to life for the 6 murder charges and an additional 50 years for the 19 counts of attempted murder, 2 weapons charges, and reckless endangerment ("Killer Gets the Maximum," 1995, p. A5).

In a recent study conducted by the National Center for Victims of Crime, 1,308 victims from four states were surveyed regarding their views of the effectiveness of victims' rights laws (Kilpatrick, Beatty, & Howley, 1998). Two of the states were chosen because they were considered "weak" in terms of victims' rights, and two states were selected because they were considered "strong" in terms of victims' rights. Researchers used four criteria to assess whether a state was considered weak or strong: a victim's right to be notified, to be present, to be heard, and to receive restitution. Among the 1,308 victims, 24% had been physically assaulted, 11% had been sexually assaulted, 10% had experienced other crimes, and 30% had lost relatives to homicide. The researchers found that victims in the two strong states were more likely than victims in the two weak states (a) to be notified of events in their cases (e.g., arrest of offender, trial scheduling, or plea bargaining), (b) to be informed of their rights as victims (e.g., right to make a victim impact statement, right to consult with prosecutor), (c) to be informed of the services available to them, (d) to report that the system was responsive to their needs (e.g., efforts to catch the offender or fairness and speed of trial), and (e) to be satisfied with the criminal justice system and its personnel. In addition, victims from strong states were more likely to exercise many of these rights, including making recommendations at a bond hearing, testifying in court, making recommendations about sentencing, and making victim impact statements. However, the researchers cautioned that even though victims from strong states were more likely to exercise their rights and to be satisfied with the justice system, over one quarter of victims from strong states were dissatisfied, indicating that legal protection does not ensure that victims' rights will be protected.

How do these participatory rights affect victims' satisfaction with the justice system and coping with victimization? Studies have produced mixed findings (Kelly & Erez, 1997). Some researchers have found that victims who participated in the justice process had higher satisfaction with the system than victims who did not participate (Erez & Tontodonato, 1992). Other studies, however, found no effects of victim participation on victims' satisfaction (Davis & Smith, 1994). Although there is little research on how increased victim participation affects the way they cope with their experiences, results suggest that increased victim participation does not directly influence their distress levels.

In one study, however, victims of nonstranger rape who received little assistance from the legal system and who encountered victim-blaming attitudes had higher posttraumatic stress scores than both victims of stranger rapes regardless of their experiences with the legal system and victims of nonstranger rapes who reported favorable receipt of services and interactions with system personnel. Furthermore, victims of nonstranger rape who received little help from the legal system and who encountered victim-blaming attitudes had the highest level of posttraumatic stress symptoms in the sample (Campbell, Sefl et al., 1999). Increased participation in the criminal justice system may indirectly help victims cope with the crime by influencing their sense of justice and fairness (Kelly & Erez, 1997).

Interaction With Mental Health Agencies

A key variable in coping with trauma is the extent to which people discuss and confront their traumatic experiences. Across several correlational studies, findings suggest that not confiding or not discussing one's experience of a traumatic event is related to worse physical health and greater psychological distress (Pennebaker & O'Heeron, 1984; Pennebaker & Susman, 1988). These findings suggest that seeking mental health services would be beneficial for crime victims.

Data from a study of the psychological consequences of criminal victimization indicate that about 1 in 6 crime victims seek professional mental health services within the first year after the crime (Norris, Kaniasty, & Scheer, 1990). In that study, victims of violent crime were more likely than victims of property crime to have sought professional mental help as well as other kinds of professional help. Almost one quarter (23%) of violent-crime victims had sought help from a mental health professional, whereas only 7% of property-crime victims had sought mental health services. Over one fifth (21%) of violent-crime victims had sought help from a clergy person compared with 7% of property-crime victims. Victims of violent crime were also more likely than victims of property crime to seek help from a lawyer or legal aid as well as from a medical doctor. Unfortunately, although slightly over half (56%) of property crime victims reported that the help they received was "very helpful," only 27% of violent-crime victims reported this degree of service satisfaction. In addition, violent-crime victims reported higher mental health services usage rates than rates reported in the general population (Norris et al., 1990), and lower satisfaction rates than service users in the general population (Norris, Kaniasty, & Thompson, 1997). In sum, whereas victims of violent crime are more likely than victims of property crime to use mental health services, they are less likely to be satisfied with these services.

Similar evidence comes from surveys of mental health professionals. A survey of a nationally representative sample of psychiatrists, psychologists, clinical social workers, mental health counselors, pastoral counselors, and marriage and family counselors indicates that annual victim-related mental health care expenditures are somewhere between $5.8 and $6.8 billion (Cohen & Miller, 1998). This survey of mental health professionals also suggests that the number of mental health care visits per year is about 25 to 30 for crime victims compared with 12 to 14 for nonvictims. In other words, crime victims appear to suffer more emotional distress, and this distress requires more professional care.

That victims of serious violent crime are more likely to seek mental health services than victims of nonviolent crimes was corroborated in a study on the mental health status and service use among 251 recent crime victims (Freedy et al., 1994). Whereas 63% of sexual assault victims and 22% of physical assault victims received mental health services, only 4% of robbery victims and 14% of burglary victims received any mental health care.

Several factors have been found to predict who among recent crime victims would use mental health services. In one study, victims with higher levels of depression and victims who had been violently victimized were more likely to seek mental health care than their respective counterparts (Norris et al., 1997). Consistent with the finding about depression, among 181 clients at an outpatient mental health clinic in a midsized city, those with PTSD were significantly more likely to use both inpatient and outpatient mental health services (Switzer et al., 1999).

Other factors that predicted mental health care use included whether the victim had had previous victimization experiences and the level of social support from family and friends. Victims who had been previously victimized were more likely than first-time victims to seek mental health care. Surprisingly, victims who reported receiving support from family and friends were more likely to seek mental health care than victims with lower levels of social support from family members and friends (Norris et al., 1997). Predicting use of mental health services following a victimization is important for intervention strategies because mental health care has been found to predict reduction in symptoms—but only when the help was sought immediately and was at least 6 months in duration (Norris et al., 1990; Norris et al., 1997).

Once victims seek treatment, the type of mental health care they may receive can vary greatly. In the past, mental health practitioners took a crisis-oriented approach (Falsetti & Resnick, 1995), which generally meant providing the victims with information and referrals. This did not entail intensive or long-term focus on the victim's psychological symptoms. For example, crisis intervention in the case of partner violence would entail helping the victim find shelter for the night and get a restraining order, and providing information on legal aid. Crisis intervention is not intended to be intensive or long-term and is thus not sufficient treatment for victims with more serious postcrime symptoms of distress. However, given that crisis intervention may be the only contact many victims have with a mental health professional, it is a viable option for those who do not need more in-depth care or could be referred elsewhere if they did require such services (Falsetti & Resnick, 1995).

Because PTSD has become a clinically diagnostic disorder and research has shown that PTSD is a common postcrime consequence, clinicians have begun to focus more on treating PTSD symptoms and not merely providing crisis intervention (Falsetti & Resnick, 1995). In recent years, several theoretically and empirically based treatments have emerged for victims of violent crime. Most of these treatment plans are known as *cognitive-behavioral interventions,* which include exposure therapy, anxiety management, and cognitive therapy (Foa & Rothbaum, 1998) and are discussed next.

Other treatments include hypnotherapy and pharmacological treatments (Foa and Rothbaum, 1998). Briefly, hypnotherapy, which can be traced back to Freud, is used to help the victim recall traumatic events. Although a few clinical case reports indicate that hypnotherapy may be useful in treating PTSD symptoms, few—if any—methodologically sound studies have been conducted on hypnotherapy's effectiveness (Foa & Rothbaum, 1998). Pharmacological treatments entail the use of medications, such as antidepressants, to help alleviate PTSD symptoms. In general, studies indicate that these drugs can have beneficial effects on PTSD symptoms (Foa & Rothbaum, 1998).

Exposure Therapy. Exposure therapy has been frequently used with Vietnam veterans and has generally been considered successful in ameliorating PTSD symptoms. In exposure therapy, clients confront their victimization experience by activating trauma memories. Exposure can occur via imagination or can entail actually confronting real situations, referred to as *in vivo exposure*. In both types of exposure therapy techniques, victims are exposed to the traumatic material in gradual steps until the PTSD symptoms decrease. This procedure has been compared to watching a scary movie repeatedly, until one is no longer frightened by it (Falsetti & Resnick, 1995). With in vivo exposure, victims may be asked to go back physically to the place where they were victimized. Falsetti and Resnick (1995) give the example of a woman raped in a parking garage who was not immediately taken back to that same parking garage but did gradually increase her exposure to cues that served as reminders of the traumatic memory. For example, a victim and her therapist may first sit in a car together in a different parking garage than the one where the attack occurred, then sit in a car together in the parking garage where the attack occurred, and then walk around together in the parking garage. Finally, the victim should be able to go to the same parking garage by herself. These steps would occur gradually until the victim felt that she had confronted her traumatic memory and no longer experienced overwhelming fear and PTSD symptoms.

In a study testing the effectiveness of exposure therapy, female rape victims were randomly assigned to exposure therapy, supportive counseling, stress-inoculation training (discussed below), or a waiting list (no treatment) (Foa, Rothbaum, Riggs, & Murdock, 1991). Females who received exposure therapy or stress-inoculation training showed reductions immediately following the treatment in all three clusters of PTSD symptoms (affective, cognitive, and arousal), whereas those who received supportive counseling showed reductions only in PTSD arousal symptoms. At follow-up, 50% of those who received exposure therapy no longer met criteria for PTSD, 50% of those who received stress inoculation training no longer had clinically significant PTSD, and 45% of those who received supportive counseling no longer had PTSD.

Another form of exposure therapy is systematic desensitization. In systematic desensitization, the therapist asks the victim to imagine the victimization experience in gradual steps, starting with the least distressing memory, while simultaneously engaging in relaxation techniques.

Stress-Inoculation Training. Stress-inoculation training first emerged in the 1970s (Meichenbaum, 1974) and is considered an anxiety management technique. That is, rather than trying to ameliorate anxiety and fear symptoms, stress inoculation attempts to train victims to manage their anxiety and fear symptoms more effectively. The technique involves three phases: education, skill building, and application. In the educational phase, the therapist describes the rationale for the treatment approach to the victim and explains how fear develops as a conditioned response to a stimulus. While practicing muscle relaxation, victims are asked to identify cues that promote fear responses. During the skill-building phase, victims are taught various strategies, including deep breathing, thought stopping, guided self-dialogue, and role-playing (Falsetti & Resnick, 1995). During the application phase, victims apply the skills they learned in the previous phase to manage fear responses.

Stress-inoculation training has been used with rape victims, and studies generally indicate that it is somewhat successful. In a study in which rape victims were given the choice of receiving stress-inoculation treatment or peer counseling, 70% chose stress-inoculation training. The study results indicated that victims who received stress-inoculation training showed significant reductions in fear, anxiety, and PTSD symptoms both immediately following the intervention and 3 months later (Veronen & Kilpatrick, 1983). No comparisons were made, however, to the peer counseling group because too few clients were in that group. In another study in which stress inoculation was compared with assertion training, supportive counseling, and a no-treatment control group, all three treatments helped reduce rape-related fears and depression and improve self-esteem. However, 6 months after the treatment, only reductions in rape-related fears were maintained (Resick, Jordan, Girelli, Hutter, & Marhoefer-Dvorak, 1988).

Cognitive Processing Therapy. Cognitive processing therapy was developed for rape victims suffering from PTSD symptoms (Resick & Schnicke, 1992). This treatment approach not only focuses on fear and anxiety symptoms but also on other cognitive effects of rape victimization, such as shame, anger, and disgust. Although cognitive processing therapy entails some elements of exposure therapy, the primary emphasis is on helping the victim accommodate cognitive schemas that were disrupted by the rape event. Individual or group sessions are used, and treatment takes the form of (a) writing assignments about the event (exposure), (b) education about how the rape may potentially alter the victim's schemas about safety, trust, power, self-esteem, and intimacy, and (c) training in identifying how these schema changes affect emotional well-being (Falsetti & Resnick, 1995; Resick & Schnicke, 1992).

In a study in which 19 sexual assault victims received cognitive processing therapy, the victim's depression and PTSD symptoms significantly decreased after the treatment relative to a waiting-list control group. PTSD rates decreased from 90% before the treatment to 0% 6 months after the treatment, and major depression rates decreased from 62% to 42% (Resick & Schnicke, 1992).

Although many psychologists have devoted much of their clinical work to survivors of victimization, data in one study conducted in Illinois indicate that mental health professionals may not be receiving adequate training on violence against women (Campbell, Raja, & Grining, 1999). These results indicate that 78% of mental health professionals surveyed have received training on child sexual abuse/incest, 56% have received training on sexual assault, 59% have received training on domestic violence, and only 36% have received training on sexual harassment. Furthermore, survey results indicate that most training is elective rather than mandatory. Last, mental health providers report having received training on referral sources for victims and on therapy modalities but not in the areas of legal and medical consequences of victimization.

SPECIAL POPULATIONS

The social and psychological effects of victimization are generally the same for most crimes although they are more serious for more serious crimes. These effects are often more complicated for certain types of victims. Here, we consider two different types of victims: children and victims of partner violence.

Children and Youths

Mortality data reveal that the burden of violent crime falls on the young. In 1996, homicide was the second leading cause of death among youths 15 to 24 years of age, the third leading cause of death among youths 1 to 4 years of age, and the fourth leading cause of death among children 5 to 14 years of age (Centers for Disease Control and Prevention, 2000).

In terms of nonfatal violent victimization among youth, approximately one third of victims of violent crime are between 12 and 19 years of age. Furthermore, although youths 12 to 24 years of age compose 23% of the U.S. population, they were victims of 49% of the violent crimes in 1994 (U.S. Bureau of Justice Statistics, 1997). Data from other national surveys reveal that approximately 1.5 million children have experienced physical abuse (Straus & Gelles, 1990), and almost a half million children are sexually abused prior to 18 years of age (Sedlak, 1991).

As with adult samples, exposure to victimization among youths is related to negative psychosocial sequelae. In a national telephone sample of youths 10 to 16 years of age, those who reported victimization experiences were more likely than their nonvictimized counterparts to manifest significant psychological and behavioral symptoms (Boney-McCoy & Finkelhor, 1995). In a study of children hospitalized on a psychiatric unit, suicidal children were more likely than their nonsuicidal counterparts to report that their fathers were abusive (Myers, Burke, & McCauley, 1985). In another study, 68 children, their parents, and their teachers were interviewed about the children's life events and current well-being. Children who had been maltreated (defined as having a record of physical abuse with protective services) were more likely than nonmaltreated children to be rated by both their parents and their teachers as having lower levels of social competence (Levendosky, Okun, & Parker, 1995). There is also evidence that children who are chronically bullied by others tend to suffer from physical and psychological problems, to have difficulty concentrating on their schoolwork, and to be afraid to go to school (Bernstein & Watson, 1997).

Sexual and physical abuse experienced during childhood not only have short-term negative consequences but also have long-term negative effects on mental health (Burnam et al., 1988; Polusny & Follette, 1995; Wolfe, Sas, & Wekerle, 1994). Most of these findings come from retrospective studies conducted with adults who were victimized as children. For example, in a sample of adult female victims of childhood sexual abuse, 87% evidenced PTSD compared with only 19% of a nonvictimized comparison group (Rodriguez, Ryan, Kemp, & Foy, 1997). Compared with their nonabused peers, sexually abused children are at 4 times the lifetime risk for any psychiatric disorder and 3 times the risk for substance abuse problems (Finkelhor & Dziuba-Leatherman, 1994a). Also, women who were sexually abused as children are at risk for revictimization in adulthood (Messman & Long, 1996). Physical abuse during childhood has been associated with high rates of depression, impaired self-esteem in adulthood, and discordant and violent adult relationships (Briere & Runtz, 1990; Fox & Gilbert, 1994).

In addition to long-term consequences on mental health, childhood maltreatment also may have long-term effects on physical health. Approximately 2,000 women 18 to 65 years of age were randomly selected from a health maintenance organization (HMO) database and were mailed questionnaires designed to assess maltreatment that had occurred in childhood (Walker et al., 1999). Using medical care use and cost data from an automated cost-accounting system of the HMO, the researchers found that women who had experienced maltreatment (scores above clinical cutoff points for either sexual abuse, physical abuse, emotional abuse, emotional neglect, or physical neglect) had median annual health care costs that were $97 greater than women who did not report maltreatment. When mental health care costs were removed from the total health costs, women who reported any maltreatment still had health care costs $55 higher than women who reported no maltreatment, and women who reported sexual abuse had health care costs $119 higher than women who were not maltreated in childhood. In terms of health care use, women who reported sexual abuse in childhood were almost twice as likely as women who did not to have visited the emergency department in the 5 years preceding the study. Women who experienced any form of child maltreatment were twice as likely as those who had not to have received mental health care during the 5 years before the study. These data indicate that the negative sequelae of child maltreatment can have long-term mental health consequences as well as long-term physical health consequences.

In one of the most scientifically rigorous studies on the effects of victimization in childhood, Widom (1989a) prospectively assessed children who had been abused or neglected. Her study used a matched cohort design, which means that both cases and controls were free of the negative outcome (e.g., delinquency) assessed at the time they were selected for study participation. All cases ($n = 908$) of physical abuse, sexual abuse, and neglect that were validated by the court were included in the sample. Controls were matched to the cases on age, sex, race, and approximate family socioeconomic status. Measures of delinquency, adult criminality, and violent criminal behavior were assessed approximately 20 years later using law enforcement records. Whereas 8% of the control subjects had been arrested for a violent offense, 16% of those who had been physically abused in childhood and 13% of those who had been neglected had been arrested for a violent offense.

A second phase of the study was then conducted, in which 79% of the original sample were interviewed in person approximately 20 years after their childhood victimizations. Results revealed that individuals who had been abused or neglected in childhood were more likely than demographically similar individuals who had not been abused to evidence violent behavior 20 years later (Weiler & Widom, 1996). Abused or neglected individuals were also more likely than controls to evidence psychological problems 20 years later, and these symptoms accounted for their relatively higher levels of violence in adulthood. Of the reinterviewed sample, 38% of those who had experienced sexual abuse in childhood, 33% of those who had experienced physical abuse in childhood, and 31% of those who had experienced neglect in childhood met diagnostic criteria for PTSD (Widom, 1999b). Results also revealed that females—but not males—who had experienced abuse or neglect in childhood were significantly more likely than controls to have substance abuse/dependence diagnoses (Widom & White, 1997). Whereas abuse or neglect in childhood was not prospectively related to drug abuse, both males and females who met diagnostic criteria for lifetime and current drug abuse/dependence were significantly more likely to report childhood histories of abuse and neglect than their counterparts who did not have substance abuse diagnoses (Widom, Weiler, & Cottler, 1999). Abuse or neglect in childhood was also, 20 years later, related to poorer academic and intellectual outcomes as well as personality disorders. Individuals who had been abused and neglected in childhood had significantly lower IQ scores (about 1 standard deviation difference) than individuals not abused or neglected in childhood (Perez & Widom, 1994). Furthermore, individuals neglected in childhood were more likely than those not neglected to be diagnosed with antisocial, borderline, narcissistic, paranoid, schizotypal, avoidant, dependent, and passive-aggressive personality disorders (Widom, 1999a). Early childhood victimization was also significantly associated with increased risk for prostitution among females but not males (Widom & Kuhns, 1996).

Partner Violence

Partner violence represents a serious public health problem in the United States. Approximately 30% of all females murdered in the United States are killed by their male partners (Federal Bureau of Investigation, 1999). The statistics for nonfatal injuries are just as staggering: 22% to 35% of women who seek medical emergency care present injuries or symptoms sustained at the hands of their male partners

(Stark & Flitcraft, 1996). Medical costs due to injuries resulting from domestic violence have been conservatively estimated at $44 million per year (Randall, 1990). These figures have particular public health significance given the high prevalence of partner abuse: 3 to 4 million women in this country are battered by male partners, and 21% to 34% of women will be physically assaulted by a male partner during the course of their lifetimes (Browne, 1993; Sassetti, 1993).

Although women are less likely than men to experience violent crimes, women are 5 to 8 times more likely than men to be victimized by intimate partners (Greenfeld et al., 1998). Also, women are approximately 4 times more likely to be killed by their male partners than by strangers (Kellermann & Mercy, 1992). Whereas partner violence accounts for 2% of the violence experienced by males, it accounts for 21% of the violence experienced by females (Greenfeld et al., 1998).

The psychological consequences of partner abuse parallel the reactions found among other types of crime victims (Council on Scientific Affairs, 1992). These psychological symptoms include depression, anxiety, suicidal ideation, low self-esteem, hopelessness, fear, social isolation, decreased trust, and PTSD (Browne, 1993; Cascardi, O' Leary, Lawrence, & Schlee, 1995; Dutton, 1992; Goodman et al., 1993; Houskamp & Foy, 1991; Kemp et al., 1991).

Many researchers have found that victims of partner violence are at risk for developing PTSD symptoms. In a study of battered women residing in a shelter, 84% of the sample met criteria for PTSD (Kemp et al., 1991). In another small-scale study of battered women, 45% showed symptoms consistent with a PTSD diagnosis, and a dose relation was found between PTSD symptoms and extent of exposure to violence; that is, women exposed to higher levels of violence manifested more symptoms associated with PTSD (Houskamp & Foy, 1991). Similarly, in a sample of predominately low-income minority women living in an urban area, women who met criteria for current PTSD were 3 times as likely as women without current PTSD to have experienced physical partner abuse within the past year. However, PTSD and nonphysical partner abuse, such as emotional and psychological abuse, were not significantly associated (Thompson, Kaslow et al., 1999). In a sample of 92 women who sought treatment for marital problems and who were physically victimized by their spouses, 30% met diagnostic criteria for PTSD, and 32% met diagnostic criteria for major depressive disorder. Women who met criteria for both disorders or PTSD only were more likely to report higher levels of fear of their partners and higher levels of physical violence than women who met criteria only for major depression. Thus, although different types of post-victimization symptoms may correlate, the factors that lead to the disorders may differ (Cascardi, O' Leary, & Schlee, 1999).

Women who are abused by their partners are more likely than nonabused women to have made suicide attempts. For example, in a large sample of women seeking medical care at hospital emergency departments (Abbott, Johnson, Koziol-McLain, & Lowenstein, 1995), those who reported experiencing prior partner violence were more likely than women who had never experienced partner violence to have made suicide attempts (26% vs. 8%). Of the women who reported prior suicide attempts, 81% had been victims of partner violence at some point in their lives (Abbott et al., 1995). In another study, 200 women who received medical care at an inner-city hospital emergency department following a nonfatal suicide attempt were approximately 4 times as likely to report being victims of physical partner abuse compared with 200 women who sought routine medical care at the same hospital (Kaslow et al., 1998).

Although victims of partner violence share many of the same psychological consequences as victims of crimes perpetrated by nonpartners, they are more likely to suffer ongoing violence. Data from the National Violence Against Women Survey (NVAWS) (Tjaden & Thoennes, 2000) indicate that among women physically assaulted by their partners, the average frequency of assaults was 7.1 incidents. Data from the NCVS also indicate high chronicity for women who have been raped by their spouses (Mahoney, 1999). Of women raped by spouses, 65% had experienced more than one similar attack in the preceding 6 months, compared with 9% of women raped by strangers, and 12% of women raped by acquaintances. Almost 20% of women raped by spouses had experienced more than 10 sexual assaults in the preceding 6 months.

Other studies have found similar results. In one study involving a random sample of 930 women in the San Francisco area, women who had been raped by strangers reported an average of 1.3 rapes each, women raped by acquaintances or friends reported an average of 1.4 rapes each, but women raped by spouses or ex-spouses reported an average of 13.2 rapes each (Russell, 1990). Similarly, Finkelhor and Yllö (1985) interviewed 50 women who had been raped by their husbands and found that half of these women had been raped at least 20 times by their spouses.

The chronicity of violence experienced by victims of partner abuse not only exacerbates the negative psychological sequelae of the trauma (Browne, 1993) but also results in increased safety concerns and increased escalation of violence severity. Data from the NVAWS (Tjaden

& Thoennes, 2000) indicate that 33% of females physically assaulted by male partners reported that their partners had threatened to harm or kill them, and 45% reported fearing bodily injury or death. Of women physically assaulted by male partners, 42% were physically injured, and 11% sought medical care. Of those who sought medical care, 9% were hospitalized for injuries inflicted by their partners (Tjaden & Thoennes, 2000). Approximately 20% of emergency department visits made by women involve partner violence (Rand & Strom, 1997).

Many people wonder why women victimized by male partners do not leave the abusive relationships. There are likely many reasons why many women stay with their abusive partner, such as a lack of material resources, social and familial pressures to stay together, love for the offender, low self-esteem, and shame. It is also important to realize that women may stay with their abusive partners because of concerns for their own safety and their children's safety. These are realistic because research suggests that women may be most at risk for injury and death when they leave or try to leave abusive partners (Wilson & Daly, 1995).

In one study, risk factors for reported physical, sexual, or acute trauma from partner abuse were assessed using data from 3,455 women who came to 1 of 11 emergency departments between 1995 and 1997. Women who had ended a relationship within the past year were 7 times more likely to have experienced physical abuse within the past year compared with women who had not recently ended a relationship (Dearwater et al., 1998). Thus, abused women find themselves in a situation in which fear of retaliation is an obstacle to extricating themselves from abusive environments, yet staying may result in experiencing increasing levels of violence due to the escalation of violence common to many abusive relationships.

SUMMARY

In this chapter, we discussed the affective, behavioral, and cognitive consequences of violent victimization on direct crime victims. First, we discussed studies that documented the increased likelihood for violent-crime victims to experience affective consequences such as PTSD, depression, anxiety, and suicidal behavior. Next, we discussed studies that found significant associations between violent victimization and behavioral consequences such as drug and alcohol problems, avoidance behavior, and medical use. Third, we discussed studies that documented some of the cognitive consequences of violent victimization such as an increased fear of crime, increased self-blame, decreased self-esteem, and decreased trust of others and meaning in the world. Whereas for most crime victims, these negative consequences of victimization gradually lessen within 6 months, in some cases, symptoms may persist for years. Next, we described some of the contextual factors that affect the outcomes of victimization. These included social support, precrime mental health functioning, crime characteristics such as the victim-perpetrator relationship and the severity of the offense, and prior victimization experiences. Finally, we discussed some of the postcrime influences on victimization consequences such as interactions with the criminal justice system and receipt of mental health services.

In the next chapter, we examine how violent victimizations affect the people with whom victims come into contact, especially their families, friends, and neighbors.

Box 4.1

DISTRESS FROM A BURGLARY VICTIMIZATION

Although this book focuses on violent crime, it is important to note that property crimes, particularly burglary, can also be stressful (Friedman, Bischoff, Davis, & Person, 1982). In 1998, there were more than 4 million household burglaries (Rennison, 1999): 3.4 million were completed crimes in which the offender entered the home unlawfully, and an additional approximately .7 million involved attempted forcible entry. Burglary rates are twice as high in households with annual incomes less than $15,000 as in households with annual incomes of more than $35,000.

In many ways, burglary victims are like victims of violent crime. Like rape victims, they often feel violated and distrusting of others (Maguire, 1980). They experience fear, anger, anxiety, sadness, surprise, and self-blame (Davis & Friedman, 1985; Waller & Okihiro, 1978). Furthermore, as the cartoon below illustrates, burglary victims often engage in counterfactual thinking, for example, by thinking that the outcome could have been much worse.

SALLY FORTH

Counterfactual Thinking After a Burglary

SOURCE: Reprinted with special permission of King Features Syndicate.

Burglary is distressing for three reasons. First, it makes people feel unsafe in the location where they have the highest expectations of being safe. Locations such as the home are called "primary territories" (Altman, 1975, p. 112), meaning that they are used exclusively by the residents, controlled on a relatively permanent basis, and central to the lives of the individuals who live there. Given that access is highly controlled and unpermitted, entry is seen as a serious violation, especially because residents' assumptions of personal invulnerability are likely to be highest when they are in their homes. Thus, when their expectations are violated, they are likely to feel especially vulnerable and fearful. Moreover, the greater the degree of territorial violation (e.g., ransacking of the home), the more victims are upset and the more vulnerable they feel (Brown & Harris, 1989). Second, burglaries often involve the loss of valuable possessions either because they are expensive or because they have high sentimental value and are irreplaceable (e.g., a grandmother's wedding ring). Third, burglary victims feel distressed because they are vulnerable to future victimization. And because burglary has the potential to develop into serious personal crimes (e.g., rape, robbery, or murder), this fear of revictimization can be strong.

Burglary victims' perceived vulnerability to future victimization makes sense. Studies from the United Kingdom and from Canada indicate a high risk of burglary revictimization within about 4 months of the first crime (Pease & Laycock, 1996). This period of increased risk is somewhat longer than for other crimes, probably because of an "insurance effect." That is, at about 4 months after a burglary, householders with insurance often have replaced their goods, and burglars can be confident that new goods will be available. Repeat burglary victimizations make sense from the perspective of the burglar because the factors that made the house an attractive target initially continue to be operating and the burglar is familiar with getting into and out of the house and with any personal property still left in the house (Pease & Laycock, 1996).

In response to burglary victimizations, victims are likely to call the police because insurance companies require a police report before reimbursing policyholders for their losses. However, because burglaries are so upsetting, victims often call the police even if the value of the stolen property is less than the insurance deductible (Ruback, Greenberg, & Westcott, 1981). If the police are supportive after the victimization (e.g., provide crime prevention information or perform a security check), victims are likely to cope better with the crime (e.g., lower fear and anger) and to have more positive attitudes toward the police (Winkel & Vrij, 1993), although some interventions may lead to greater fear of a future victimization (Van den Bogaard & Wiegman, 1991). In addition to calling the police, burglary victims may also take action to prevent the reoccurrence of the crime, including installing security systems that include burglar bars, alarms, and lighting.

Aside from installing security systems, burglary victims may be more likely to stay inside their homes. One effect of this behavior may be less surveillance of the streets, which, in turn, may mean that criminals are less fearful of being caught. Thus, with fewer "eyes on the street," the neighborhood may be less safe (Shotland & Goodstein, 1984). There is also some evidence that burglaries in a neighborhood may increase the likelihood that people will move (Dugan, 1999).

▣ DISCUSSION QUESTIONS

1. Most of the research on the consequences of victimization uses PTSD as the outcome measure. Why? Should future research include measures of other outcomes?

2. Determining the effects of victimization on distress can be difficult because it can be unclear whether the victimization caused the distress, the distress caused the victimization, or some other factor caused both the distress and the victimization. How can this problem be overcome? Related to this same issue is the question of how to measure the long-term effects of childhood victimization. Most studies have been retrospective, whereas Widom's research was a prospective study that followed abused children for 20 years.

3. After being victimized, not all crime victims seek help, either from family and friends or from mental health care professionals. What characteristics predict who is likely to seek mental health care? Should all victims be encouraged to seek such help?

4. One of the unique features of partner violence is the chronicity of the violence at the hands of the same perpetrator. What are the effects of this chronicity on women victimized by partners?

5. Why should victims have the right to testify at sentencing? Are some victims worth more than others? Does it really make any difference whether victims testify at sentencing or parole hearings?

5 ⠿

Secondary Victimization

The Effects of Violence on Family Members, Friends, Neighbors, and Professionals

Although there has been extensive research on the psychological consequences of violent crime on direct victims, less attention has been given to the consequences of violence on secondary or indirect victims (e.g., spouses of war and rape victims, family members of homicide victims, and witnesses of violence). In this chapter, we first provide a general overview of secondary victimization. Second, we discuss the effects of violent crime on secondary victims, including family members, friends, neighbors, and coworkers of victims of nonhomicidal crimes; family members of homicide victims; children who witness domestic and community violence; and professionals who work with crime victims. As in Chapter 4, we discuss the effects of secondary victimization on affect, cognitions, and behaviors.

SECONDARY VICTIMIZATION

It is not surprising that violent crimes affect more people than just the direct victims. Given the prevalence of violent crimes (see Chapter 1), people are likely to encounter situations in which someone they love or know is criminally victimized or to witness the victimization of another (Figley & Kleber, 1995). Common sense would tell us that when we witness victimization or know someone who has been victimized, we will experience adverse consequences.

This phenomenon is referred to variously as "secondary victimization," "indirect victimization," "vicarious victimization," "the ripple effect," and "emotional contagion." The psychological symptoms experienced from knowing someone who has been victimized or from witnessing someone being victimized are referred to as "secondary traumatic stress symptoms" (Figley & Kleber, 1995).

The American Psychiatric Association's definition of a traumatic event used for diagnosing posttraumatic stress disorder (PTSD) illustrates that one need not be a direct or primary victim of a violent victimization to experience posttraumatic stress:

> A traumatic stressor involving direct personal experience of an event that involves actual or threatened death or serious injury, or other threat to one's physical integrity, or witnessing an event that involves death, injury, or a threat to the physical integrity of another person or learning about unexpected or violent death, serious harm, or threat of death or injury experienced by a family member or other close associate. (1994, p. 424)[1]

From this definition, it is clear that witnessing a traumatic event or learning about a trauma experienced by another can lead to symptoms of posttraumatic stress disorder. Furthermore, research shows that secondary or indirect victimization has the same potential to lead to chronic PTSD symptoms as a primary or direct experience with violence. For example, in a random sample of more than 1,000 adults, indirect traumatic experiences, such as receiving the news of a violent death or injury of a close friend or relative, were just as likely as direct traumatic experiences, such as physical and sexual assault, to lead to long-lasting PTSD symptoms (Breslau & Davis, 1992). Below, we review the research on how crime affects the victims' families, neighbors, and coworkers, those who witness violent crime, and the professionals who interact with crime victims.

EFFECTS OF NONHOMICIDAL
CRIMES ON FAMILY MEMBERS,
FRIENDS, NEIGHBORS, AND COWORKERS

Secondary Effects of War-Related
Trauma on Families of Veterans

Most of the research on how family members are affected by the victimization of another family member has been conducted with families of war veterans. For example, using medical records and questionnaire data from 382 Israeli war veterans who had suffered stress reactions during the 1982 Lebanon war, Solomon and her colleagues found that wives of veterans with PTSD had significantly higher levels of psychological and social dysfunction than wives of veterans without PTSD (Solomon, Waysman, Avitzur, Enoch, 1991; Solomon, Waysman, Levy, Fried, Mikulincer, Benbenishty et al., 1992). Furthermore, marital relationships of Israeli combat veterans with stress reactions were characterized as more conflicted, less intimate, less satisfying, and less cohesive than marital relationships of veterans without war-related stress symptoms (Solomon, Waysman, Levy, Fried, Mikulincer, & Enoch, 1992).

Similar results have been reported from families of Vietnam veterans. In a study of 23 female partners of Vietnam veterans receiving treatment for PTSD, the more PTSD symptoms the veteran manifested, the lower his partner's self-esteem and the poorer her coping skills (Verbosky & Ryan, 1988). In addition, in a national random survey of Vietnam veterans, in which veterans and their families were interviewed, wives of veterans with PTSD reported significantly more psychological distress than wives of veterans without the disorder. Furthermore, there were more marital problems and family violence in families of veterans with PTSD than in families of veterans without the disorder. Lastly, the children of veterans with PTSD evidenced significantly more behavioral problems than children of veterans without the disorder (Kulka et al., 1991).

Secondary Effects of Sexual and
Nonsexual Assault on Victims' Significant Others

These secondary effects of war trauma have analogous effects in the case of crime victims. For instance, the clinical literature suggests that partners of rape victims may experience anger, guilt, and shame following the rape of their significant others (Silverman, 1978). In a descriptive study of spouses of rape victims, the couples in the study reported marital difficulties, including problems in communication, sexual relations, emotional support, and understanding (Miller, Williams, & Bernstein, 1982). In a study of 152 support providers of robbery, assault, and burglary victims, 80% reported an increased fear of crime (Friedman, Bischoff, Davis, & Person, 1982). Of the sample, 20% installed new locks or took other precautions to protect their residences from break-ins. The increase in fear and precautionary behavior doubled if the victim and respondent were family members or lived in the same neighborhood. Among 138 female victims of completed or attempted rape or aggravated assault, partners and friends or family members of the victims were interviewed about their levels of distress and fear of crime (Davis, Taylor, & Bench, 1995). Indirect victims' distress levels were unrelated to distress levels of the direct victims or to whether the crime was a sexual or a nonsexual assault. Interestingly, the sex of the indirect victim was significantly related to their distress levels, with female family members or friends showing more distress than male partners, family members, or friends. This study, however, was limited by not having a control group.

Secondary Effects of Crime on Neighbors of Victims

The secondary effects of victimization have also been found to occur among those living in the same neighborhood as the victim. This research has typically found that when a neighbor, friend, acquaintance, or coworker is victimized, hearing about the victimization can lead to increased fear and anxiety (Covington & Taylor, 1991; Taylor & Hale, 1986). Skogan and Maxfield (1981) proposed a three-step model to explain the indirect effect of victimization on others' fear levels. First, the higher the perception of community-level crime, the greater the likelihood that neighbors will talk to each other about crime-related information. Second, the more residents are connected with the neighborhood (e.g., belonging to a neighborhood association), the greater the likelihood that neighbors will talk to each other about crime. Third, the more neighbors talk to each other about crime, the greater their fear of crime. Ironically, in this model, neighborhood integration, which is thought to be related to lower crime rates (see

Chapter 6), may actually promote higher fear levels. Consistent with their model, Skogan and Maxfield (1981) found that people who talked with other neighbors about community crime problems were more likely to know of people in their neighborhood who had experienced rape, physical assault, burglary, or theft. In turn, those who knew about the victimization experiences of others in their community reported higher fear of crime.

Worker-Related Secondary Stress

Workers in occupations at high risk for being targeted by criminals are vulnerable to experiencing the indirect effects of victimization. For example, Figley and Kleber (1995) describe several ways that a bank robbery can have indirect negative effects on employees at the bank who may not even have been present at the time of the robbery. These effects include an increasing sense of insecurity and hypervigilance, increasing workload when direct victims take time off following the robbery, and increasing social tensions at the bank.

Summary of Effects of Nonhomicidal Crimes on Family Members, Friends, Neighbors, and Coworkers

Most of the research on the effect of nonhomicidal crimes on secondary victims has been conducted with families of war veterans. These studies indicate that wives of veterans with PTSD tend to have significantly higher levels of psychological and social dysfunction, more conflicted marital relationships and family violence, lower self-esteem, and poorer coping skills than wives of veterans without PTSD. Children of veterans with PTSD may also be at greater risk for behavioral problems than children of veterans without the disorder. Research also indicates that partners of rape victims are at risk for experiencing secondary traumatic stress symptoms such as anger, guilt, shame, and marital difficulties. Fear of crime is also likely to result from knowing someone who has been victimized or from knowing of a neighbor who has been criminally victimized. Finally, coworkers of violent crime victims may be at risk for experiencing symptoms of secondary traumatic stress such as feelings of insecurity and hypervigilance.

FAMILY MEMBERS OF HOMICIDE VICTIMS

Approximately 20,000 people lose their lives to homicide each year in the United States (Maguire & Pastore, 1999, Table 3.114). Consequently, many more than 20,000 are affected by this loss annually. Using a national probability sample, researchers estimate that 5 million adults have lost an immediate family member to criminal or vehicular homicide, and 16 million have lost an immediate family member, other relative, or close friend to homicide (Amick-McMullan, Kilpatrick, & Resnick, 1991). Several studies of family members of homicide victims, termed "homicide survivors," indicate that survivors experience myriad posttrauma symptoms across affective, behavioral, and cognitive domains (Amick-McMullan et al., 1991; Bard, Arnone, & Nemiroff, 1980; Thompson, Norris, & Ruback, 1998).

Affective Consequences

Most, if not all, studies of family members of homicide victims have found elevated rates of psychological distress, such as PTSD, depression, and anxiety. In a national sample representing the noninstitutionalized U.S. adult population, 19% of those who had lost an immediate family member to criminal homicide met criteria for lifetime PTSD (they had experienced PTSD symptoms during their lifetimes), and 5% met criteria for current PTSD (they had experienced PTSD symptoms within the last few months) (Amick-McMullan et al., 1991). In a study of 150 family members of homicide victims, homicide survivors reported significantly higher occurrences of PTSD symptoms than a group of 108 demographically similar individuals who had experienced other types of traumatic events (e.g., robbery, physical assault, or sexual assault) within the past 5 years (Thompson et al., 1998). In another study, occurrences of PTSD symptoms were significantly higher among homicide survivors than among rape victims and individuals who had lost significant others to nonhomicide deaths (Amick-McMullan, Kilpatrick, Veronen, & Smith, 1989). The occurrence of PTSD among family members of homicide victims is illustrated by the words of a father whose daughter was murdered: "Every time something is on television or in the newspapers about the crime, it opens up all the hurt and brings back all the bad memories" (Cook, 1995, p. G4). Similarly, a friend who watched his friend being murdered said, "There's no feeling like holding your friend while he dies in your arms. But then again, you really don't feel. There's just numbness" (R. Russell, 1994, p. D6).

TABLE 5.1 Sample Means and Standard Deviations on
Distress Measures of Homicide Survivors Compared
With Published Norms

	Homicide Survivors (N = 150)	Nonpatient Adults (N = 341)	Psychiatric Outpatients (N = 576)	Violent Crime Victims (N = 175)
Depression				
M	.91[a][b]	.28	1.80	.91
SD	.76	.46	1.08	.88
Anxiety				
M	.87[a][b]	.35	1.70	.93
SD	.80	.45	1.00	.81
Somatization				
M	.78[a][b]	.29	.83	.62
SD	.82	.40	.79	.73
Hostility				
M	.50[a][b][c]	.35	1.16	.85
SD	.53	.42	.93	.73

SOURCE: Thompson, Norris, and Ruback (1998). Reprinted with permission of Kluwer Academic Publishers.
NOTE: Brief Symptom Inventory (BSI) norms for nonpatient and outpatient adults were taken from Derogatis and Spencer (1982); those for violent crime victims were taken from Norris and Kaniasty (1994).
a. Homicide sample significantly different from nonpatient adults ($p < .05$).
b. Homicide sample significantly different from psychiatric outpatients ($p < .05$).
c. Homicide sample significantly different from recent violent crime victims ($p < .05$).

Homicide survivors also evidence high levels of other types of psychological distress, such as depression. In the study of 150 family members of homicide victims mentioned above, homicide survivors scored significantly higher on depression, anxiety, hostility, and somatization than the norms for general population nonpatient adults. Of the homicide sample, 26% showed scores in the clinically significant range on either depression, anxiety, hostility, or somatization compared with only 3% of the no-trauma group (see Table 5.1).

Behavioral Consequences

In addition to affective consequences, the loss of a family member to homicide results in negative behavioral consequences, some of which come from interacting with the criminal justice system following the murder. Homicide is a crime that almost always comes to the attention of the police. Thus, homicide survivors typically have some involvement with criminal justice system personnel.

When family members of homicide victims deal with the criminal justice system following the murder of their loved ones, their involvement can exacerbate many of the psychological wounds brought on by the homicide. In the words of a man whose mother was one of the 168 people killed in the Oklahoma City bombing, "The last year or so, we have been able to kind of put it out of our minds because of all of the other things going on. But with the trial starting up again, it kind of brings it all back. . . . It reopens the scab" (Casey, 1997, p. A10). In the words of another homicide survivor, "You never bury a loved one who's been murdered, because the justice system keeps digging them up" (Schlosser, 1997, p. 52).

Prior to the homicide, most survivors probably perceived the criminal justice system as a process whereby justice would be meted out. When these expectations are violated, the survivors are likely to feel vulnerable and helpless. When someone dies suddenly, family members encounter a series of people whose involvement is "officially determined." The quality of these contacts after a homicide are critical for successful coping (Bard & Connolly, 1982). When family members are treated sensitively by justice system personnel, they can start to trust in society again. However, if they have unsatisfactory experiences with the justice process, they are likely to have pessimistic and cynical attitudes regarding justice and equality (Frieze, Hymer, & Greenberg, 1987; Greenberg, Ruback, & Westcott, 1983).

For example, in the Oklahoma City bombing case against Terry Nichols, family members and relatives of bombing victims were disappointed and angry that the jury did not convict Nichols of first-degree murder charges and did not sentence him to the death penalty. They were also distraught over comments made by the jury forewoman, who announced to reporters that the case against Nichols was circumstantial. Family members likely felt that the justice process did not do "justice" for their loved ones who were killed, thereby exacerbating their distress over their loved ones' murders (Hillman, 1998).

Providing information to family members such as whether the offender has been caught, prosecutors' specific plans for the case, and when court cases will be heard can help improve the quality of survivors' interactions with the criminal justice system. When a police officer does not take the time to explain to family members what happened to their loved ones, family members are likely to feel ignored and unimportant. When a defense attorney paints a portrait of their loved ones as having brought about the crimes, family members are likely to be hurt and angered. When a plea bargain takes place without their knowledge, family members are likely to feel devalued. One woman whose son was murdered was so distraught over the lack of information and action provided by the police that she started looking for the killers herself. "I was down there every weekend . . . doing my own investigation. . . . Every time I went down there, I hoped that someone would shoot me. I wasn't fearful. My only child, all I had in my life, was gone" (McDonald, 1995, p. B2).

In one study, although 80% of homicide survivors reported feeling that the justice system should provide them with legal assistance and information on the status of the case, only 33% reported that they had received this service (Riggs & Kilpatrick, 1990). More than 80% also believed that the system should provide an advocate, yet only 27% reported that they were adequately served in this area. Of the sample, 80% also believed that the courts should provide personal protection for family members, but only 10% reported receiving this service. In this study, those who reported the most psychological distress were the least satisfied with the criminal justice system. Their feelings of dissatisfaction and cynicism about the criminal justice process are illustrated by the words of a woman who lost her husband to murder:

> I would love to be able to put this in the past and go on, but the laws of our justice system don't allow me to do that. Regardless of how many years go by, I have to relive this every time he [the murderer] is up for parole. (Oglesby, 1997, p. F8)

Another behavioral consequence that may be experienced by family members of homicide victims is avoidance of things that serve as reminders of the homicide or the deceased (Burgess, 1975). For example, in a study conducted with 200 parents who had lost children to murder, one respondent was quoted as saying, "I stay at home all the time now. I'm scared to death to go for a walk in my own neighborhood" (Rinear, 1988, p. 313). In another study, a woman who had lost a brother to an unsolved homicide said she was afraid to let people walk behind her (Burgess, 1975).

Cognitive Consequences

As with direct victims of crime, research has shown that family members of homicide victims evidence negative consequences in several cognitive domains following the murder, including cognitions of fear and vulnerability, mistrust and loss of control, and blame. Because homicide is typically the result of intentional maliciousness on the part of one person toward another, family members of the victim are likely to experience feelings of fear and vulnerability. In some cases, survivors may literally fear for their lives if a suspect has not been apprehended. For example, in a study of 200 parents who had lost children to homicide, a quarter of the parents reported fears about their safety and the safety of their surviving children and other family members (Rinear, 1988). One respondent interviewed was quoted as saying, "I am much more concerned about the safety and life of my remaining daughter. Before, I never thought anything like this could happen to us . . . we're still scared that what happened once might happen again" (Rinear, 1988, p. 313).

Another common response experienced by homicide survivors is a mistrust of others. Because murder has the potential to undermine one's faith in the world, survivors who are able to restore order and reduce their sense of helplessness are able to cope better than those who cannot (Burgess, 1975). On a related note, losing a family member to homicide is an event that most people don't expect will happen to them. When it does, feelings of a lack of control over one's life and world are likely to follow. One friend of a homicide victim expressed the changes in his cognitive schema this way: "He showed me that there's no special profile for a target. He wasn't running with the type of people that were into illegal activity or gang-related activity" (Willis, 1994, p. D7). The mother of a friend of the same homicide victim said she thought of the victim as an angel who died for some reason.

> And I think he was put here to show kids that they don't have to be so angry, and so hard and all of this crazy stuff. Then he was taken away to show these kids that all of this anger and hate is snuffing out the nicest and kind young men, as well as the angry ones. (B. Russell, 1994, p. D6)

Another consequence of loss of a family member to homicide is the need for family members to blame someone for the murder, including the perpetrator, the criminal justice system, society at large, and sometimes even the victims or themselves (Burgess, 1975; Rinear, 1988). In a study of parents of murdered children, parents reported a high amount of self-blame for the murder (Rinear, 1988). For example, one parent was cited as saying, "I helped him to buy the Corvette that attracted the murderers to him" (Rinear, 1988, p. 313). Another parent was quoted as saying, "I should have insisted that he wear a bulletproof vest since there was danger in one of the neighborhoods where he delivered papers" (Rinear, 1988, p. 313). Although these statements may not sound rational, they exemplify many of the self-blame and "if only" counterfactual thinking often observed among trauma victims (Roese, 1997). As discussed in Chapter 4, when a crime is unusual or rare, victims are more likely to engage in counterfactual thinking. Because homicide is less prevalent than any other type of crime, family members of homicide victims may be most vulnerable to counterfactual thinking. That is, they may imagine outcomes of the crime that are worse than those that actually occurred or imagine things that they could or should have done differently (Roese, 1997).

Summary of Homicide Survivors

In summary, losing a family member to homicide can have negative affective, behavioral, and cognitive consequences. Most of this research has focused on the affective consequences of losing a family member to murder. These studies are fairly uniform in finding high levels of negative psychological symptoms among homicide survivors, especially PTSD. Behavioral consequences of loss of a family member to homicide may involve the desire to avoid reminders of the homicide. Last, the cognitive consequences of loss of a family member to homicide include fear of crime, feelings of a loss of control, and the need to blame someone or something for the murder. Thus, as in the case of direct experience with crime, losing a family member to murder can negatively affect the indirect victim in multiple ways.

WITNESSING VIOLENCE

Aside from being a homicide survivor, individuals might also be affected by violence if they witness violence in their family or in their neighborhood. Most of the research that has examined the psychological consequences of witnessing violence has been conducted with children and adolescents. Until the past decade, very little was known about how witnessing violence affects the psychological well-being of youths. But recently there have been several studies of the secondary victimization of youths, particularly on two topics: children who witness domestic violence and children exposed to community violence.

Children Who Witness Domestic Violence

Researchers estimate that every year, about 3 million to 10 million children witness violence in their households. About one third of children have seen their parents engage in violence at least once, and most have witnessed multiple incidents (Straus, 1992, as cited in Edleson, 1999). Parents are likely to underestimate the extent to which their children witness violence, because they may think the children were sleeping or playing outside while the abuse was occurring (Edleson, 1999).

Although there are dozens of studies on the topic, there are problems in using them to determine whether witnessing violence per se has detrimental effects (Edleson, 1999). First, many studies do not differentiate between children who have been abused and those who were not abused but witnessed domestic violence. Second, many of the children who have been interviewed in these studies have come from shelters for battered women, which means not only that they have witnessed violence but also that they have been removed from their homes and neighborhoods. Thus, it is not clear whether problems the children report relate to witnessing violence or to the disruptions in their lives. Third, most studies of children's responses to witnessing violence have relied on mothers' reports of their children's experiences rather than on the children's reports of their own experiences.

In general, interviews with battered women and their children indicated that children had seen or heard nearly all of the abuse incidents despite the fact that parents had often tried to shield their children from being exposed to their fighting. Exposure to domestic violence took the form of witnessing verbal threats of injury, suicide attempts, threats and actual use of guns and knives, verbal assaults on their parents' characters, objects being thrown across rooms, and physical contact, such as hitting (Rosenberg, 1987).

Children of battered women are at increased risk for sustaining physical and sexual abuse themselves as well as myriad affective, behavioral, and cognitive problems related to witnessing violence that is typically chronic in nature. Children who have witnessed domestic violence are significantly more likely than children who have not to evidence emotional distress, poor cognitive and social problem-solving skills, low self-esteem, behavioral problems, use of violence as a conflict resolution strategy, and poor peer relations (Jaffe, Hurley, & Wolfe, 1990; Kashani, Daniel, Dandoy, & Holcomb, 1992; Kolbo, 1996; McCloskey, Figueredo, & Koss, 1995; O'Keefe, 1994; Rosenberg, 1987; Wolfe, Jaffe, Wilson, & Zak, 1985).

Affective Consequences. Children who witness domestic violence between spouses or between parents and their partners suffer negative affective consequences. A sample of 1,452 undergraduates completed questionnaires about their exposure to parental physical aggression before the age of 16 and about their current psychological functioning. Results indicated that young adults who had been exposed to domestic violence reported more general distress, more internalizing distress (e.g., depression or anxiety), and more externalizing distress (e.g., delinquency or aggression) than young adults who had not witnessed parental violence. The frequency of witnessed interparental conflict was also associated with distress symptoms in young adulthood, even after controlling for variables measuring physical abuse, parental alcoholism, divorce, and socioeconomic status. Those who had witnessed their same-sex parents as the victims of physical aggression evidenced the highest distress scores (Henning, Leitenberg, Coffey, Bennett, & Jankowski, 1997). In a sample of 198 children, those living in a violent family were more than twice as likely as children living in nonviolent families to have clinically significant child adjustment problems (Wolfe et al., 1985).

Work by researchers at the University of Arizona suggests that witnessing family violence affects children's psychological functioning across several different affective domains. That is, rather than showing a specific form of psychopathology such as depression, the affective outcomes of children of battered women are quite heterogeneous and affect both internalizing and externalizing behaviors (McCloskey et al., 1995). PTSD has also been noted among child witnesses of family violence. Among 84 children recruited from battered-women's shelters, more than half (56%) met criteria for PTSD. The duration of the domestic violence witnessed by a child as well as the number of male role models a child witnessed engaging in domestic violence against his or her mother increased the likelihood for developing PTSD (Lehmann, 1997).

Behavioral Consequences. Witnessing domestic violence affects not only children's emotional well-being but also their behavioral well-being. In a study of 47 children living with their mothers in battered-women's shelters, children who witnessed domestic violence showed developmental delays and behavioral problems as evidenced by parent and teacher reports of communication skills, conduct problems, learning problems, and hyperactivity (Gleason, 1995). In another study, children of battered women residing in shelters had significantly lower scores on social competence than children from nonviolent homes and than children who had been exposed to family violence in the preceding 6 months but were no longer living in violent homes (Wolfe, Zak, Wilson, & Jaffe, 1986). Recency of witnessing family violence is also related to children's social competence such that children recently exposed to family violence report fewer social activities, lower school performance, and fewer interests (Wolfe et al., 1986).

Based on a review of 31 studies, Edleson (1999) found that children who witness domestic violence show a number of behavioral problems, including aggression, anxiety, and depression. And in the long term, witnessing adult domestic violence as a child is related to reports of depression and low self-esteem in adult women and to reports of trauma-related symptoms in both adult women and adult men. Boys generally respond to witnessing parental violence with externalized behavior, particularly hostility and aggression, whereas girls respond with internalized problems, such as depression (Stagg, Wills, & Howell, 1989). However, some research suggests that girls who witness parental violence are especially likely to be violent themselves. Younger children who witness parental violence seem to be especially likely to show problems. Despite the research showing that children who witness parental aggression are more likely to show aggressive behavior, there is evidence that some children raised in these conditions cope successfully and show few negative reactions.

Cognitive Consequences. Witnessing family violence also affects children's cognitive well-being, including cognitions about the acceptability of aggression as an appropriate conflict resolution strategy (Jaffe et al., 1990). Based on estimates from a national probability sample, young boys who witness their fathers' aggressive behavior are 10 times more likely than young boys who are not exposed to family violence to abuse their wives when they become adults (Straus, Gelles, & Steinmetz, 1980).

Additional Consequences/Caveats. Many children who suffer secondary victimization by witnessing domestic violence may also be primary victims of violence. Thus, researchers who study the effects of witnessing violence on children must pay special attention to untangling these effects. In one study, researchers compared abused children who had also witnessed violence between their parents (a) with nonabused children who had witnessed parental violence and (b) with nonabused children who had not witnessed parental violence. Children who witnessed parental violence and were victims of physical abuse had the highest distress scores, followed by children who were not themselves primary recipients of abuse but had witnessed parental violence.

Children who had neither been abused nor witnessed parental violence had the lowest level of distress (Hughes, 1988).

Summary on Children
Witnessing Domestic Violence

In summary, children who witness violence at home are more likely than their peers to evidence myriad negative consequences. As with direct victims of crime, these symptoms can be affective, behavioral, and/or cognitive. Most of the relevant research has focused on the psychological consequences for children who have witnessed domestic violence. These children show both internalized distress, such as depression and anxiety, and externalized distress, such as increased aggression and delinquency.

Exposure to Community Violence

Aside from seeing violence inside their home, children may also be exposed to community violence. For example, a survey of 9th and 10th graders at a New York City high school revealed that approximately 50% reported knowing someone who had been murdered, 31% had witnessed a stabbing, 37% had witnessed a shooting, 59% had witnessed a beating, and 61% had witnessed a robbery (Pastore, Fisher, & Friedman, 1996). In a study of children and their families residing in disadvantaged neighborhoods, Dubrow and Garbarino (1989) found that in one community, all children interviewed had witnessed a shooting before the age of 5. In another study conducted in a large southeastern city, mothers of elementary school children 9 to 12 years old living in or near one of the largest housing developments in the United States were interviewed regarding their children's exposure to violence. More than one fourth of the mothers (26%) reported that their children had witnessed a shooting, 19% reported that their children had witnessed a stabbing, 72% reported that their children had witnessed the use of weapons, 40% reported that their children had seen a dead body, and 6% of the mothers reported that their children had witnessed a murder (Osofsky, Wewers, Hann, & Fick, 1993). More and more, researchers are using phrases such as "war zones" (Garbarino, Kostelny, & Dubrow, 1991) and "battle zones" (Lorion & Saltzman, 1993) to describe the environments in which many children are being raised today.

Research indicates not only that the exposure to violence in the community is widely prevalent but that exposure to community violence has negative psychological consequences on affect, behavior, and cognition (Boney-McCoy & Finkelhor, 1995; Garbarino et al., 1991; Martinez & Richters, 1993; Pynoos et al., 1987).

Affective Consequences. Among children exposed to violence, PTSD symptoms are the most commonly reported effects. In a study of more than 200 African American youths aged 7 to 18, witnessing violence was significantly related to higher PTSD symptoms, even after controlling for personal victimization experiences (Fitzpatrick & Boldizar, 1993). Similarly, in an in-depth clinical study of 10 children aged 5 to 17 who had witnessed the sexual assaults of their mothers, 9 of the 10 children had PTSD symptom scores in the severe range, and one of them had PTSD symptom scores in the moderate range. Interviews with 159 children following a sniper attack at an elementary school found that more than one third of the children had moderate to severe levels of PTSD symptoms, and one fifth had mild symptoms of PTSD (Pynoos et al., 1987).

In addition to being at risk for PTSD, youths exposed to community violence are at risk for other distress symptoms. Elementary school children who are exposed to higher levels of violence show increased stress symptom scores, particularly internalized types of distress such as depression and anxiety (Osofsky et al., 1993). A study of 6- to 10-year-old children living in a low-income neighborhood found that children with severe distress (75th percentile and above) were significantly more likely than children with distress levels below the 75th percentile to have seen drug deals, people being arrested, someone carrying an illegal weapon, and someone being hit, slapped, or punched by a family member (Martinez & Richters, 1993).

Behavioral Consequences. Exposure to violence is also related to behavioral problems such as conduct disorder, suicidal behavior, and alcohol and drug use. Several researchers have noted conduct problems among youths exposed to violence (Durant, Cadenhead, Pendergrast, Slavens, & Linder, 1994; Guerra, Tolan, Huesmann, Van Acker, & Eron, 1995; Osofsky, 1995; Widom, 1989a). In a study of 2,000 ethnically diverse children in second, third, and fourth grades, children who reported higher levels of stress due to neighborhood violence were significantly more likely to be named by their peers as engaging in aggressive behavior (Guerra et al., 1995). Similarly, black adolescents— living in or around public housing projects in a city in the southeast— who had been exposed to high levels of community violence were more likely to have engaged in violence themselves than those who had not been exposed to community violence (Durant et al., 1994). A more recent study of the behavioral consequences of exposure to violence was a longitudinal examination of ninety-seven 9- to 10-year-old boys (Miller, Wasserman, Neugebauer, Gorman-Smith, & Kamboukos, 1999). In this study, boys who had witnessed more community violence showed more changes in antisocial behavior 15 and 30 months later, even after controlling for parental monitoring, parental involvement, and parent-child conflict.

In terms of suicidal behavior, 9th- and 10th-grade students at a high school in New York City who knew someone who had been murdered were almost 4 times more likely to report having attempted suicide than their counterparts who did not know anyone who had been murdered. Students who had witnessed a stabbing were almost 3 times as likely to have attempted suicide than students who had not witnessed a stabbing (Pastore et al., 1996). Youths exposed to community violence are also more likely than their counterparts to evidence significant problems with alcohol. The 9th and 10th graders in New York City who reported witnessing shootings were twice as likely to report significant alcohol use than students who had not witnessed shootings (Pastore et al., 1996).

A link has also been found between exposure to community violence and psychophysiological disturbances among youths. Children who reported more exposure to community violence also reported more sleep deprivation and lower resting pulse rates (Cooley-Quille & Lorion, 1999). These results suggest that children who are exposed to high levels of community violence may be adapting physiologically to this stressor.

Cognitive Consequences. Researchers have also discussed how children's cognitions may be affected by exposure to community violence. Most of the 10 children who had witnessed the sexual attacks of their mothers reported hypervigilant concerns about personal safety, increased fears about leaving the house, feelings of guilt, and increased anger (Pynoos & Nader, 1988). One child stayed up every night past 3:00 A.M. because that was the time the rapist had come. Another child felt regret at not having tried to hit the attacker with his baseball bat. Other researchers have discussed how a child growing up in a violent environment may adopt a worldview that is dysfunctional in nonviolent settings. For example, a child may become hypervigilant in reacting to perceived slights or insults. This behavior is maladaptive in a school setting and will probably cause the child problems academically and socially. Conversely, a child may react to chronic exposure to violence by withdrawing emotionally from the environment and others (Garbarino et al., 1991).

Summary of Community Violence Exposure

In summary, exposure to community violence among youths is quite prevalent. Furthermore, exposure to community violence has negative sequelae on their affective, behavioral, and cognitive well-being. PTSD symptoms and conduct problems are common consequences of exposure to community violence. In addition, hypervigilant concerns and fears about personal safety are common cognitive consequences of exposure to violence in the community.

PROFESSIONALS' SECONDARY TRAUMATIZATION

Until recently, the vicarious effects of violent crime on professionals who work with victims had not been studied. In 1991, the National Organization of Victim Assistance (NOVA) delineated 9 categories of trauma workers: immediate responders (e.g., police officers), later responders (e.g., medical personnel), unexpected responders (e.g., bystanders and witnesses), emergency room personnel, body recovery and burial personnel, crisis intervenors (e.g., mental health professionals), voluntary personnel (e.g., Red Cross), remote responders (e.g., equipment maintenance personnel), and emergency support personnel (e.g., dispatchers). A 10th category, victim advocates, has also been suggested. Although all of these trauma workers can potentially play a role in cases of violent victimization, crisis intervenors (e.g., mental health workers) and unexpected responders (e.g., witnesses) are particularly likely to be called on in cases of victimization. In this section, we focus on professional mental health workers' reactions to working with victims of violent crime.

The phrase "compassion fatigue" has been used to describe the secondary traumatic stress symptoms professionals who interact with victims of trauma often experience (Figley, 1995). In describing his interest in the topic, a leading investigator in this area of research wrote that he had experienced considerable dismay over seeing numerous colleagues abandon their clinical practices with traumatized individuals because they had difficulty dealing with the pain of others

(Figley, 1989). To help identify therapists at risk for developing compassion fatigue, Figley developed the 66-item Compassion Fatigue Self-Test for Psychotherapists, which asks therapists to rate characteristics about themselves and their current clinical situations on a 5-point scale (Figley, 1995). The following are sample items:

1. I think that there is no one to talk with about highly stressful experiences.
2. Working with those I help brings me a great deal of satisfaction.
3. I am preoccupied with more than one person I help.
4. I feel like I have the tools and resources that I need to do my work as a helper.
5. I find it difficult separating my personal life from my helper life.

Based on responses to the scale, clinicians and others who work with trauma victims can be classified by their potential for compassion satisfaction, risk for burnout, and risk for compassion fatigue (Figley, 1995). Four factors may explain why some professionals are at increased risk for developing compassion fatigue as a result of their interactions with traumatized clients: (a) empathy the provider feels toward his or her client, (b) the trauma history of the therapist, (c) any unresolved trauma of the therapist, and (d) working with traumatized child clients (Figley, 1995).

Other researchers have also studied the effects on professional therapists of working with trauma victims. These researchers have elucidated specific potential indicators of secondary traumatic stress, which include affective symptoms, behavioral problems, and changes in cognitive schema (Dutton & Rubinstein, 1995). Examples of how each of these three domains of secondary traumatic stress may be manifested are presented next.

Affective Consequences

Several types of affective symptoms resulting from secondary traumatic exposure have been reported in the literature (Boylin & Briggie, 1987; Figley & Kleber, 1995; McCann & Pearlman 1990), many of which are consistent with PTSD. For example, professionals working with trauma victims may feel distressing emotions, such as grief, depression, rage, and anxiety. Professionals may also experience intrusive imagery, such as nightmares, and numbing or dissociation as manifested by an avoidance of working with the traumatic material brought up by the client. Also consistent with PTSD symptoms, professionals may experience somatic problems, such as sleep difficulties, headaches, and gastrointestinal problems, and other physiological arousal symptoms, such as heart palpitations.

Behavioral Consequences

Behavioral problems noted in the literature on professionals' vicarious victimization include the following: (a) disturbances with relationships; (b) addictive behavior, such as substance abuse and workaholism; and (c) impairment of daily functioning manifested by feeling alienated in relationships and neglecting work responsibilities. Relationship problems may encompass both personal and professional relationships. Personal relationships may become compromised due to trust and intimacy issues that arise from being faced with the client's victimization experience (Boylin & Briggie, 1987).

The professional relationship with the client can also be affected negatively by the professional's secondary traumatic stress. One possible reaction is detachment, which may be used as a coping strategy to ward off negative thoughts about the therapist's own vulnerability or memories of personal traumas. Conversely, overidentification with the patient is another possible reaction, which may be used as a coping strategy to try to overcome feelings of loss of control or feelings of heightened vulnerability elicited by the client's victimization experience (Dutton & Rubinstein, 1995). Clinicians have suggested several signs that may indicate that a therapist is experiencing secondary traumatic stress resulting in relationship disturbances (Pearlman & Saakvitne, 1995). These include withdrawing socially, feeling different from others or feeling like one knows something others do not know, feeling emotionally exhausted, feeling alienated from sexual partners and/or intimates, and being unable to enjoy common forms of entertainment (e.g., movies).

Other behavioral consequences of secondary exposure to violence may include seeking mental health care and coping with the trauma by using alcohol. A survey was conducted of rescue workers and body handlers who worked for the Medical Examiner's Office during the aftermath of the bombing of the Alfred P. Murrah Federal Building in Oklahoma City. Results indicated that 14% of those surveyed reported seeking mental health treatment and 10% reported increasing their use of alcohol in the 2 months following the bombing (Tucker, Pfefferbaum, Nixon, & Foy, 1999). However, these results should be interpreted with some caution because only 38% of the 135 workers who were mailed surveys completed the questionnaires.

Cognitive Consequences

Examples of cognitive shifts that occur as a result of secondary traumatic stress include suspicion of others (Courtois, 1988; McCann & Pearlman, 1990), "clinician guilt" (Silver, 1986), and victim blaming (Silver, 1986). Generally, research on direct victims of trauma (see Chapter 4) has delineated five domains of cognitive schemas that may be affected by an experience with violence (McCann, Sakheim, & Abrahamson, 1988): safety, trust, esteem, control, and intimacy. It has been proposed that therapists can also have these same cognitive schemas undermined by secondary traumatization elicited by the client's sharing of his or her violent experience. This notion was supported by a study in which researchers found that therapists who reported more exposure to clients' "trauma material" manifested more disruptions in their cognitive schema of esteem for others (Pearlman & Saakvitne, 1995).

Summary of Professionals' Secondary Traumatization

In sum, researchers have only recently started to examine how working with victims of violence may affect professional therapists. This research has found that indirect exposure to traumatic events may cause secondary traumatic stress symptoms. The symptoms encompass affective reactions such as depression and anxiety, behavioral consequences such as relationship disturbances, and cognitive reactions such as mistrust. High empathy with the client, a personal history of unresolved trauma, and working with child victims are factors that increase the likelihood of compassion fatigue.

SUMMARY

In this chapter, we discussed the effects of violence on secondary victims. It now should be clear that direct victims are not the only ones adversely affected when a crime occurs. Witnessing violence and knowing someone who has been victimized can also lead to adverse affective, cognitive, and behavioral consequences. We reviewed the literature on the effects of nonhomicidal crimes on family members, friends, neighbors, and coworkers and described how these groups can experience the same affective, cognitive, and behavioral consequences that victims suffer. Likewise, the effects of a homicide on family members and the effects on youths of witnessing domestic violence or of witnessing violence in the community are similar to the consequences that direct crime victims experience. Finally, we discussed secondary victimization among various types of professionals who deal with crime victims, including mental health providers and emergency workers. These professionals are at increased risk of compassion fatigue, relationship disturbances, and guilt.

∷ DISCUSSION QUESTIONS

1. Why are family members likely to engage in counterfactual thinking about the death of a family member, especially a child? Should they be discouraged from doing so?

2. How does the criminal justice system affect the psychological recovery of family members of homicide victims? What kind of training should police officers receive about how to deal with homicide survivors? Should there be additional resources, such as specialized mental health groups, for these survivors?

3. The research on the effects on children of witnessing violence in the home and in the community is relatively recent. What are the limitations of this research? How can this research be improved? To what extent is the research on children growing up in war situations relevant?

4. That family, friends, and professional mental health workers experience compassion fatigue is not surprising. What sorts of support mechanisms could be implemented to reduce this problem?

NOTE

1. Reprinted with permission from the *Diagnostic and Statistical Manual of Mental Disorders, Fourth Edition.* Coyright © 1994, American Psychiatric Association.

6 ⚏

The Effects of
Violent Victimization
on Communities

Although individuals suffer the most immediate and visible effects of violent victimizations, neighborhoods and communities are also harmed by violent crimes. Like individuals, communities are generally resilient and can recover from problems, even chronic problems, related to high rates of violence. However, sometimes these violence-related problems can destroy a community. That is, in the same way that victimization devastates an individual's illusion of invulnerability, positive self-view, and perception of the world as a meaningful place (Janoff-Bulman & Frieze, 1983), high levels of crime can shatter people's perceptions of their community as a place where they believe they can live safely and happily.

This chapter discusses how that process occurs, focusing on the effect of violent victimizations on three community-level factors: (a) fear of crime, (b) residents' informal social control over their community, and (c) formal social control mechanisms, including the criminal justice system. The chapter also discusses the long-term effects of violent victimization on a community, particularly in terms of the economic costs and neighborhood change. Finally, the chapter discusses interventions that might successfully be used to combat the negative effects of high rates of violence on the life of a neighborhood.

CHARACTERISTICS OF NEIGHBORHOODS

Because neighborhoods are more than a collection of individual residents, it is important to understand the factors that characterize these communities and differentiate them from each other. Some of these factors put neighborhoods at risk for future violence, whereas others protect neighborhoods from violent crime.

Neighborhoods differ on structural characteristics such as social and economic stratification, family status (e.g., percentage of female-headed households), residential stability (how long families stay in the community and percentage of families that own their homes), racial composition, and level of urbanization (Sampson, 2001). In general, communities characterized by low socioeconomic status and residential instability have high rates of violence. This general finding is consistent with research and theory from the 1930s suggesting that large crowded cities with heterogeneous populations undermine the links between family, friends, and neighbors and that, as a result of these pressures, individuals have more superficial, anonymous, and transitory relationships (Wirth, 1938). In the absence of informal social control, incivilities and crime increase, and there is a greater need to rely on formal social control mechanisms, such as the criminal justice system. The same loss of a sense of neighborhood that contributes to an increase in crime also leads to a decreased reliance on others and an increased fear of crime.

In the past 20 years, some inner-city neighborhoods have experienced a concentration of poverty and disadvantage (Wilson, 1987), largely because of the relocation of manufacturing jobs away from central cities (Wilson, 1996). In particular, some urban areas have high proportions of poor blacks living in female-headed families with children, one factor that increases the likelihood of high rates of crime.

However, some neighborhoods with these characteristics have lower rates of violence than would be expected. What seems to be true of these neighborhoods is that they have high *collective efficacy*. This concept refers to "mutual trust [among neighbors] and the willingness to intervene for the common good," specifically to supervise children and maintain public order (Sampson, Raudenbush, & Earls, 1997, p. 919). Specifically, residents of neighborhoods with high collective efficacy are likely to agree that statements such as the following characterize their neighborhoods: "People around here are willing to help their neighbors"; "This is a close-knit neighborhood"; and "People in this neighborhood can be trusted." They are also likely to say that their neighbors would intervene in situations such as children painting graffiti on walls or skipping school.

In a study of 343 neighborhood clusters in Chicago that involved interviews with 8,782 residents as well as analyses of census data and police reports, researchers found that neighborhoods with high collective efficacy had crime rates 40% lower than neighborhoods with low collective efficacy (Sampson et al., 1997). Although neighborhoods with low collective efficacy tend to be those with high levels of poverty, high levels of ethnic and linguistic heterogeneity, and low levels of residential stability, collective efficacy is an important predictor of crime rates even when these other factors are held constant statistically.

EFFECTS OF VIOLENT CRIME ON COMMUNITIES

Violent crime can affect communities both directly and indirectly. The most important direct effects are on fear of crime and informal social control. That is, the amount of violence in a neighborhood can affect residents' perceptions of crime and risk of victimization. In addition, violence can affect residents' willingness to control disorder and incivilities in their neighborhood. In turn, incivilities and fear of crime can affect the stability of the community because individuals and businesses are likely to want to leave high-crime neighborhoods. Even if they do not leave the neighborhood, individuals are likely to change their behaviors because of the high crime. In addition to these effects, violent crime can indirectly change a community because men from the neighborhood are removed, thus leaving fewer people to exercise informal social control.

Fear of Crime

Fear of crime generally refers to a fear of being attacked, suffering physical harm, or enduring some intrusion that destroys privacy and dignity (Brantingham & Brantingham, 1995) rather than to a fear of losing property. Fear of crime is related to physical vulnerability (e.g., because of age or lack of physical strength) and to lack of perceived control over the situation (e.g., being in an unknown area, being out at night, or being afraid of encountering "scary" individuals). As illustrated by the cartoon in Figure 6.1, fear of crime depends on both individual and contextual factors.

Figure 6.1. Fear of Crime Is Based on Individual and Contextual Factors
SOURCE: Copyright © 1994. G. B. Trudeau.

Fear of crime has important implications at both the individual and community levels. For individuals, fear of crime leads to anxiety and affects their willingness to go places outside their home, although this process is reciprocal in that fear leads to avoidance, and avoidance, in turn, leads to fear (Liska, Sanchirico, & Reed, 1988). For communities, fear of crime is a determinant of the quality of life in the neighborhood and is thus related to economic activity (e.g., the number and success of businesses), to the amount of pedestrian and automobile traffic, and ultimately, to the life or death of the community.

More than 30 years ago, the President's Commission on Law Enforcement and Administration of Justice (1967) commented on how the fear of crime can affect activity in a community:

> People stay behind the locked doors of their homes rather than risk walking in the streets at night. Poor people spend money on taxis because they are afraid to walk or use public transportation. Sociable people are afraid to talk to those they don't know. (p. 52)

That fear of crime causes people to go outside less means that there are likely to be fewer individuals who serve as "eyes on the street." Consistent with this notion, burglaries, larcenies, and motor vehicle thefts are less likely to occur when there are witnesses than when there are not (Pope, 1977).

An extremely high level of fear of crime shared by most of the community is often characterized as a "crime wave." Perceptions of crime waves are not always related to actual increases in crime. Rather, they may be partly related to the way the police and the media report crime statistics. Often during crime waves, individuals who ordinarily are not afraid (e.g., nonminorities or the better-educated) become more fearful, and their increased fear is partly due to lower confidence in the ability of the police to deal with the crime problem (Baker, Nienstedt, Everett, & McCleary, 1983).

The disparity between fear of crime and the risk of actual victimization can be quite large. For example, elderly individuals have high levels of fear of crime but low risks of victimization, whereas teenagers and young adults have low levels of fear of crime but high risks of victimization (see Chapter 2). Dark and isolated areas are generally the most feared as sites for crime, although they tend to evidence relatively low frequencies of crimes committed (Brantingham & Brantingham, 1995). Similarly, locations marked by vandalism, litter, and graffiti produce the highest levels of fear of crime even though these incivilities do not usually mark areas with the highest rates of serious crime. In other words, fear of crime is often more closely tied to high levels of noise and traffic, the presence of alcoholics, panhandlers, teenagers, and contact with individuals who are "different" than to high rates of serious crime. Subway riders who are most concerned for their safety are also likely to be most concerned about the presence of drunks, loiterers, and public urination in subway cars and on train platforms (Kenny, 1987).

Conversely, areas in which people feel safe may actually be locations where crime is likely. For example, people generally feel safe on busy shopping streets, but these are locations where robberies are most likely to occur. At universities, crimes are most likely to occur in libraries, student unions, and dormitory laundry rooms—locations where individuals report feeling safe (Brantingham & Brantingham, 1995). Similarly, auto thefts and thefts from autos are concentrated in locations that people consider safe, such as parking lots and exposed locations (e.g., on a street near their home).

Regarding the effect of place on crime, Brantingham and Brantingham (1995) distinguished between *crime generators* and *crime attractors*. Crime generators are areas that attract large numbers of people. They can produce crime by bringing large concentrations of people (potential victims) into contact with potential offenders who, even though they did not come to the area with the explicit intent to commit crimes, will notice and take advantage of any available criminal opportunities, most often minor property crimes. Crime prevention techniques for crime generator areas are likely to reduce the amount of crime because potential offenders are motivated only by opportunity and removing the opportunity should prevent the crime from occurring.

Crime attractors draw criminal offenders who are strongly motivated to commit particular types of crimes because they provide well-known opportunities for committing those crimes. These areas include streets where prostitutes walk, known drug markets, large shopping malls, and neighborhoods with high concentrations of bars. Crime prevention techniques in crime attractor areas are unlikely to reduce the amount of crime because potential offenders who are motivated to commit crimes travel to the crime attractors where there are known opportunities. Removing the opportunity should mean that potential offenders merely travel to other locations that have the crime-attracting qualities.

Some demographic factors are not related to the risk of crime, but race is. In general, blacks are more afraid of crime than whites are (Skogan & Maxfield, 1981), probably because their actual risk of victimization is higher. They are more likely to live in communities with violent offenders, and they are more likely to believe that they cannot rely on the police to keep their neighborhoods safe (DiIulio, 1994). Moreover, blacks are more likely than whites to live in neighborhoods that have incivilities, and these signs of neighborhood disorder probably increase their perceived risk of victimization.

Fear of crime also appears to be linked to the racial composition of a neighborhood. In particular, some research suggests that fear of crime increases for both blacks and whites—but more so for whites—

when blacks live nearby (Liska, Lawrence, & Sanchirico, 1982). In an examination of residents of Tallahassee, Florida, Chiricos, Hogan, and Gertz (1997) found that white residents' fear of crime was positively related to the numbers of black individuals they perceived to be living within a mile of them. This correlational finding could mean that the perception of the numbers of black people living nearby produces higher fear, or it could mean that higher fear produces the perception that greater numbers of blacks live nearby. Or, underlying racism may cause both the fear and the perception (Chiricos et al., 1997). However, white residents' fear of crime was unrelated to the actual proportion of blacks living within their census block. For both whites and African Americans, fear of crime was determined primarily by respondents' perceived risk that they would be victimized. Research conducted in urban Baltimore (Covington & Taylor, 1991), which has more people, higher population density, and higher levels of incivilities than Tallahassee, found that the racial composition of their neighborhoods affected fear of crime levels for both blacks and whites. That is, whites were most afraid of crime when they lived in predominantly black neighborhoods, and blacks were most afraid of crime when they lived in predominantly white neighborhoods.

Victimization and Fear. Although most studies have found that crime victims are more afraid of crime than nonvictims are (Dubow, McCabe, & Kaplan, 1979; Skogan & Maxfield, 1981), other studies have found that crime victims are not more afraid (Agnew, 1985; Van der Wurff & Stringer, 1989) or are actually less afraid than nonvictims. Victimization may not cause an increase in fear of crime because victims use "neutralization techniques" to cope with the crime (Agnew, 1985). In this way, victims minimize the harm they experienced (e.g., "not as bad as I imagined"), increase their gain from the victimization (e.g., "smartened me up"), or use the victimization to avoid future crimes (e.g., "now I know what to do to be safe"). Moreover, although victims are likely to feel vulnerable and to be open to following advice about crime prevention, these feelings are likely to exist for only a relatively short period after a crime (Weinstein, 1989).

In addition, being victimized does not necessarily make people more afraid and more careful because citizens' ideas about crime, such as their judgments about the rate of crime and demographic characteristics of offenders, are strongly influenced by mass media reports of crime (Tyler, 1984). This result makes sense, given that 10% of network television news, 19% of local television news, and 18% of the front pages of newspapers are concerned with crime and criminal justice. Despite this high rate of coverage, however, mass media reports of crime have little effect on citizens' perceived risks of being crime victims for three reasons (Tyler, 1984). First, people may not find these reports very informative because the media tend to overreport serious crimes, underreport more common but less serious crimes, and focus only on high-crime areas in certain neighborhoods. By reporting only extreme cases of crime, the media might actually make individuals feel less afraid (Schwarz, 1999). Second, many people may not be upset by media reports of crime because they do not see a connection between themselves and the victims in the reports. Finally, people have an illusion of invulnerability. That is, they underestimate their own objective risks of victimization (see Chapter 4).

Breakdown of Informal Social Control

One of the effects of violence in a community is a breakdown of social control mechanisms, both formal and informal, which bring the behavior of individuals into line with a group's norms or rules. Social control refers to the ways in which individuals are motivated to conform to normative behavior patterns and are restrained from behaving in violation of those norms. Formal social control refers to the written law, which is enforced by the police and courts. Informal social control refers to unwritten rules of conduct, which include both local customs and conventions and more universally observed norms for behavior, such as moral codes. Informal social control is enforced by individuals within a community, who use behaviors such as watching, warning, rebuking, and rejecting (Rosenbaum, Lurigio, & Davis, 1998, p. 37). For example, adults in a community with a high level of informal social control would feel mutually responsible for their neighborhood and would probably say something to neighbors' children if, for instance, they were playing too loudly on the street. Informal social control can also be enforced through community groups affiliated with local institutions such as schools, churches, and businesses (Hunter, 1985).

Research suggests that violence in a community can affect informal social control. A breakdown in informal social control is evidenced by the presence of disorder and incivilities. Violent crime can also indirectly affect informal social control; for example, individuals arrested for violent behavior are removed from the community and therefore cannot enforce local norms.

Disorder and Incivilities. The "crime problem" is more than the eight index crimes the FBI uses to track serious crimes in the United States (murder, robbery, rape, aggravated assault, burglary, larceny, motor vehicle theft, and arson). The crime problem also includes disorder, fear, and urban decay (Kelling & Coles, 1996, p. 5). Disorder refers to crude and threatening behavior that violates the sense of civility necessary for urban dwellers to feel safe as they conduct much of their daily lives in the presence of strangers (Kelling & Coles, 1996, p. 14). This disorder includes signs such as dirt, graffiti, noise, abandoned cars, public drunkenness, homeless people, beggars, unlicensed vending and peddling, harassment, public urination and defecation, street prostitution, and youth gangs. One of the most important effects of disorder is that it leads to more disorder, in the same way that littering leads to more littering (Cialdini, Kallgren, & Reno, 1991). Wilson and Kelling (1982) described this process in terms of broken windows:

> If a window in a building is broken *and left unrepaired,* all the rest of the windows will soon be broken. . . . [O]ne unrepaired broken window is a signal that no one cares, so breaking more windows costs nothing. (p. 31)

These signs of disorder may lead to the perception that residents are less likely to participate in maintaining order, for example, by calling the police or intervening directly to get teenagers to stop harassing neighborhood citizens. The process then feeds on itself as offenders become more emboldened to commit crimes, and residents become even more likely to withdraw from public areas. At some point, residents may simply move out of the neighborhood, leaving behind housing that is more likely to be rental than owner occupied and more likely to be vacant than occupied (Skogan, 1990).

Moreover, a declining neighborhood is likely to see changes in the racial, ethnic, and socioeconomic composition of the community. Although physical incivilities are related to crime and to the fear of crime, the exact extent to which they contribute independently to neighborhood crime is not clear because incivilities are related to unemployment rates and nonresidential land uses, both of which are also related to crime.

In his analysis of surveys of 13,000 individuals in 40 neighborhoods in Atlanta, Chicago, Houston, Philadelphia, Newark, and San Francisco, Skogan (1990) found that residents generally agreed about the level of disorder in their community. Skogan also found that signs of social and physical disorder were significantly related to the perceived crime problems in the area even after controlling for the area's level of poverty, racial composition, and stability of the population.

However, based on his analyses of robbery victimizations in 30 neighborhoods, Skogan concluded that economic and social conditions did not have direct effects on the level of crime. Rather, they affected the level of disorder in the communities, and this level of disorder affected the amount of crime in the area. Disorder in a neighborhood was also related to the decline of the area. In neighborhoods with high levels of disorder, residents were afraid and moved out, real estate prices dropped, businesses failed, and no new businesses moved in.

Thus, because disorder seems to be related both to crime and to the fear of crime, police departments have placed more emphasis on reducing signs of disorder in communities. For example, one of the points of emphasis in most community-oriented policing projects is to reduce disorder. And reducing incivilities and disorder does appear to reduce crime; one study found robbery rates in 156 cities were reduced when police focused on reducing disorder, as indicated by increased arrests for disorderly conduct and driving under the influence (Sampson & Cohen, 1988).

Absence of Men in the Community. An indirect way that violent crime can affect a community is the extent to which the reaction of the criminal justice system disrupts informal social control in the community. According to social disorganization theories, ecological characteristics such as poverty, residential mobility, ethnic heterogeneity, and population density disrupt the organizational structures of communities, thereby reducing residents' ties to other residents and to the community and making it difficult for those communities to regulate themselves. In an extension of this idea, Rose and Clear (1998) argued that formal public controls may actually make more public controls necessary. Although arresting and imprisoning offenders removes these dangerous individuals from the neighborhood, which should make the community safer, under some circumstances, this practice may damage neighborhood structure and produce more social disorganization: Sending men to prison means, according to Rose and Clear, that families are disrupted, children are not supervised, and property is not guarded. Thus, according to this hypothesis, even sending violent offenders to prison can have some negative effects on the community.

Breakdown in Formal Social Control

In addition to these effects on informal mechanisms of social control within a community, violent crime can also affect community residents' reliance on formal social control. Although formal and informal social control mechanisms are distinct, formal social control cannot operate effectively without informal social control (Hunter, 1985). That is, police and the criminal justice system generally can function only if they are aided by citizens. Violence in a community can affect formal control in three ways: victims' willingness to report crimes to the police, police officers' willingness to record crimes, and victims' and witnesses' willingness to testify at trial.

Victims' Willingness to Report Crimes. Violence in communities is likely to lead to a norm of not calling the police because individuals fear negative reactions from others in the community and because community residents do not trust the police (Rosenbaum et al., 1998, p. 237). For example, based on his ethnographic research on the culture of youth violence in inner-city Philadelphia, Anderson (1999, p. 321) suggested that "residents sometimes fail to call the police because they believe that the police are unlikely to come or, if they do come, may even harass the very people who called them." Such a norm means not only that individuals are less likely to call the police themselves but also that they would be less likely to advise victims to call the police.

Consistent with this idea, neighborhoods appear to differ in how respondents view the appropriateness of calling the police. For example, Klinger and Bridges (1997) used observational data from 60 neighborhoods in 24 cities across the United States in which police-citizen interactions were coded in three ways: (a) when the police were first made aware of the problem, (b) when the police officers arrived at the scene, and (c) when the police actually encountered the problem. They found that the data contained extensive false positives (calls that were initially classified as crimes that turned out to be noncrimes), false negatives (calls that were initially classified as noncrimes that turned out to be crimes), and misclassification errors (calls that were initially classified as one type of crime that turned out to be another type of crime). These errors were associated with factors correlated to crime in certain neighborhoods. Specifically, calls for service undercounted total crimes in neighborhoods where residents experienced higher rates of victimization, were more afraid of crime, and believed the police responded more slowly to their calls.

Police Officers' Willingness to Record Crimes. Police officers' decisions to record incidents as crimes are relatively invisible because there is no written account for the community and courts to review (Warner, 1997). There is some evidence to suggest that the decision to record or not to record an incident may be related to the type of community in which the incident occurred. In particular, it has been suggested that police are less likely to record incidents in neighborhoods with high percentages of poor or minority populations because the police view a crime in these neighborhoods as less serious (Kress, 1980) and view the victims as people who "deserve what they get" (Stark, 1987, p. 902). Moreover, in areas with high rates of crime, the police are likely to focus only on those comparatively more serious crimes that are beyond what is normal for the neighborhood because they do not have the resources to respond to all crimes.

In her analysis of calls for service in 61 neighborhoods in Boston in 1990, Warner (1997) found that police were less likely to record burglaries in poor neighborhoods. This finding could be due to police officers' devaluing residents of these neighborhoods. For example, because they are poor or because they are perceived to be morally unworthy, police may assume that they are also more criminal.

Victims and Witnesses Are Less Likely to Testify. Related to fear of crime is community residents' reluctance to report crimes or to testify about crimes that police and prosecutors would like to prosecute in the criminal justice system. In many cases, this fear of intimidation is justified because victims and witnesses, particularly in cases involving domestic violence or organized crime, are sometimes threatened or assaulted to discourage them from testifying (Healey, 1995). More recently, intimidation has occurred in the context of an entire community in which gangs, especially those involved in drug selling, create an atmosphere of fear to prevent any witness cooperation.

In addition to being afraid, victims and witnesses are reluctant to testify because of strong ties to their community and a basic distrust of the police. In particular, these individuals may be unwilling to testify if the offenders are neighbors, classmates, members of the same church, or children of friends (Healey, 1995). Intimidation is probably more likely to occur if (a) the initial crime involved violence, (b) there was some relationship between the victim and the offender, (c) the defendant lives near the victim, and (d) the victim is a member of some group that is easily victimized, such as the very young, the elderly, and illegal immigrants (Healey, 1995).

Intimidation can take several forms, but it is usually expressed directly as actual or threatened physical violence or indirectly, for example, by parking outside the victim's house or making nuisance telephone calls. Victims and witnesses also report having their property damaged or being intimidated in the courtroom when large numbers of gang members sit in to demonstrate support for the defendant, often by wearing black armbands or by making threatening hand signals to the victims and witnesses.

In serious cases of intimidation, prosecutors and police must relocate witnesses on a short-term basis, and in extreme cases, they must even provide witnesses with new identities and move them to new locations. In less serious cases, prosecutors and police can reduce victims' and witnesses' perceived intimidation by providing them with protected transportation to and from the courthouse and with separate and secure waiting rooms in the courthouse. Moreover, to ensure safety within the courthouse, many jurisdictions have installed metal detectors and covered windows. They have also installed cameras to videotape individuals as they enter the courtroom. Because a condition for most individuals on probation or parole is to refrain from associating with known gang members, documentation of such association might result in revocation of parole or probation, thus deterring gang members from attending the trial.

Long-Term Effects of
Violence on the Community

With few exceptions, the effects of high rates of violence on a community have not been examined directly. Investigations have been conducted on the impact of disorder on community stability and change (Skogan, 1990). Given that disorder is related to both actual victimization rates and perceived victimization risks, it is probably not unwarranted to assume that the effects of violence are similar to the effects of disorder.

Whether crime and disorder cause neighborhoods to decline depends on the stability of the neighborhood. Neighborhoods are stable to the extent that (a) about the same number of people move in as move out, (b) the people who move in are similar to those who move out, (c) the housing is repaired and rebuilt, and (d) the prices for the housing remain appropriate for the quality of the housing and the social class of the residents in the area (Skogan, 1990, p. 12). In stable communities, potential problems (such as individuals outside carryout liquor stores who harass women, litter the street with bottles, and publicly urinate) are immediately dealt with by residents.

In contrast, in declining communities, residents are dissatisfied with their neighborhoods, withdraw from community life, and want to move. Shops and businesses are likely to fail in such communities because few people want to shop in areas that have high levels of disorder (Skogan, 1990, p. 13). Although many individuals might want to move, generally only those who are more affluent, better educated, and have families actually do. In Chicago, individuals who moved out of the city were more likely to be white, middle class, and family oriented despite the fact that blacks, the poor, and single individuals were more dissatisfied with their neighborhoods (Skogan & Maxfield, 1981).

Aside from the expenses involved in actually moving to a new home, moving a household in response to a crime can be costly because of additional expenses such as costs associated with breaking a lease, getting a new mortgage, and taxes (Dugan, 1999). Moreover, there are social and psychological costs associated with moving because the person is likely to be isolated from former neighbors and therefore more likely to experience stress, anxiety, and depression.

To test the hypothesis that criminal victimization increases the likelihood that victims will move, Dugan (1999) used data from the National Crime Survey for the years 1986 to 1990 to examine 22,375 addresses over a 3-year period. Of this sample, about 23% moved during the 3 years, roughly 8% per year. Dugan found that individuals who had been victimized within a mile of their homes were more likely to move after the victimization than to stay but that crimes committed more than a mile from their homes did not affect their likelihood of moving. However, there was also evidence that multiple victimizations predicted moving, meaning that residents did not move immediately after there was a crime in the neighborhood. In other words, it appears that victims use moving as a strategy to prevent crime, although they probably try other less costly crime prevention measures before moving.

The type of individuals who move because they have been victimized can affect the nature of communities because the individuals who leave are likely to have more economic resources than those who stay (Cullen & Levitt, 1997, as cited in Dugan, 1999) and are more likely to be white than minority (Liska & Bellair, 1995). In addition to this selective out-migration, there is likely to be selective in-migration because more affluent households are less likely than poor ones to move into high-crime neighborhoods. This pattern makes sense in that high crime rates lower property values and decreasing crime rates raise property values (Hellman & Naroff, 1979). Thus, crime-ridden neighborhoods are likely to be poorer and have higher percentages of nonwhites than neighborhoods with lower crime rates. High crime rates might also undermine the relationships of the individuals who remain in the neighborhood (Agnew, 1999).

Once neighborhoods enter a spiral of decline, it is difficult to reverse the process because the individuals who remain and those who move in are generally not active members of community organizations concerned about preventing and responding to crime. The individuals who remain are likely to be elderly and long-time residents who do not want to move or who cannot afford to move (Skogan, 1990, p. 79). Such individuals are unlikely to participate in community groups not only because they are elderly and generally less active but also because their new neighbors are likely to be unfamiliar and different from those neighbors who characterized their community when they chose to move into it. Individuals who move into declining communities are also unlikely to join community groups to improve the neighborhoods because they tend to be renters, single parents, young, poor, and not very well educated. In other words, these individuals tend to be the opposite of the kind of people who characteristically make up community crime prevention programs.

Businesses tend to leave declining communities because they face higher costs of doing business. For example, in high-crime areas, insurance may be prohibitively expensive, or it may not be available at all. Because businesses in declining communities often have high expenses related to security, such as the need to hire off-duty police officers, they often have to charge high prices, which customers may find too expensive and which may force them to shop elsewhere. Moreover, to preserve profit margins, businesses may decide that it is not worthwhile for them to repair and rehabilitate their buildings because they believe that at some point they will simply leave. When businesses leave a community, residents have to go farther to do their shopping, and the neighborhood itself loses some of its cohesive structure. In addition, the city tax base suffers because a closed business does not pay property taxes, and the absence of customers probably means lower sales tax revenues for the city (Skogan, 1990).

Generally, the research on the effects of crime and disorder on communities suggests that the relationship is more complex than that poverty and high rates of residential mobility lead to higher rates of crime (Shaw & McKay, 1942). Rather, the evidence on the effects of disorder and crime on decline in communities suggests that crime can be an important factor in causing decline. That is, there is evidence to suggest that crime causes poverty.

COMMUNITY INTERVENTIONS
TO REDUCE VIOLENT CRIME

Crime prevention refers to reducing the actual incidence of crimes, the incidence of incivilities, and fears about crimes and incivilities. Several types of interventions, both from within and from outside communities, have been tried to reduce violent crime. One type is community organization. A second type is third-party policing. A third type involves changing design features of the physical environment.

Organized Community Efforts to Combat Crime

Although violence is more likely to occur in communities characterized by poverty, ethnic heterogeneity, and high turnover, such communities are also likely to have low rates of participation in community crime prevention programs (Skogan, 1988). Community crime efforts tend to be concentrated in white middle-class, low-crime neighborhoods because such individuals are more likely to join voluntary formal organizations of any type and because they are more likely to have an economic commitment to the community (Greenberg, Rohe, & Williams, 1985). In addition, there are likely to be differences in mutual trust between high-crime and low-crime areas. Residents of high-crime neighborhoods are less likely than residents of low-crime neighborhoods to trust their neighbors because their neighbors and their neighbors' children might be precisely the criminal offenders they are afraid of (Rosenbaum et al., 1998, p. 24). The exception to the general finding that community organization is greatest in white middle-class communities was evidenced by the reactions of individuals in lower-class, largely black neighborhoods plagued by drug dealing (Davis, Smith, Lurigio, & Skogan, 1991, as cited in Rosenbaum et al., 1998, p. 106).

Organized efforts aimed only at preventing crime are rarely successful; effective groups address general community affairs as well as fear of crime (Skogan & Maxfield, 1981). It is also the case that factors that lead to the formation of community efforts to combat crime such as a fear-arousing crime or series of crimes are not the same as factors such as civic-mindedness and resources that increase the probability that those efforts will continue (Rosenbaum et al., 1998, p. 27).

Community efforts to reduce crime might be effective in reducing fear for three reasons (Rosenbaum et al., 1998, p. 44). First, these efforts may operate directly to reduce crime and disorder, and this cleaner, more ordered environment might make residents feel better.

Second, working with others in their community to clean up incivilities might work indirectly to reduce fear by increasing residents' familiarity and mutual trust. Third, residents who themselves clean up the incivilities might gain a perception that they can control aspects of their lives, and this perceived control reduces their fear of crime.

Despite these reasons, however, much research indicates that community crime prevention programs are often not effective in reducing crime and might actually have several negative effects (Rosenbaum et al., 1998, p. 239). One of the problems with community crime prevention programs is that they have lower rates of participation than other types of voluntary organizations, probably because they involve activities that only a small group of people are likely to be interested in and that are unlikely to show clear results (Rosenbaum et al., 1998, p. 22). Some of the negative effects come from crime prevention efforts such as barbed wire fences and guard dogs, which indicate to residents that the area is not safe, that they should not trust their neighbors, and that they should avoid certain areas. These beliefs make residents less likely to think of their neighborhood as a community and less willing to enforce community norms through informal control mechanisms.

One of the possible downsides of organizing residents of a community, either formally or informally, is that these individuals might believe they need to police areas themselves and even to dispense justice themselves. For example, citizen patrol organizations, such as the Guardian Angels, often make residents feel safer even though there is no evidence that they reduce violent crime rates (Rosenbaum et al., 1998, p. 49). Police agencies are generally supportive of such groups as long as they act only as the "eyes and ears" of law enforcement.

The fear, however, is that these citizen patrol organizations might turn into vigilante groups. This fear is not unreasonable given the evidence of spontaneous vigilante activities in which citizens apprehend suspects and immediately punish them, completely outside the criminal justice system (Shotland, 1976). Consider the following example of spontaneous vigilantism (Claiborne, 1973, as cited in Shotland, 1976):

> At 4:45 P.M. September 3, Robert Mayfield, 38, was driving his 1967 Cadillac along Morningside Avenue at West 127th Street when he became involved in an argument with another motorist.
>
> According to police, Mayfield became enraged at the taunting of a small crowd, pulled a gun and fired blindly into the crowd, mortally wounding a 4-year-old boy and injuring another man.
>
> A woman began screaming, "He killed my baby," and an off-duty policeman, Earl Robinson, ran up and ordered Mayfield to drop his gun. Mayfield fired once, hitting Robinson in the chest.

Suddenly, according to Robinson's account, the crowd of by-standers closed in on Mayfield, knocking him to the ground, and kicking him relentlessly. . . . Mayfield was taken to Knicker-Bocker Hospital where he was admitted with cerebral hemorrhage, multiple contusions and internal injuries. (p. 31)

Spontaneous activities such as these are especially likely to occur in high-crime areas, often where there are high concentrations of minorities who believe that the legal system has not dealt adequately with the crime problem. For example, of the 71 police precincts in New York City, the 5 precincts with the most vigilante activity ranked 1st, 2nd, 7th, 9th, and 18th in rates of robbery (Shotland, 1976).

Third-Party Policing

Traditionally, police react to crime by apprehending individual offenders for past or present illegal actions. In contrast, preventing crime requires the police to focus on future events and on individuals other than the potential offender (Buerger & Mazerolle, 1998).

Effective crime prevention consists of both individual and collective responses. Individual responses refer to the generally voluntary actions of individual persons to prevent potential victimizations of themselves and their families. These responses primarily involve (a) target hardening (e.g., using dead bolt locks, installing alarm systems, or learning self-defense techniques and carrying protective devices such as chemical sprays or firearms) and (b) avoidance (e.g., changes in routine activities to avoid certain places some or all of the time). Collective responses refer to the actions of groups of people, which are primarily voluntary (block watches and citizens' patrols), and can also include the design of buildings and neighborhoods in an effort to reduce criminals' opportunities to commit crimes. Generally, these types of situational responses are aimed at making criminal activity riskier, more time-consuming, and less rewarding (Buerger & Mazerolle, 1998). Collective responses may also include government-sponsored activities and government-imposed responses (Gauthier, Hicks, Sansfaçon, & Salel, 1999).

One type of government-imposed response is *third-party policing,* which police use to persuade or coerce individuals to change their environment in ways that will reduce the probability that crime will occur (Buerger & Mazerolle, 1998). This type of intervention is modeled after police use of the civil law to impose obligations on noncriminal third parties as a way of reducing deviant behavior. For example, in many jurisdictions, parents can be penalized if their children are truant from school or violate curfews. Thus, the government assumes that by threatening punishment against parents, parents will act as enforcers to make their children go to school during the day and to be at home at night.

In the same way, police use third-party policing to induce ordinary citizens to supplement existing informal social controls that shape individual behavior and to take better care of their properties (Buerger & Mazerolle, 1998). Third-party policing can have a larger impact than the criminal law because the threat of the criminal law is weakened by (a) low probabilities of being caught, (b) plea bargaining to avoid severe sentences, (c) long delays before the sentence is imposed, and (d) early release from prison because of overcrowding in the system (Buerger & Mazerolle, 1998). In contrast, third-party policing gives police the power to impose penalties that have direct and immediate detrimental effects on the person, including, for example, use of land and running of businesses. Third-party policing forces landowners, caretakers of apartments, and business managers to enforce the law for those who use their property or patronize their businesses.

For example, in Oakland, California, the police developed a program called "Beat Health," in which police officers identified locations with high rates of citizen complaints and reported crimes (Buerger & Mazerolle, 1998). The work was then passed on to a team consisting of five police officers, five police service technicians, and a community liaison officer supervised by a police sergeant and working with three attorneys in the city attorney's office. The team worked on locations with drug problems by focusing on the enforcement of municipal housing, fire, sewer, and safety codes. In almost all cases, property owners worked with the police team to remedy these problems and to screen tenants more effectively rather than go to court. The police closed the case when no drug arrests or drug-related emergency calls had been made for 3 months.

In Minneapolis, city officials initially did not have municipal ordinances with which to impose minimum conditions on landlords of residential property. As a result, the police had to rely on appeals to the landowners about increasing profitability (e.g., through fewer repair bills for tenant-caused damage), to political figures, and to the public through the news media.

Generally, forcing landlords (through threat of inspection and penalties) to meet health, safety, and building code regulations not only brings rental housing up to the minimum standards but also serves a larger function of crime prevention. Several studies suggest that such threats against landlords of privately owned rental housing can reduce drug dealing and crime (Green, 1995; Sherman et al., 1997).

One of the problems with police-focused interventions to prevent crime is that blocking opportunities at some times or in some situations may, if potential offenders are not deterred, simply move the crime rather than prevent it (Buerger & Mazerolle, 1998). Crime can be displaced to other locations (spatial displacement) or other times (temporal displacement), it can be committed in another way (tactical displacement), or converted into another crime (target displacement).

Although third-party policing may yet develop into a more comprehensive method of crime prevention, there are possible limitations to its widespread development (Buerger & Mazerolle, 1998). In particular, the local ordinances used to threaten landowners may be challenged and overturned in court. Moreover, if the police were to be involved in an abuse of the procedure (e.g., an overly aggressive attack on an innocent landowner), there might be widespread backlash against the concept.

Environmental Design

Just as there is some evidence that the physical environment might be related to crime causation, there is also evidence that environmental factors are related to crime prevention. For example, convenience stores are less likely to be robbed if there are other businesses nearby, if the safe is inaccessible, and if the outside area is well lighted. This emphasis on environmental design to prevent crime can be effective with some types of crime because it attempts to prevent criminal behavior before it occurs, rather than trying to deal with a crime problem after a crime occurs.

In the urban renewal of the 1960s, many public housing high-rises were built, with accommodations for hundreds of families. These building designs resulted in very high crime rates, especially in interior public spaces such as lobbies, hallways, elevators, stairwells, laundry rooms, and basements. These areas were often deserted, many of the apartments were empty, and some buildings, such as the Pruitt-Igoe project in St. Louis, were simply blown up because they were failures as public housing.

Newman (1972) argued that architects could design buildings that created private and semiprivate spaces that families would feel belonged to them and that they would therefore keep under surveillance and defend against intruders who did not belong there. Newman suggested that defensible spaces include apartment buildings with semiprivate entrances for five or six families rather than for hundreds. These ideas were supported in analyses of archival data from the New York City Housing Authority (Newman, 1973).

Newman also suggested that defensible space include neighborhood streets, where access could be limited by making through streets into dead ends (Cose, 1994). This idea has been used in the Five Oaks neighborhood in Dayton, Ohio, a transitional area that had gone from 3% to 43% black over a 20-year period (Cose, 1994). Accompanying this change was an increase in prostitution, drug dealing, and poverty in the area of about a half square mile. The police department called Newman in to implement changes to create defensible neighborhoods that would make anonymous crimes more difficult to commit. These changes included installing speed bumps, closing streets and alleys, and placing brick-and-metal gates decorated with the neighborhood logo. After a year, traffic had declined 67% within the neighborhood, and crimes had fallen by 26%.

Aspects of the physical environment might affect the chances of a crime occurring because they influence how potential offenders perceive and evaluate a possible crime site (Taylor & Harrell, 1996). Assuming that potential offenders act rationally, they will choose to commit crimes that require the least amount of effort, that are likely to provide the most benefits, and that have the fewest risks of being caught. Thus, according to this rational-offender perspective, offenders would decide whether or not to commit a crime in a particular location depending on factors such as (a) how easy it would be to enter the location, (b) how vulnerable the targets are, (c) how likely the offender is to be seen, and (d) how easy it would be for the offender to leave the location after the crime is completed.

The emphasis on environmental factors related to crime has produced a large area of literature called environmental criminology, which focuses on environmental factors related to the fear and incidence of crime, because fear is not necessarily related to the actual occurrence of crime. Clarke (1995) proposed a general model of situational crime prevention, which assumes that potential offenders act rationally and would therefore be less likely to commit crimes if they had to exert more effort, if they faced greater risks of getting caught, and if there were fewer rewards for committing the crime. As shown in Table 6.1, Clarke described four strategies within each of these three general motivational concerns.

TABLE 6.1 Situational Crime Prevention Strategies

Increase the Effort	Increase the Risks	Reduce the Rewards
Harden the target	Entry/exit screening	Target removal
Access control	Formal surveillance	Identify property
Deflect offenders	Surveillance by employees	Reduce inducements
Control facilitators	Natural surveillance	Rule setting

SOURCE: Clarke, R. V. (1995). Situational Crime Prevention. In M. Tonry & D. P. Farrington (Eds.), *Building a Safer Society: Strategic Approaches to Crime Prevention: Vol. 19. Crime and Justice: A Review of Research* (pp. 91-150). Chicago: University of Chicago Press. Reprinted with permission.

If the effort required to commit a crime is too great, potential criminals who are thinking rationally should decide that the crime is not worth committing. One way to increase potential offender effort is to harden the target by using physical barriers or reinforced materials. Putting steering locks on cars and safeguarding bus drivers with protective screens are examples of target hardening. Access control is a second way to increase potential offender effort. If these individuals cannot easily get into apartments or office buildings because entry requires an identification badge or a doorman to open the door, they might be kept out, in the same way that a moat and a drawbridge regulated access in medieval castles. Deflecting potential offenders is a third way to increase their effort; their behavior is channeled so that unacceptable behavior becomes more difficult. For example, rival soccer fans might be physically separated and their arrivals and departures scheduled so that there would be no long periods of waiting. A final way of increasing effort is to control facilitators—that is, to restrict factors that increase the likelihood of a crime occurring. For example, in the Old West, customers in saloons often had to give up their weapons when they entered, to lower the risk of drunken gunfights. Many bars serve beer in plastic mugs rather than glass, to make them less likely to be used as weapons.

In addition to considering effort, rational criminals are attuned to the risk of getting caught. Presumably, if the risks are greater, potential offenders are less likely to commit crimes. One way to increase this risk is to use entry/exit screening—that is, to increase the risk of detecting individuals who illegally carry objects. A good example of this strategy is the screening of airline passengers and baggage for weapons and explosives. Formal surveillance by police officers or monitoring devices are other ways to increase potential offenders' risks of getting caught. If, for example, there are closed-circuit television cameras in a public transit station monitored by transit police, potential offenders may be deterred because they know that their behavior will be observed and recorded. Surveillance by employees is a third way to increase the risks of catching an offender. For example, individuals such as hotel doormen increase the likelihood that criminals will be seen and caught. A final way to increase the risk of detection is to rely on natural surveillance. That is, individuals in their everyday activities can serve as deterrents to crime. This strategy would include programs such as Neighborhood Watch and would argue that factors that increase natural surveillance, such as better street lighting, would increase deterrence.

In addition to considering the amount of effort involved in a crime and the risk of getting caught, a rational criminal is concerned about the potential rewards. Measures that reduce the rewards should reduce crime. One way to reduce the rewards is to remove the valuable target completely. For example, requiring exact-change fares for buses dramatically reduced robberies (Chaiken, Lawless, & Stevenson, 1974, as cited in Clarke, 1995) because potential criminals knew that bus drivers did not carry change and did not have access to fares. Identifying property is a second way to reduce the rewards of crime. Property marked with their owners' social security numbers and auto parts with vehicle identification numbers are more difficult to sell because they can be traced, and therefore should reduce the rewards of the crime. Removing inducements is a third way to reduce the rewards of crime. For example, the New York City subway system had a policy of immediately cleaning any of its 6,245 subway cars that had been painted with graffiti because this deprived offenders of the opportunity to see their work on display. A final way to reduce the rewards of crime is to set rules so that there is no ambiguity about the acceptability or unacceptability of conduct. For example, several colleges and universities have established rules about appropriate sexual conduct to make it clear to potential offenders that sexual behavior without consent is wrong.

Although some of these strategies have been effective in preventing crime, there is evidence that the primary effect of many of these strategies is to displace crime to other targets rather than to prevent crime completely. Moreover, many of these strategies have not produced much vigilance. For example, closed-circuit television systems permit continuous monitoring of all individuals on subway platforms, but if they are not monitored, their presence may not deter crime. Similarly, the assumption of Neighborhood Watch programs that people pay attention to what is occurring outside their homes is almost certainly overstated. Moreover, although some of these strategies may be effective, they make life inconvenient and are therefore often subverted. For example, apartment residents sometimes prop open self-locking doors so that their friends can enter, but in doing so, they also allow others, including potential criminals, to enter the building.

It is important to note that although changes in design might be effective in reducing crime and the fear of crime, these changes in the environment may actually increase crime and disorder. For example, potential victims can have more perceived control over locations if there is more lighting, if their view is not obstructed, if there are no hiding places, and if they can choose paths that allow them to avoid areas or people they do not want to encounter. These changes might make potential victims less cautious when they venture outside their homes, thus increasing their risk of victimization (Brantingham & Brantingham, 1995).

Similarly, alterations in the environment designed to reduce fear might have the counterintuitive result of increasing crime. For example, increased street lighting, viewing angles, and escape routes may increase crime because potential victims are more likely to use the areas. These fear-reduction techniques mean that potential offenders are also more likely to use the area. For example, prostitutes generally prefer well-lighted areas so that they can be seen by potential customers and by others on the street, because greater visibility probably means they are safer.

Moreover, it may be that changes made to protect property actually work to further signs of physical disorder. For example, following the riots of the late 1960s and early 1970s, many businesses installed solid-metal, pull-down security gates to cover their store windows at night. These gates do make the stores more resistant to break-ins through the windows, although they have no effect on break-ins through the back door or the roof, which may be more common. Moreover, the solid-metal gates mean that the store's lights cannot illuminate the streets and police cannot use their flashlights to inspect store interiors. Finally, because the solid metal curtains give the impression of a fortress, which limits economic development (e.g., because pedestrians cannot window-shop), many city planners and business groups have proposed bans on them (Pacelle, 1996).

SUMMARY

In this chapter, we examined the effects of violent victimizations on communities. At the community level, violent crime leads to increased fear and breakdown of both informal and formal social control. In addition, violent crime leads indirectly to the breakdown of communities because individuals and businesses are likely to move, if possible, to avoid the dangers of violent crime. Three types of community-level interventions have been used to reduce the effects of violent crime: organized community efforts to prevent crime, third-party policing, and changes in the design of the built environment.

■ DISCUSSION QUESTIONS

1. In what ways can residents be given more control over their neighborhood? Are these interventions effective in reducing crime? What role can the police play in reversing the spiral of decay and increasing community cohesion?

2. The idea that taking offenders out of the community might reduce informal social control is nonintuitive. Might there be some types of crime for which this effect would be most true?

3. Is it acceptable for police in high-crime neighborhoods to record citizen reports of crime at a lower rate than police in low-crime neighborhoods do? Should police focus only on the most serious crimes in these neighborhoods?

4. Is third-party policing ethical, or does it amount to government-sponsored extortion?

7

Summary and
Implications

A traditional concern of the criminal justice system is the reintegration of offenders into the community as productive members of society (Braithewaite, 1989). At the same time, however, the criminal justice system has not been very concerned with reintegrating *victims* back into society and restoring them to their circumstances prior to the crime (Fletcher, 1995, p. 202). For the most part, this lack of concern reflects the attitude that crimes are offenses against the state rather than against individuals and that for several centuries, victims have been important to the prosecution only insofar as they can serve as witnesses against the defendants. In the past 30 years, however, victims have gained some rights regarding their role in the criminal justice system, and there has been increased concern about their welfare.

In this last chapter, we examine those changes, both governmental and nongovernmental, in terms of their success in meeting the problems of victims and communities discussed in the earlier chapters and briefly summarized below. In addition, we argue that victims' informal social networks and the formal legal system should be more supportive of victims not only because victims need help but also because such a policy would benefit the operation of the criminal justice system. We also discuss policies by which these goals could be achieved and point out ways that these policies might be harmful to the system. Our discussion of implications focuses on individual-level interventions and system-level interventions.

THE EFFECTS OF VICTIMIZATIONS
ON INDIVIDUALS AND COMMUNITIES

In this book, we have made three arguments about violent victimizations: (a) They cause physical harm and psychological distress to victims, (b) they cause psychological distress to victims' families and friends, and (c) they harm neighborhoods and communities.

Victims of interpersonal violence often suffer physical injuries which, in a small percentage of cases, require medical care and even hospitalization. Much more commonly, victims are likely to experience psychological distress, including depression, anxiety, and PTSD, and to experience cognitive consequences such as increased self-blame, lowered self-esteem, and greater fear of crime. Behaviorally, violent victimization is likely to result in withdrawal and is associated with increased drug and alcohol use.

Victims' friends and relatives also suffer indirect victimization because of violent crimes. At an extreme, these individuals may suffer secondary traumatic stress, which refers to those psychological symptoms typical of PTSD. More common are heightened fear of crime and greater avoidance of situations presumed to be risky.

Finally, neighborhoods and communities suffer because of violent crimes. High levels of violent crime result from and contribute to further breakdowns in both informal and formal social control. Violent crime causes individuals and businesses to withdraw from community life and, if it is feasible, to leave the community.

INDIVIDUAL-LEVEL INTERVENTIONS

For individual victims, interventions relate to reducing psychological distress, reducing the risk of future victimizations, and gaining restitution for their losses.

Reducing Psychological Distress

As discussed in Chapter 3, how victims cope depends to a great extent on their experiences immediately after the crime, including their interactions with the police, with families, friends, and strangers, and with formal victim service agencies. Individual-level interventions to reduce victims' distress thus need to involve all three of these groups.

Police. Police officers who respond to victims supportively are more likely to gain victims' trust, which means that victims will probably be more willing to provide information to these officers and to participate in any subsequent investigation and prosecution. Because of their important role, agencies have recently begun to focus on how police can be more sensitive to victims' needs. One of these agencies is the Office for Victims of Crime, an agency within the U.S. Department of Justice.

According to the Office for Victims of Crime (2000), police officers must understand that crime victims have three major needs: a need to feel safe, a need to express their emotions and tell their stories, and a need to know "what comes next" after their victimizations. Some of the suggestions from the Office for Victims of Crime about how police officers should interact with victims appear in Table 7.1.

In the case of victims with special needs, such as the elderly, child victims, and victims of sexual assault, the Office for Victims of Crime urges police to be aware that these groups are likely to suffer higher levels of physical and mental injuries than other types of victims.

Families and Friends. Although police officers can affect victims' recovery, other individuals, particularly families and friends, are likely to have even more influence on victims' short-term and long-term reactions. As suggested in Chapter 3, others can influence whether victims label an event as a crime, their view of how serious the crime is, what coping options they choose, and how they recover from the crime. Crime victims often consult with others, and the information and advice they receive from these advisers strongly influence their decision to call or not to call the police, even if this advice comes from a stranger (Greenberg & Ruback, 1992).

In terms of social influence on victims' recovery, victims often rely on lay individuals or professionals or both for social support (Davis, Brickman, & Baker 1991; Norris, Kaniasty, & Scheer, 1990). A key variable in how people cope with trauma is the extent to which they discuss and confront their traumas; victims who confide in others about a traumatic event have less psychological distress and better physical health (Pennebaker & Beall, 1986).

Because victims often turn to their families and friends for social support, it is important that the potential advisers to victims (i.e., all of

TABLE 7.1   Tips to Law Enforcement Officers for Responding to
              Victims' Three Primary Needs

Victims' need to feel safe

- Ask victim to tell you in just a sentence or two what happened. Ask if they have any physical injuries.
- Take care of their medical needs first.
- Offer to contact a family member, friend, or crisis counselor for victims.
- Provide a "safety net" for victims before leaving them. Make telephone calls and pull together personal or professional support for the victims. Give victims a pamphlet listing resources available for help or information. This pamphlet should include contact information for local crisis intervention centers and support groups; the prosecutor's office and the victim-witness assistance office; the state victim compensation/assistance office; and other nationwide services, including toll-free hotlines.

Victims' need to express their emotions

- Assure victims that their emotional reactions to the crime are not uncommon. Sympathize with the victims by saying things such as "You've been through something very frightening. I'm sorry"; "What you're feeling is completely normal"; "This was a terrible crime. I'm sorry it happened to you."
- Counter any self-blame by victims by saying things such as "You didn't do anything wrong. This was not your fault."
- Ask open-ended questions. Avoid questions that can be answered by "yes" or "no." Ask questions such as "Can you tell me what happened?" or "Is there anything else you can tell me?"

Victims' need to know "what comes next" after their victimization

- Briefly explain law enforcement procedures for tasks such as the filing of your report, the investigation of the crime, and the arrest and arraignment of a suspect.
- Tell victims about subsequent law enforcement interviews or other kinds of interviews they can expect.
- Counsel victims that lapses of concentration, memory losses, depression, and physical ailments are normal reactions for crime victims. Encourage them to reestablish their normal routines as quickly as possible to help speed their recovery.

SOURCE: Abridged from Office for Victims of Crime (2000).

us) understand the ways they may help victims. For example, a community-based, spousal abuse education program in a low-income community on the outskirts of Mexico City includes information for both victims and community members (Fawcett, Heise, Isita-Espejel, & Pick, 1999). An example of a campaign message for community members describes victims' needs for social support and tells individuals exactly what actions they should take.

The Abused Woman Needs You
Approach her and ask her what is wrong
Support her by listening and establishing trust
Help her, she may be in danger
Accompany her to victim support centers
(Fawcett et al., 1999)[1]

Victim Service Agencies. In addition to social support from families and friends, victims may also need professional help (e.g., clergy, mental health, or legal aid). Today, there are more than 10,000 victim services programs in the county, including over 2,000 that serve battered women and more than 2,000 rape crisis centers (Office for Victims of Crime, 1998). In addition to crisis and mental health counseling, these agencies assist victims with shelter, information, emergency financial assistance, and advocacy.

Crime victims are more likely to use mental health services if violence was used during the crime, if they had previously been criminally victimized, and if they had received informal social support from families and friends. Predicting who is most likely to use mental health services following a victimization is important for intervention strategies because the use of mental health care services is related to a reduction in symptoms—but only when the help is sought immediately and is at least 6 months in duration (Norris, Kaniasty, & Thompson, 1997). Data from a study on the psychological consequences of victimization have shown that approximately 1 in 6 crime victims seek professional mental health services within the first year after the crime. Furthermore, violent-crime victims reported higher mental health services usage rates than the rates reported in the general population (Norris et al., 1990).

Once victims seek treatment, the type of mental health care they receive can vary. In the past, most victims would have received a crisis-oriented treatment approach (Falsetti & Resnick, 1995). Crisis counseling is short-term and entails providing the victims with information and referrals. Currently, other longer-term treatment options are available, most of which are *cognitive-behavioral interventions.* Examples of these longer-term treatments include exposure therapy, stress-inoculation training, and cognitive therapy (see Chapter 4). Exposure therapy entails having victims confront their victimization experiences by activating trauma memories, either through imagination or confronting real-life situations. Exposure occurs in gradual steps until the PTSD symptoms decrease. Stress-inoculation training is an anxiety management technique. Rather than trying to ameliorate anxiety and fear symptoms, stress inoculation attempts to train victims to manage their anxiety and fear symptoms more effectively through education, skill building, and application. Cognitive processing therapy not only focuses on fear and anxiety symptoms but also on the cognitive effects of victimization, such as shame, anger, and disgust. Cognitive processing is similar to exposure therapy, but the primary focus is to help victims accommodate their cognitive schemas that were disrupted by the victimization event. All these treatment approaches have shown some success in ameliorating PTSD symptoms of victims.

Victims often require support and help and so do many of their family members and friends. Unfortunately, there has been little, if any, empirical research on the mental health needs of and appropriate treatment for victims' families and friends. However, given the stresses they experience (see Chapter 5), we suspect that such research will take place in the next few years.

Reducing Revictimizations

A small percentage of people account for a disproportionately large number of criminal victimizations. Given this high rate, it is not surprising that the best predictor of future victimization is past victimization, and thus from a policy perspective, it makes sense to focus crime prevention efforts on these high-risk individuals.

The Risk of Revictimization. Several studies indicate that revictimization is most likely to occur soon after the victimization (Farrell, 1995), and this finding appears to be true for different types of crime (burglary, property crime, racial assaults, and domestic violence). One study in England, for example, found that the risk of a repeat victimization is particularly likely within 11 days (Lloyd, Farrell, & Pease, 1994). The fact that repeat victimizations are likely to occur so soon after prior victimizations means that prevention efforts should be in place within 24 hours to maximize prevention (Farrell, 1995). Furthermore, given that crime prevention resources are limited, it makes sense to focus efforts on those places with the highest risk. Thus, after the period of the highest revictimization risk has passed, those resources (e.g., a portable alarm or security guards) should be moved to persons or areas with higher risks because they have been more recently victimized.

Interventions to Prevent Revictimization. There have been some experimental investigations of the possibility of educating victims to prevent revictimization. In an experimental study of whether victims can lower their risk of subsequent crime by learning crime prevention skills, Davis and Smith (1994) assigned robbery, burglary, and assault victims either to a control group that received a single session of traditional crisis counseling, primarily psychological support and information about the criminal justice system, or to an experimental group that received both traditional crisis counseling and crime prevention training. This included a discussion with a counselor on specific techniques they could use to prevent crime in the context of their daily living patterns, a film on strategies for crime avoidance, and the opportunity for a free home security survey. As would be expected, the experimental group was more knowledgeable about crime prevention training, more positive about the usefulness of crime prevention techniques, and more likely to engage in precautionary behaviors. However, the experimental group was not less afraid of crime. Indeed, individuals who took more precautions were more likely to be afraid of crime, possibly because information about crime and the need for taking precautions might have increased people's fear. There was no difference between the experimental and control groups in terms of revictimization over the next year.

Based on the success of intervention programs in Great Britain to prevent partner-violence revictimizations, a similar program was established in New York City (Davis & Taylor, 1997). Under this program, the Domestic Violence Intervention Education Project (DVIEP), a two-person team consisting of a social worker and a police officer visits the victims and perpetrators. Victims are told how to obtain restraining orders, seek counseling, move to a shelter, or apply for financial assistance. They receive information about the use of social services, and all victims are encouraged to report violence if it occurs again. Perpetrators are told that they are being monitored by the police and may be referred to treatment groups for batterers.

To test the effects of these interventions on victims' use of services, calls to the police, and partner violence, Davis and Taylor (1997) conducted an experiment in which (a) households were randomly assigned to receive or not to receive a follow-up visit from the police officer-social worker team and (b) housing projects in the area were randomly assigned to receive or not to receive public education about partner violence (which included leaflets, pamphlets, and informational presentations). It was expected that households receiving either of these treatments compared with households that did not would be more likely to report acts of violence to the police, to report violence sooner, and to use social services for partner violence.

Neither intervention affected the level of subsequent violence in the homes, based on self-reports by victims. However, reports to the police of new violence were increased by both intervention strategies. That is, homes that received follow-up visits were more likely than those that did not receive such visits to report violence to the police, and homes in projects that received the education programs were more likely to report violence than homes in projects that did not receive the programs. These effects were stronger for homes with more serious histories of violence. Thus, the two programs might have increased victims' confidence that the police would be able to do something (e.g., arrest the offender) that ultimately would lead to a lessening of the violence.

These experimental investigations (Davis & Smith, 1994; Davis & Taylor, 1997) suggest that it is possible to give victims important information that might decrease their risk of revictimization. However, even though victims are more knowledgeable, they are not necessarily less afraid of crime or less likely to be victimized again. Future research is clearly needed.

Civil Litigation

A different type of intervention with victims is to have them file civil litigation against the perpetrator and negligent third parties, because most criminal acts are also tortious acts (i.e., civil wrongs) that constitute grounds for a civil lawsuit. For example, the parents of victims Nicole Brown Simpson and Ron Goldman successfully brought a civil suit against O. J. Simpson for wrongful death.

Lawsuits Against Perpetrators. One advantage of civil litigation over criminal prosecution is that the burden of proof in civil lawsuits (a preponderance of the evidence) is lower than that for criminal cases (beyond a reasonable doubt). Moreover, in civil litigation, the victim can present evidence that would be inadmissible in a criminal case. For example, in civil cases, the victim is able to bring in evidence of prior similar crimes committed by the perpetrator and can force the perpetrator to testify. A final advantage of civil litigation is that it gives victims a sense of control. In their dealings with the criminal justice system, many victims feel powerless, because the system is designed to protect the interests of the larger society rather than those of the victim (Brien, 1992). Even when victims are consulted about plea bargaining agreements, the prosecutor still has complete discretion to accept the offender's plea to a lesser charge, because the victim's wishes are only one of many factors the prosecutor must consider (e.g., the strength of the evidence, the cost of a trial, or the likelihood of a conviction by the jury).

Although a victim can proceed with a civil suit completely independently of the criminal action, in most cases it makes more sense for the victim to wait until after the criminal action has been resolved. Waiting serves two strategic functions (Brien, 1992). First, if the victim files a civil action suit against the defendant in a criminal case before the case is resolved, the victim's credibility is likely to be undermined because the victim's willingness to testify against the defendant will probably be seen as being prompted by a desire to win monetary damages in the civil suit. Second, if the defendant is found guilty in the criminal trial, the victim will not need to prove that a tort occurred because a conviction in criminal court is usually sufficient to establish civil liability. Although there are advantages for the victim waiting before filing suit, the victim generally should not wait too long because the statute of limitations requires that suits be filed within a reasonable time (often 2 years) after the tort occurred.

Despite the potential advantages of a civil lawsuit against the offender, it should be noted that there are also potential costs (Brien, 1992). It is possible, given the vagaries of trials, that even victims with strong cases can lose their lawsuits. Other disadvantages include the stresses from being in a lawsuit and of having to testify and confront the offender, the potential delay of several years in getting a court decision because of case backlogs, and the costs of filing fees, court expenses, and attorneys. Moreover, there is the possibility that the offender has no assets and no insurance; therefore, even if the plaintiff-victim wins the lawsuit, the victim will not be able to collect at all on the judgment or will be able to receive only minimal compensation. Nevertheless, in such cases, victims may still benefit psychologically by having a court validate that they were wronged.

Lawsuits Against Third Parties. Because of problems associated with suing the offender, victims often sue negligent third parties, such as the owners of the property where an assault, robbery, or sexual assault occurred (a procedure that is analogous to third-party policing; see Chapter 6). Such lawsuits can not only help individual victims of crime but can also promote greater safety and encourage crime prevention measures. For instance, these kinds of lawsuits have led to what are now relatively standard security features, such as peepholes in doors to hotel rooms and adequate lighting in the common areas of apartment complexes (Brien, 1992).

Since the early 1980s, more and more crime victims living in apartments have sued their landlords for failing to provide them with safe places to live (e.g., inadequate locks and windows) and for failing to inform them about past instances of crime in the apartments (Soto, 1993). In these suits, crime victims generally present evidence of prior similar crimes that should have put the property owner on notice to make conditions safer. To be applicable, the prior incidents must have been of the same type and nature as the most recent crime and must have occurred with enough frequency that it was reasonable for the owner to have expected a crime to occur (Premises Liability, 1990). For example, a victim raped at an apartment building would probably be able to recover financially if she could show that rapes had previously occurred there. Instead of the *prior similar incidents* test, some states use a *totality of the circumstances* test. That is, based on all of the circumstances, the test determines whether it was reasonable to expect the owner to take precautions. Under a "totality" test, prior similar incidents are just one type of factor that affects the reasonableness of expecting the owner to have taken precautions to prevent the crime.

Since 1983, courts have made it easier for victims to sue landowners, so that the average settlement (before trial) in these cases was $600,000, whereas the average jury verdict was $1.3 million. As a result of these suits, many landlords now make it a policy to immediately notify tenants of any crimes on the premises so that tenants cannot claim that they did not know of the danger. In addition, some companies have required tenants to sign forms in which they agree not to hold the landlord liable for criminal acts on the property. Although such waivers are probably not valid, statements in them, such as agreeing to report the crimes and to work with the police, do place some responsibility on the tenants.

Courts in several states have concluded that retail stores have a duty to take reasonable actions to protect customers from criminal acts in parking lots which, based on prior crimes, are reasonably foreseeable (Lee, 1997). The problem has become acute because parking lots have gotten larger and stores are open 24 hours a day. Because parking lots are private property, the police cannot be expected to do anything more than routinely patrol the area. It is up to the stores to exercise reasonable care to protect their customers. The parking lot owner's responsibility will depend on whether the area is a high-crime area (e.g., whether it is frequented by drunks or drug users), whether the owner was aware of criminal activity in the area, and whether prior criminal activity had taken place on the parking lot. The owner's duty to customers may be especially high if, as is the case with automatic teller machines and night depositories, the use of the facilities carries some risk.

In sum, the advantages of civil lawsuits against criminal perpetrators are monetary compensation, punishing the perpetrator, encouraging third parties to take measures to prevent crime, and giving victims control over legal matters involving them.

NEIGHBORHOOD-LEVEL
INTERVENTIONS

At the neighborhood level, interventions have been aimed at modifying the environment, helping the police respond to crime more effectively, and crime prevention.

Environmental Interventions

Four different approaches related to features of the physical environment have been used to reduce the amount of crime and the perception of crime in homes and neighborhoods: (a) changing the design of housing and the layout of city blocks, (b) changing traffic and land use patterns, (c) encouraging the use of territorial markers, and (d) reducing the signs of physical deterioration. Housing design and block layout refer to physical features that make these areas more defensible. In the case of public housing, this redesign has meant constructing low-rise rather than high-rise buildings, clearly delineating private spaces through fences and similar types of markers, and providing unimpeded lines of sight.

A second approach to crime reduction through environmental design relates to changing boundaries, land uses, and traffic patterns. In general, low-crime neighborhoods have features that lead to less traffic (e.g., one-way streets, narrower streets, and a lower percentage of commercial property). In part, this lower level of crime in low-traffic areas may occur because residents in neighborhoods with high levels of automobile and pedestrian traffic (both of which are associated with commercial land use) tend to use their front yards less and interact less with their neighbors (Appleyard, 1981; Baum, Davis, & Aiello, 1978). Related to this lower use and less frequent interaction is a general reduction in informal social control, meaning that residents are less likely to enforce the norms of their neighborhood or the formal laws. Thus, for example, residents are less likely to intervene if they see possible offending.

A third approach to crime reduction through environmental design is to increase residents' use of territorial markers (e.g., name plates or fences) because such markers serve as a signal to outsiders that residents are likely to respond to threats of crime. Studies indicate that the more markers there are in the neighborhood, the safer residents feel. Because of the value of creating spaces that residents can watch and defend, many communities have encouraged neighborhood cleanup, beautification programs, and urban gardening programs.

The fourth approach to crime reduction through environmental design concerns controlling signs of physical deterioration (e.g., trash, graffiti, broken windows, or abandoned buildings), because these signs of *incivilities* indicate to residents that government officials and agencies do not care about the neighborhood (see Chapter 6). That perception, in turn, means that residents are less likely to participate in maintaining order, for example, through calling the police or intervening directly to get teenagers to stop harassing neighborhood citizens. This process then feeds on itself, as offenders become more emboldened to commit crime and residents become even more likely to withdraw from public areas. At some point, residents may simply move out of the neighborhood, leaving behind housing that is more likely to be rented than owner occupied and more likely to be vacant than occupied (Skogan, 1990).

Police Response to Crime

There have been three periods of policing in the United States (Kelling & Moore, 1988): political, professional, and community. During the 19th century, local politicians controlled the police. In this political era, police officers knew the neighborhoods well and maintained order, but this period was also marked by corruption and the abuse of civil rights, particularly those of immigrants. From 1900 to the early 1970s, the professional period of policing, police focused their efforts on crime, relying heavily on technology such as patrol cars, radios, and 911 emergency telephone systems to help them catch offenders. The community-policing era, which began in the 1970s, changed the focus of police efforts from rapid response to citizens' calls about crime, regardless of the urgency, to a problem-solving approach to crime prevention in which citizens were seen as partners.

One focus of community-policing efforts has been to work with community residents to develop block watch programs and to clean up neighborhoods, including painting over graffiti and removing abandoned vehicles (Fleissner & Heinzelmann, 1996). These programs can lower fear not only because the signs of community decay (the "broken windows") are removed but also because residents develop a trusting relationship with the police. Further joint activities can address other problems in the community, which will also increase residents' beliefs that they can control their neighborhood. Moreover, these efforts at improving police-community relations are presumed to improve communication and trust with community residents, a necessary condition if police are to be able to solve crimes.

In addition to working with neighborhood residents, community-policing efforts also involve multiagency partnerships with educational, social, and other governmental agencies. Together, all of these groups work to identify problems, identify possible solutions, implement responses, and evaluate the effectiveness of the responses. Many of these efforts involve dealing with the environment, such as closing drug houses and redirecting traffic around the neighborhood as happened in a demonstration of community policing in Hartford, Connecticut (Fleissner & Heinzelmann, 1996). The program also included citizen patrols of the neighborhoods, increased lighting, cleanup campaigns, and increased control over juveniles' activities (e.g., setting opening and closing times of public parks). Such actions can not only reduce the fear of crime and perhaps crime itself but can also increase residents' informal social control (e.g., they have some control over who can enter their neighborhood) and the quality of their lives.

Community policing, through its emphasis on multiagency solutions to social problems of housing, unemployment, and education, helps to deal with factors that are highly correlated with crime. A second way that community policing reduces crime is through better police-community relations. Poor police-community relations prevent crimes from being solved because police need leads to do so.

Community-based crime prevention requires fundamental changes in how problems are characterized, how the roles of citizens and criminal justice professionals are defined, and how solutions are proposed and implemented (Kelling & Coles, 1996). Traditionally, the criminal justice system has focused on the most serious crimes, reacting to them when notified by citizens but otherwise not becoming involved in community life. In contrast, community-based crime prevention is primarily citizen focused. Neighborhood-based groups are expected to determine priorities and to work to control disorder, fear, and crime. Police and other criminal justice agencies are expected to work with citizens in identifying and solving larger problems that cause individual criminal actions. The research in Chicago on collective efficacy (see Chapter 6) is consistent with the suggestion that community policing might be an effective means of helping communities develop mechanisms of informal social control to combat violence in their neighborhoods.

The movement toward community policing reflects frustration with traditional societal responses to violent crime as well as recognition that there should be an emphasis on preventing violence (Roth & Moore, 1995). Work within the public health field parallels the movement toward community policing. This approach assumes that the same epidemiological methods that were useful in identifying and reducing unintentional injuries (e.g., by determining that seat belts could reduce the number of fatal automobile accidents) could be used to determine patterns of violence and to indicate ways to prevent violence that complement the criminal justice system (e.g., teaching young men to resolve disputes nonviolently or changing the trigger mechanisms on guns). Both the community-policing and public health approaches emphasize prevention, especially prevention achieved through changing the physical and social environment rather than individual behavior. Moreover, both approaches assume that significant decreases in violence are most likely to be achieved from finding and solving many specific problems, each of which produces a small reduction in violence.

SYSTEM-LEVEL INTERVENTIONS

In addition to interventions at the individual and neighborhood level, there have been interventions that affect the entire system. One type of system-level intervention focuses on the enforcement, prosecution, and punishment of crimes that have not previously been punished. An example of this type of system-level intervention is the change in response to partner violence. A second type of system-level intervention focuses on the needs of victims.

Responses to Partner Violence

Historically, in the United States, women have had little recourse for help and protection from domestic violence (Fagan, 1996). Beginning in the 1960s, however, partner violence was recognized as an important social issue, although social norms and legal barriers still limited the actions women could take against abusive spouses. By

1980, 47 states had laws giving women more protection under restraining orders and allowing police to make arrests without warrants for misdemeanor domestic assaults. This change in statutory law was accompanied by changes in procedures, and many police agencies developed mandatory arrest policies, many prosecutors' offices developed special units for domestic violence, and many probation offices developed special treatment programs for abusive husbands.

One set of reforms begun in the 1960s and 1970s was aimed at making criminal justice procedures easier and less onerous to use so that battered women would be more likely to use them (Fagan, 1996). Another set of reforms was aimed at stopping the violence by punishing and therefore deterring offenders, making offenders undergo treatment, and protecting women by giving them the power to seek protective orders and prosecution. One of these reforms was a pro-arrest policy in all domestic assault cases, which came about as the result of three pressures (Jones & Belknap, 1999): (a) successful lawsuits against the police for failing to protect women who had reported prior assaults, (b) feminists' calls for more effective police response, and (c) the results from the initial Minneapolis Domestic Violence Experiment suggesting that mandatory arrest reduces subsequent assaults.

Although the original Minneapolis study had indicated that arrest was effective for everyone, subsequent replications in five cities suggested that arrest was much more of a deterrent for employed than for unemployed individuals and may actually increase crime among the jobless. In three cities, arrests appeared to have a deterrent effect for about a month, but after that period, arrests seemed to be related to an increase in subsequent violence, particularly for unemployed and unmarried men. Rather than institute mandatory arrest policies, as many jurisdictions have done, Sherman (1992) has suggested that police officers be given a list of options from which they must choose, including taking the victim to a shelter for battered women, conveying intoxicated offenders and victims to alcohol detoxification treatment centers, and giving the victim's opinion more weight in the decision to make an arrest.

In addition to police intervention, several cities have established special prosecution units to focus resources on domestic violence. These units differ from most prosecutors' offices in that prosecutors' decisions do not have to be based only on traditional criteria for the severity of the victim's injury and the strength of the evidence against the defendant. Prosecutors in these special units can use other criteria, such as protecting the victim. Allowing these other criteria to affect prosecution builds on the fact that victims often have other goals, such as obtaining property, getting money, or forcing offenders to partici-pate in counseling (Fagan, 1996).

In addition to specialized prosecution units, some jurisdictions have established specialized courts for family violence. These courts were established because domestic violence cases are often viewed as less important than other types of cases; thus, they are often lower pri-ority when cases are scheduled for hearing and when resources are allocated for punishment, particularly compared with violence involv-ing strangers.

Responses to the Needs of Victims

Since 1982, 32 states have added victims' rights amendments to their constitutions, giving victims the right to be informed about the status of their case, to be present at the trial, and to be heard at the sen-tencing hearing. In some states, these constitutional amendments also give victims the right to be informed about and to attend bail hearings, plea negotiations, and parole hearings.

Victims have used these rights to play greater roles in bail hearings, plea agreements, and parole decisions. For example, in 1993, an Ari-zona appeals court threw out a parole board decision to release a rapist from prison because the board had not allowed the victim to testify at the parole hearing, a right guaranteed by an amendment to the Arizona Constitution (Lambert, 1995). When the second hearing was held, the parole board did not release the rapist from prison.

The initial goal of a large segment of the victims' rights movement in the United States was to combat crime by making it easier to convict suspected offenders. Later, the movement focused on having the gov-ernment treat crime victims in the same way that it treats victims of nat-ural disasters (Fletcher, 1995, pp. 188-189). That is, the focus was on having the government compensate victims whose lives had been dis-rupted by violent crime. A third concern of the victims' rights move-ment has been to increase victim participation in the criminal justice process, primarily as a means of giving the victim control and dignity. Our discussion of system-level interventions centers on three goals of the victims' rights movement: providing assistance, gaining monetary reparation (both in terms of compensation from the state and restitu-tion from the defendant), and increasing victim participation in the legal process.

Victim Assistance Programs.   The idea that the government should pro-vide assistance to crime victims is less than 30 years old (Sebba, 1996).

In 1974, the Law Enforcement Assistance Administration funded eight such programs. Ten years later, the federal Victims of Crime Act provided federal funding to states, which was then passed on to eligible crime victim assistance programs. The 1989 Victims of Crime Act provided $43 million to local victim service programs. Other funding for victim assistance programs comes from fines and specific fees paid by convicted offenders. Today, there are almost 10,000 victim assistance programs in the country (Young, 1997).

Most of these programs are aimed at helping victims overcome the negative effects of the victimization and at helping both victims and the criminal justice system by making more effective use of victims and witnesses (Sebba, 1996, pp. 251-273). Typically, these programs provide crisis and follow-up counseling, make referrals to other agencies, help victims file claims, accompany victims to court, and educate the public about crime and victim assistance. These programs generally reach only a small fraction of victims; in Britain, it is estimated that only 5% of victims who reported their crimes and only 1% of all victims receive victim assistance services (Maguire, 1989, as cited in Sebba, 1996, p. 257). These programs have sometimes been criticized because they emphasize psychological counseling rather than tangible assistance, such as a place to stay, and many of the programs are more concerned with making victims good witnesses for the prosecution than with improving their welfare (Davis, 1983).

Victim Compensation Programs. Victim compensation programs are state-funded plans by which "innocent victims" of violent crimes and "reasonably acting" good Samaritans can receive help for medical costs, counseling, lost wages, and funeral expenses. According to most of these laws, the applicants cannot receive compensation if their expenses were covered by health insurance, car insurance, sick leave, disability insurance, or regular salary. In most states, victims must report the crime within 72 hours of the crime or have a good reason for not doing so. In addition, claimants must file an application for compensation within some time period, often 6 months, to the state agency administering the program. Moreover, victims cannot recover damages if they were involved in illegal activities at the time of their injuries.

Victim compensation was first proposed in 1951, by an English magistrate inspired by a victim who had been blinded during an assault (Stark & Goldstein, 1985, p. 103). In the United States, the first victim compensation scheme was established in California in 1965. In most states, victims have the right to be informed about compensation, and in many states, police departments and prosecutors' offices are required to have crime victim liaisons and victim witness coordinators.

The money in the victim compensation fund comes from court costs paid by defendants in criminal cases. For example, in Texas, defendants pay $45 in felony cases, $35 for Class A and Class B misdemeanors, and $15 for Class C misdemeanors. This fund covers victims' uninsured losses and expenses arising out of violent crimes, including medical services, counseling, lost wages, child care, and crime scene cleanup. The maximum payment under the law is $25,000, although the amount can be increased to $50,000 in the case of catastrophic injury (Dietz, 1997).

In addition to benefiting victims, the compensation fund in Texas also provides funds for intervenors who help victims or who are injured while trying to prevent crime or catch offenders. Members of the victims' immediate families and households may be eligible for funds to pay for counseling. Under some conditions, individuals who pay victims' debts may be reimbursed.

In Texas, victims must meet four requirements. First, they must be innocent of any responsibility for the crime. Second, they must report the crime to the police within 72 hours, although there are exceptions for "extraordinary circumstances" and for child victims. Third, they must cooperate with criminal justice personnel in the prosecution of the case, if there is one. Fourth, they must file the application for compensation within a year of the crime, although again there are exceptions for "good cause" and for child victims.

Despite the existence of compensation programs, many have criticized them for giving "too little, too late, to too few of the crime victims" (van Dijk, 1984, as quoted in Sebba, 1996, p. 233). These programs help only a small percentage of victims because most eligible victims do not apply for the funds, possibly because only about a third of all victims know there is compensation available. However, knowing about the program is just the first hurdle. In almost all states, compensation is limited to (a) violent crimes in which the victim suffered injuries, (b) only certain kinds of expenses (medical care, hospitalization, lost wages, or mental health care), and (c) to a certain amount (most often $10,000). Aside from these restrictions, to receive compensation, the victim must have reported the crime to the police, must cooperate with the prosecutor about the case, must not have precipitated the crime, and must not be related to or have an ongoing relationship with the offender. Assuming that the victim has passed these hurdles, processing the award can take many months (or even years) because the agency needs to check for possible fraud and may still refuse to grant compensation to the victim. Because most crime victims do not benefit from the compensation programs, many have criticized them for being symbolic of the government's interest in victims but not actually providing any substantive benefits.

In addition to state-funded compensation, many states now require offenders to provide restitution to victims. This restitution order is a statement by the court that the offender has a duty to restore the victim to his or her circumstances prior to the crime. Findings from one study suggest that a judge's imposition of restitution is predicted primarily by the ease of quantifying harm rather than by factors that make offenders "good risks" (Outlaw & Ruback, 1999). This effect may indicate either that judges are willing to order restitution only when it is easy for them to do so or that they consider quantification a reasonable indicator of victim deservedness. In the majority of cases, offenders paid most of what they were ordered to pay. However, there was also a substantial minority (41%) who paid nothing or less than half of their restitution orders. Importantly, the research suggested that offenders who paid their ordered restitution had lower rearrest rates than those who did not pay, and this effect of payment seemed especially strong for offenders who were more integrated in the community (i.e., those who were married, employed, and older). In addition, analyses revealed that the payment of fines to the government had little or no effect on recidivism. Thus, it seems that the effects of restitution were specific to the act of repairing damage to the victim rather than being an artifact of payment.

Enhancing the Role of the Victim in the Criminal Process

There have been three suggestions about increasing the victim's role in the criminal justice system (Sebba, 1996, Chap. 12): (a) private prosecutions, which are used in many European countries; (b) an indirect role (e.g., through victim impact statements), which is becoming more common in the United States; and (c) informal dispute resolution, which is still relatively new.

Private Prosecutions. One possible way to increase the role of the victim in the criminal justice system is to permit them to bring private prosecutions against offenders, as is allowed in Canada and many European countries and as was the case in the American colonies prior to independence. For example, in Germany, the victim has the right, through a lawyer, to join the proceedings as a private prosecutor, both to further the criminal prosecution and to pursue a civil remedy for damages. (*German Code of Criminal Procedure,* as cited in Fletcher, 1995, p. 194). Generally, private prosecutions are not viewed favorably in the United States because they may lead to unjustified prosecutions (e.g., victims may prosecute based on vindictive motives or private prosecutions will not take the "public interest" into account) and because there may not be prosecutions even when there should be (e.g., it is too costly or too much trouble for victims to bring a private prosecution). Moreover, it may be that private prosecution is unconstitutional (e.g., *Young v. U.S. ex rel. Vuitton et Fils,* 1987).

Indirect Role. A second possible way to increase victims' participation in the criminal justice system is to give them indirect roles, such as providing victim impact statements at sentencing or at parole hearings (see Chapter 4). There are several arguments for and against victim participation in sentencing hearings (Kelly & Erez, 1997). The arguments in favor of victim participation relate (a) to the victim, by promoting psychological healing, treating the victim as an important part of the proceeding, producing greater satisfaction with the system and therefore greater cooperation; (b) to the offender, by promoting rehabilitation because the offender must face the harms the victim suffered; and (c) to the system, by producing sentences that more fairly and accurately indicate the harms done and that also better reflect the community's response to crime. The arguments against victim participation relate both (a) to the victim—the process may be traumatic and may create expectations that will not be met, or victims may not want to be responsible for the defendant's sentence and (b) to the system—the system may become overwhelmed by a large number of victims who want to testify, the presence of victims in court puts pressures on judges that may be inconsistent with justice, and if judges take victim impact statements into account, sentencing would not necessarily be predictable. This, in turn, would undermine plea bargains and prosecutors' ability to control cases and caseloads.

Consistent with the arguments against victim participation, research on victim impact statements generally suggests that on balance, they have no effect on sentencing (Kelly & Erez, 1997). That is, in some cases, the sentence might be more severe (e.g., if the harm was especially egregious), and in other cases, the sentence might be less severe (e.g., if there was no harm). In most cases, the impact statement has no effect because most sentences are based on the severity of the offense and the offender's prior record, factors that are known before the sentencing hearing. Although emotional appeals might make the victim feel better, judges prefer to rely on objective information (e.g., the extent of physical injury) and are not generally influenced by impassioned requests. Thus, it appears that victim impact statements almost never add any new information beyond what is already in the record, meaning that the hearings are simply symbolic occasions in which victims have an opportunity to speak but do not have any real impact on the final sentence.

Rather than participating in sentencing and parole hearings, victims are sometime called on to participate in plea bargaining, because that is where the important decisions regarding the number and severity of charges are actually made: "The power that could make a difference in the life of victims lies not at the end of the process but at the beginning" (Fletcher, 1995, p. 248).

But even if victims were given the right to participate in plea bargaining, in no jurisdiction do they (or would they) have the right to force decision makers to act in a certain way. For example, the Texas Constitution provides that victims have "the right to confer with a representative of the prosecutor's office," but they do not have the right to veto the prosecutor's decision. Nor do victims have "the standing to participate as a party in a criminal proceeding" (Texas Constitution, art. 1, sec. 30).

Informal Dispute Resolution. A third way to increase the victim's role is to move the processing from the criminal justice system to informal dispute resolution mechanisms (Sebba, 1996, Chap. 11). In these informal hearings, the presiding officer is generally not a judge, lawyers are usually not permitted, and the traditional rules governing trials (e.g., the rules of evidence) are not applied. Instead, the parties are urged to come to a voluntary agreement or to be bound by a decision reached by a larger forum of community members.

Informal processing serves several goals. First, it saves the system money and time, because judges do not have to hear every case. Second, informal processing increases community solidarity and reduces the general level of social tension. Third, informal processing gives victims access to justice. Victims who participate in informal processing, such as victim-offender mediation, are likely to be more satisfied than victims who go through the traditional criminal court process (Umbreit & Greenwood, 2000a).

In particular, informal processing might make sense in cases in which the victims engaged in some behavior that suggests they were partly to blame for the crime. In such cases, police and prosecutors are likely to believe that criminal prosecution may not be worth the resources, because juries may not convict and judges may not sentence harshly. Fattah (1997) has argued that mediation and restitution make more sense than criminal prosecution for these kinds of cases.

Today, there are more than 300 victim-offender mediation programs (Umbreit & Greenwood, 2000a). Most of these programs (65%) are run by private, community-based or church-based agencies. The programs run by government agencies (35%) are located in probation departments, correctional facilities, prosecuting attorneys' offices, and victim services agencies. About 45% of the programs work only with juvenile offenders, almost 9% work only with adult offenders, and about 47% work with both juvenile and adult offenders (Umbreit & Greenwood, 2000b). On average, each of these programs has 136 annual case referrals and conducts 106 mediation sessions. The primary goals of the mediators in these sessions are to encourage discussions between victims and offenders, to make the parties feel comfortable, and to negotiate plans for victims to receive restitution.

An Appropriate Balance

Although we have repeatedly emphasized our concern for individual victims, it is important to recognize that too much concern for the victim might have detrimental effects on the operation of the criminal justice system, effects that are counterproductive. At one extreme, concern about the costs of interaction with the criminal justice system (the *second victimization*) might keep victims and those who advise them from reporting crimes, from giving evidence to police and prosecutors, or from testifying at trial—because they wish to avoid the lost time and potential humiliation of working with the criminal justice system. Although this result may be good for individual victims, society may suffer if offenders believe they can commit crimes without fear of being caught or punished.

At the other extreme—overinvolvement—victims may be so concerned with gaining retribution against the offender that they interfere with other goals of the criminal justice system, including system efficiency, offender rehabilitation, and reintegration of offenders into the community. Many of the recent changes in state statutes and constitutions have been aimed at giving victims a greater role in the criminal justice system and, at a minimum, informing victims of the status of their case. Although evidence to date suggests that this increased role has not overly burdened the criminal justice system, many individuals in the system still have fears that the victim's single-minded pursuit of punishment might disrupt the operation of the system.

As we stated at the beginning of this book, directly or indirectly, violent crime touches everyone. Victims and their families have been ignored too long, and the social and psychological costs of victimization on individuals and communities have not been adequately addressed. The criminal justice system needs victims to play an active role in reporting crimes, preventing crimes, and ensuring that offenders receive justice for their crimes. But punishment is just one of several goals of the criminal justice system. One of the clear implications of concern for victims is that there should be an appropriate balance between the needs of the victim and the needs of society.

■■ DISCUSSION QUESTIONS

1. What policies can be implemented to reduce victimization? To what extent is crime prevention the responsibility of individuals rather than of government? How much money are we as a society willing to spend to reduce crime?

2. The research on mandatory arrests from the Minneapolis Domestic Violence Experiment and the five replication sites presents an interesting example of whether research findings should be used to set policy. Current evidence seems to indicate that, at least for some men, mandatory arrest increases the likelihood that they will beat their spouses or girlfriends in the future. Should that finding mean that mandatory arrests should not be instituted?

3. Are lawsuits justified against third parties, such as owners of apartment buildings? Do these lawsuits produce behavior that deters future victimizations, or are they simply a way for victims (and their lawyers) to receive compensation?

4. Victim compensation programs have been criticized for making it too difficult for victims to receive payments. Does the government have an obligation to compensate victims? To what extent is it necessary for the government to impose hurdles on this compensation (e.g., to prevent fraud)?

5. Across the country, there are more than 27,000 victim-related state statutes, and 29 states have victim rights constitutional amendments. What changes in the law still need to be made? The provision of victim services is the most direct way that society can meet victims' needs. How can victim services be improved in a cost-effective manner? You might want to look at the report of the Office for Victims of Crime (1998).

NOTE

1. Copyright © 1999 by the American Psychological Association. Reprinted with permission of the APA and the author.

References

Abbott, J., Johnson, R., Koziol-McLain, J., & Lowenstein, S. R. (1995). Domestic violence against women: Incidence and prevalence in an emergency department population. *Journal of the American Medical Association, 273,* 1763-1767.

Abramson, L. Y., Seligman, M. E. P., & Teasdale, J. (1978). Learned helplessness in humans: Critique and reformulation. *Journal of Abnormal Psychology, 87,* 49-74.

Agnew, R. (1992). Foundation for a general strain theory of crime and delinquency. *Criminology, 5,* 47-88.

Agnew, R. (1999). A general strain theory of community differences in crime rates. *Journal of Research in Crime and Delinquency, 36,* 123-155.

Agnew, R. S. (1985). Neutralizing the impact of crime. *Criminal Justice and Behavior, 12,* 161-180.

Altman, I. (1975). *The environment and social behavior.* Monterey, CA: Brooks/Cole.

American Psychiatric Association. (1987). *Diagnostic and statistical manual of mental disorders* (3rd ed., Rev.). Washington, DC: American Psychiatric Association.

American Psychiatric Association. (1994). *Diagnostic and statistical manual of mental disorders* (4th ed.). Washington, DC: American Psychiatric Association.

Amick-McMullan, A., Kilpatrick, D., & Resnick, H. (1991). Homicide as a risk factor for PTSD among surviving family members. *Behavior Modification, 15,* 545-559.

Amick-McMullan, A., Kilpatrick, D., Veronen, L., & Smith, S. (1989). Family survivors of homicide victims: Theoretical perspectives and an exploratory study. *Journal of Traumatic Stress, 2,* 21-35.

Amir, M. (1971). *Patterns in forcible rape.* Chicago: University of Chicago Press.

Anderson, E. (1999). *Code of the street: Decency, violence, and the moral life of the inner city.* New York: Norton.

Annest, J. L., Mercy, J. A., Gibson, D. R., & Ryan, G. W. (1995). National estimates of nonfatal firearm-related injuries. *Journal of the American Medical Association, 273,* 1749-1754.

Appleyard, D. (1981). *Livable streets.* Berkeley: University of California Press.

Archer, J. (2000a). Sex differences in aggression between heterosexual partners: A meta-analytic review. *Psychological Bulletin, 126,* 651-680.

Archer, J. (2000b). Sex differences in physical aggression to partners: A reply to Frieze (2000), O' Leary (2000), and White, Smith, Koss, and Figueredo (2000). *Psychological Bulletin, 126,* 697-702.

Atkeson, B., Calhoun, K., Resick, P., & Ellis, E. (1982). Victims of rape: Repeated assessment of depressive symptoms. *Journal of Consulting and Clinical Psychology, 50,* 96-102.

Attorney General's Task Force on Family Violence. (1984). *Final report.* Washington, DC: Author.

Babbie, E. (2000). *The practice of social research* (9th ed.). Belmont, CA: Wadsworth.

Bachman, R. (1994). *Violence against women: A national crime victimization survey report.* Washington, DC: U.S. Bureau of Justice Statistics.

Bachman, R. (2000). A comparison of annual rates and contextual characteristics of intimate partner violence against women from the National Crime Victimization Survey (NCVS) and the National Violence Against Women Survey (NVAWS). *Violence Against Women, 6,* 839-867.

Bachman R., & Saltzman, L. (1995). *Violence against women: Estimates from the redesigned survey* (U.S. Bureau of Justice Statistics special report; Publication No. NCJ-154348). Washington, DC: U.S. Department of Justice.

Bachman, R., & Taylor, B. M. (1994). The measurement of family violence and rape by the redesigned National Crime Victimization Survey. *Justice Quarterly, 11,* 499-512.

Baker, M. H., Nienstedt, B. C., Everett, R. S., & McCleary, R. (1983). The impact of a crime wave: Perceptions, fear, and confidence in the police. *Law & Society Review, 17,* 319-335.

Baker, T. C., Burgess, A. W., Brickman, E., & Davis, R. C. (1990). Rape victims' concerns about possible exposure to HIV infection. *Journal of Interpersonal Violence, 5,* 49-60.

Bard, M., Arnone, H., & Nemiroff, D. (1980). Contextual influences on the post-traumatic stress adaptation of homicide survivor-victims. In C. Figley (Ed.), *Trauma and its wake: Vol. 2. Traumatic stress theory, research, and intervention* (pp. 292-304). New York: Brunner/Mazel.

Bard, M., & Connolly, H. (1982). *A retrospective study of homicide adaptation.* Rockville, MD: National Institute of Mental Health.

Bard, M., & Sangrey, D. (1986). *The crime victim's book* (2nd ed.). New York: Brunner/Mazel.

Baum, A., Davis, A. G., & Aiello, J. R. (1978). Crowding and neighborhood mediation of urban density. *Journal of Population, 1,* 266-279.

Bennett, A. (1995, January 5). Apples & oranges: Is Tallahassee really as plagued by crime as New York City? *Wall Street Journal,* pp. A1, A16.

Bernstein, J. Y., & Watson, M. W. (1997). Children who are targets of bullying: A victim pattern. *Journal of Interpersonal Violence 12,* 483-498.

Bernstein, N. (1996a, May 6). Behind some fraternity walls, brothers in crime. *New York Times,* pp. A1, B6.

Bernstein, N. (1996b, May 5). Colleges campuses hold court in shadows of mixed loyalties. *New York Times,* pp. 1, 16.

Bettleheim, B. (1979). *Surviving and other essays.* New York: Vintage.

Black, D. J. (1970). The production of crime rates. *American Sociological Review, 35,* 733-748.

Bleakley, F. R. (1997, December 17). Ultimate renovation project: Two 110-story towers. *Wall Street Journal,* pp. B1, B12.

Block, R., & Skogan, W. G. (1986). Resistance and non-fatal outcomes in stranger-to-stranger predatory crime. *Violence and Victims, 1,* 241-253.

Blumstein, A., & Rosenfeld, R. (1999). Trends in rates of violence in the U.S.A. *Studies on Crime & Crime Prevention, 8,* 139-167.

Boney-McCoy, S., & Finkelhor, D. (1995). Psychosocial sequelae of violent victimization in a national youth sample. *Journal of Consulting and Clinical Psychology, 63,* 726-736.

Bowker, L. (1984). Coping with wife abuse: Personal and social networks. In A. R. Roberts (Ed.), *Battered women and their families: Intervention strategies and treatment programs.* New York: Springer.

Bownes, I., O'Gorman, E., & Sayers, A. (1991). Assault characteristics and posttraumatic stress disorder in rape victims. *Acta Psychiatrica Scandinavica, 83,* 27-30.

Boylin, W. M., & Briggie, C. R. (1987). The healthy therapist: The contribution of symbolic-experiential family therapy. *Family Therapy, 14,* 247-256.

Braithewaite, J. (1989). *Crime, shame, and reintegration.* Cambridge, UK: Cambridge University Press.

Brandl, S. G., & Horvath, F. (1991). Crime-victim evaluation of police investigative performance. *Journal of Criminal Justice, 19,* 109-122.

Brantingham, P. J., & Brantingham, P. L. (1995, March). *Understanding and controlling crime and fear of crime: Conflicts and trade-offs in crime prevention planning.* Paper presented at the annual meeting of the Academy of Criminal Justice Sciences, Boston.

Breslau, N., & Davis, G. (1992). Posttraumatic stress disorder in an urban population of young adults: Risk factors for chronicity. *American Journal of Psychiatry, 149,* 671-675.

Brien, V. O. (1992). Civil legal remedies for crime victims. *Office for Victims of Crime Bulletin.* Washington, DC: U.S. Department of Justice.

Briere, J., & Runtz, M. (1987). Post sexual abuse trauma: Data and implications for clinical practice. *Journal of Interpersonal Violence, 2,* 367-379.

Briere, J., & Runtz, M. (1990). Differential adult symptomatology associated with three types of child abuse histories. *Child Abuse and Neglect, 14,* 357-364.

Brown, B. B., & Harris, P. B. (1989). Residential burglary victimization: Reactions to the invasion of a primary territory. *Journal of Environmental Psychology, 9,* 119-132.

Browne, A. (1993). Violence against women by male partners: Prevalence, outcomes, and policy implications. *American Psychologist, 48,* 1077-1087.

Browne, A., & Williams, K. R. (1992, November). *Are women as violent as men? Research on "domestic violence" and considerations for the field.* Paper presented at the annual meeting of the American Society of Criminology, New Orleans.

Buerger, M. E., & Mazerolle, L. G. (1998). Third-party policing: A theoretical analysis of an emerging trend. *Justice Quarterly, 15,* 301-327.

Burgess, A. (1975). Family reactions to homicide. *American Journal of Orthopsychiatry, 45,* 391-398.

Burgess, A., & Holmstrom, L. (1976). Coping behavior of the rape victim. *American Journal of Psychiatry, 13,* 413-417.

Burgess, A., & Holmstrom, L. (1979). Adaptive strategies and recovery from rape. *American Journal of Psychiatry, 136,* 1278-1282.

Burnam, M., Stein, J., Golding, J., Siegel, J., Sorenson, S., Forsythe, A., & Telles, C. (1988). Sexual assault and mental disorders in a community population. *Journal of Consulting and Clinical Psychology, 56,* 843-850.

Buss, T. F., & Abdu, R. (1995). Repeat victims of violence in an urban trauma center. *Violence and Victims, 10,* 183-194.

Calhoun, K., Atkeson, B., & Resick, P. (1982). A longitudinal examination of fear reactions in victims of rape. *Journal of Counseling Psychology, 29,* 655-661.

Campbell, R., Raja, S., & Grining, P. (1999). Training mental health professionals on violence against women. *Journal of Interpersonal Violence, 14,* 1003-1013.

Campbell, R., Sefl, T., Barnes, H. E., Ahrens, C. E., Wasco, S. M., & Zaragoza-Diesfeld, Y. (1999). Community services for rape survivors: Enhancing psychological well-being or increasing trauma. *Journal of Consulting and Clinical Psychology, 67,* 847-858.

Cascardi, M., O' Leary, D., Lawrence, E., & Schlee, K. (1995). Characteristics of women physically abused by their spouses and who seek treatment regarding marital conflict. *Journal of Consulting and Clinical Psychology, 63,* 616-623.

Cascardi, M., O'Leary, D. K., & Schlee, K. A. (1999). Co-occurrence and correlates of posttraumatic stress disorder and major depression in physically abused women. *Journal of Family Violence, 14,* 227-249.

Cascardi, M., Riggs, D., Hearst-Ikeda, D., & Foa, E. (1996). Objective ratings of assault safety as predictors of PTSD. *Journal of Interpersonal Violence, 11,* 65-78.

Casey, P. (1997, April 25). For survivors at home, trial "reopens the scab." *Atlanta Journal/Constitution,* p. A10.

Centers for Disease Control and Prevention. (2000). Web-Based Injury Statistics Query and Reporting System: WISQARS [Online]. Available: http://www.cdc.gov/ncipc/wisqars [1999, Dec. 20].

Chiricos, T., Hogan, M., & Gertz, M. (1997). Racial composition of neighborhood and fear of crime. *Criminology, 35,* 107-131.

Cialdini, R. B., Kallgren, C. A., & Reno, R. R. (1991). A focus theory of normative conduct: A theoretical refinement and reevaluation of the role of norms in human behavior. In M. P. Zanna (Ed.), *Advances in experimental social psychology* (Vol. 24, pp. 201-234). San Diego, CA: Academic Press.

Clarke, R. V. (1995). Situational crime prevention. In M. Tonry & D. P. Farrington (Eds.), *Building a safer society: Strategic approaches to crime prevention: Vol. 19. Crime and justice: A review of research* (pp. 91-150). Chicago: University of Chicago Press.

Cluss, P., Boughton, J., Frank, E., Stewart, B., & West, D. (1983). The rape victim: Psychological correlates of participation in the legal process. *Criminal Justice and Behavior, 10,* 342-357.

Coates, D., Wortman, C. B., & Abbey, A. (1979). Reactions to victims. In I. H. Frieze, D. Bar-Tal, & J. S. Carroll (Eds.), *New approaches to social problems.* San Francisco: Jossey-Bass.

Cohen, L. E., & Felson, M. (1979). Social change and crime: A routine activity approach. *American Sociological Review, 44,* 588-608.

Cohen, L. J., & Roth, S. (1987). The psychological aftermath of rape: Long-term effects and individual differences in recovery. *Journal of Social and Clinical Psychology, 5,* 525-534.

Cohen, M. A. (1988). Pain, suffering, and jury awards: A study of the cost of crime to victims. *Law and Society Review, 22,* 537-555.

Cohen, M. A., & Miller, T. R. (1998). The cost of mental health care for victims of crime. *Journal of Interpersonal Violence, 13,* 93-110.

Coker, A. L., Smith, P. H., Bethea, L., King, M. R., & McKeown, R. E. (2000). Physical health consequences of physical and psychological intimate partner violence. *Archives of Family Medicine, 9,* 451-457.

Cook, R. (1995, May 14). The long wait for justice. *Atlanta Journal/Constitution,* p. G4.

Cooley-Quille, M., & Lorion, R. (1999). Adolescents' exposure to community violence: Sleep and psychophysiological functioning. *Journal of Community Psychology, 27,* 367-375.

Cose, E. (1994, July 11). Drawing up safer cities. *Newsweek,* p. 57.

Council on Scientific Affairs, American Medical Association. (1992). Violence against women: Relevance for medical practitioners. *Journal of the American Medical Association, 267,* 3184-3189.

Courtois, C. (1988). *Healing the incest wound: Adult survivors in trauma therapy.* New York: Norton.

Covington, J., & Taylor, R. B. (1991). Fear of crime in urban residential neighborhoods: Implications of between- and within-neighborhood sources for current models. *Sociological Quarterly, 32,* 231-249.

Craig, K. M., & Waldo, C. R. (1996). So, what's a hate crime anyway? Young adults' perceptions of hate crimes, victims, and perpetrators. *Law and Human Behavior, 20,* 113-129.

Craven, D. (1996). *Female victims of violent crime* (U.S. Bureau of Justice Statistics selected findings; Publication No. NCJ-162602). Washington, DC: U.S. Department of Justice.

Darley, J., & Latané, B. (1968). Bystander intervention in emergencies: Diffusion of responsibility. *Journal of Personality and Social Psychology, 8,* 377-383.

Davidson, J., Hughes, D., George, L., & Blazer, D. (1996). The association of sexual assault and attempted suicide within the community. *Archives of General Psychiatry, 53,* 550-555.

Davis, C. G., Lehman, D. R., Wortman, C. B., Silver, R. C., & Thompson, S. C. (1995). The undoing of traumatic life events. *Personality and Social Psychology Bulletin, 21,* 109-124.

Davis, C. G., Nolen-Hoeksema, S., & Larson, J. (1998). Making sense of loss and benefiting from the experience: Two construals of meaning. *Journal of Personality and Social Psychology, 75,* 561-574.

Davis, R., Taylor, B., & Bench, S. (1995). Impact of sexual and nonsexual assault on secondary victims. *Violence and Victims, 10,* 73-84.

Davis, R. C. (1983). Victim/witness noncooperation: A selected look at a persistent phenomenon. *Journal of Criminal Justice, 11,* 287-299.

Davis, R. C., Brickman, E., & Baker, T. (1991). Supportive and unsupportive responses of others to rape victims: Effects on concurrent victim adjustment. *American Journal of Community Psychology, 19,* 443-451.

Davis, R. C., & Friedman, L. N. (1985). The emotional aftermath of crime and violence. In C. R. Figley (Ed.), *Trauma and its wake: The study and treatment of posttraumatic stress disorder* (pp. 90-112). New York: Brunner/Mazel.

Davis, R. C., & Smith, B. (1994). The effects of victim impact statements on sentencing decisions: A test in an urban setting. *Justice Quarterly, 11,* 453-469.

Davis, R. C., Taylor, B., & Lurigio, A. (1996). Adjusting to criminal victimization: The correlates of postcrime distress. *Violence and Victims, 11,* 21-37.

Davis, R. C., Taylor, B., & Titus, R. (1997). Victims as agents: Implications for victim services and crime prevention. In R. C. Davis, A. J. Lurigio, & W. G. Skogan (Eds.), *Victims of crime* (2nd ed., pp. 167-179). Thousand Oaks, CA: Sage.

Davis, R. C., & Taylor, B. G. (1997). A proactive response to family violence: The results of a randomized experiment. *Criminology, 35,* 307-333.

Dearwater, S. R., Coben, J. H., Campbell, J. C., Nah, G., Glass, N., McLoughlin, E., & Bekemeier, B. (1998). Prevalence of intimate partner abuse in women treated at community hospital emergency departments. *Journal of the American Medical Association, 280,* 433-438.

Derogatis, L., & Spencer, P. (1982). *The Brief Symptom Inventory (BSI): Administration, scoring, and procedures manual—I.* Baltimore: Author.

Dietz, E. D. P. (1997, April). The Texas crime victims' compensation act. *Texas Bar Journal, 60,* 320-322, 324.

DiIulio, J. J. (1994, Fall). The question of black crime. *The Public Interest, 117,* 3-32.

Dillman, D. A. (1978). *Mail and telephone surveys: The total design method.* New York: Wiley.

Dubow, F., McCabe, E., & Kaplan, G. (1979). *Reactions to crime: A critical review of the literature.* Washington, DC: National Institute of Justice.

Dubrow, N., & Garbarino, J. (1989). Living in the war zone: Mothers and young children in a public housing development. *Child Welfare, 68,* 3-20.

Dugan, L. (1999). The effect of criminal victimization on a household's moving decision. *Criminology, 37,* 903-930.

Durant, R. H., Cadenhead, C., Pendergrast, R. A., Slavens, G., & Linder, C. W. (1994). Factors associated with the use of violence among urban black adolescents. *American Journal of Public Health, 84,* 612-617.

Dutton, M. (1992). Assessment and treatment of post-traumatic stress disorder among battered women. In D. Foy (Ed.), *Treating PTSD: Cognitive-behavioral strategies* (pp. 69-98). New York: Guilford.

Dutton, M., Burghardt, K., Perrin, S., Chrestman, K., & Halle, P. (1994). Battered women's cognitive schemata. *Journal of Traumatic Stress, 7,* 237-255.

Dutton, M. A., & Rubinstein, F. L. (1995). Working with people with PTSD: Research implications. In C. R. Figley (Ed.), *Compassion fatigue: Coping with secondary traumatic stress disorder in those who treat the traumatized* (pp. 82-100). New York: Brunner/Mazel.

Easterbrook, J. A. (1959). The effect of emotion on cue utilization and the organization of behavior. *Psychological Review, 66,* 183-201.

Edleson, J. L. (1999). Children's witnessing of adult domestic violence. *Journal of Interpersonal Violence, 14,* 839-870.

Elias, R. (1984). Alienating the victim: Compensation and victim attitudes. *Journal of Social Issues, 40*(1), 103-116.

Elias, R. (1986). *The politics of victimization.* New York: Oxford University Press.

Ellingworth, D., Farrell, G., & Pease, K. (1995). A victim is a victim is a victim? Chronic victimization in four sweeps of the British Crime Survey. *British Journal of Criminology, 35,* 360-365.

Ellis, E., Atkeson, B., & Calhoun, K. (1981). An assessment of long-term reactions to rape. *Journal of Abnormal Psychology, 90,* 263-266.

Epstein, S. (1980). The self-concept: A review and the proposal of an integrated theory of personality. In E. Staub (Ed.), *Personality: Basic issues and current research.* Englewood Cliffs, NJ: Prentice Hall.

Erez, E., & Tontodonato, P. (1992). Victim participation in sentencing and satisfaction with justice. *Justice Quarterly, 9,* 393-417.

Erikson, E. H. (1963). *Childhood and society* (2nd ed.). New York: Norton.

Fagan, J. (1996). *The criminalization of domestic violence: Promises and limits* (National Institute of Justice Research Report; Publication No. NCJ-157641). Washington, DC: U.S. Department of Justice.

Fagan, J., Piper, E. S., & Cheng, Y. (1987). Contributions of victimization to delinquency in inner cities. *Journal of Criminal Law and Criminology, 78,* 586-609.

Falsetti, S., & Resnick, H. (1995). Helping the victims of violent crime. In J. Freedy & S. Hobfoll (Eds.), *Traumatic stress: From theory to practice* (pp. 263-285). New York: Plenum.

Farrell, G. (1995). Preventing repeat victimization. *Crime and Justice, 19,* 469-532.

Farrell, G., & Pease, K. (1993). *Once bitten, twice bitten: Repeat victimization and its implications for crime prevention.* London: Home Office Police Department.

Farrell, G., Phillips, C., & Pease, K. (1995). Like taking candy: Why does repeat victimization occur? *British Journal of Criminology, 35,* 384-399.

Fattah, E. A. (1997). Toward a victim policy aimed at healing, not suffering. In R. C. Davis, A. J. Lurigio, & W. G. Skogan (Eds.), *Victims of crime* (2nd ed., pp. 257-272). Thousand Oaks, CA: Sage.

Fawcett, G. M., Heise, L. L., Isita-Espejel, L., & Pick, S. (1999). Changing community responses to wife abuse: A research and demonstration project in Iztacalco, Mexico. *American Psychologist, 54,* 41-49.

Federal Bureau of Investigation. (1999). *Crime in the United States 1998: Uniform crime reports.* Washington, DC: U.S. Department of Justice.

Federal Bureau of Investigation. (2000). *National incident-based reporting system.* Retrieved December 27, 2000, from the World Wide Web: www.fbi.gov/ucr/nibrs/faqs.htm

Felson, M. (1998). *Crime and everyday life* (2nd ed.). Thousand Oaks, CA: Sage.

Felson, R. B., & Tedeschi, J. T. (1995). A social interactionist approach to violence: Cross-cultural applications. In R. B. Ruback & N. A. Weiner (Eds.), *Interpersonal violent behaviors: Social and cultural aspects* (pp. 153-170). New York: Springer.

Figley, C. (1989). *Helping traumatized families.* San Francisco: Jossey-Bass.

Figley, C. (1995). *Compassion fatigue: Coping with secondary traumatic stress disorder in those who treat the traumatized.* New York: Brunner/Mazel.

Figley, C., & Kleber, R. (1995). Beyond the "victim": Secondary traumatic stress. In R. Kleber, C. Figley, & B. Gersons (Eds.), *Beyond trauma: Cultural and social dynamics* (pp. 75-98). New York: Plenum.

Finkelhor, D., & Asdigian, N. L. (1996). Risk factors for youth victimization: Beyond a lifestyles/routine activities theory approach. *Violence and Victims, 11,* 3-19.

Finkelhor, D., & Dziuba-Leatherman, J. (1994a). Children as victims of violence: A national survey. *Pediatrics, 94,* 413-420.

Finkelhor, D., & Dziuba-Leatherman, J. (1994b). Victimization of children. *American Psychologist, 49,* 173-183.

Finkelhor, D., & Yllö, K. (1985). *License to rape: Sexual abuse of wives.* New York: Holt, Rinehart, & Winston.

Fischer, C. (1984). A phenomenological study of being criminally victimized: Contributions and constraints of qualitative research. *Journal of Social Issues, 40*(1), 161-178.

Fitzpatrick, K. M., & Boldizar, J. P. (1993). The prevalence and consequences of exposure to violence among African-American youth. *Journal of the American Academy of Child and Adolescent Psychiatry, 32,* 424-430.

Fleissner, D., & Heinzelmann, F. (1996). *Crime prevention through environmental design and community policing* (Report No. NCJ-157308). Washington, DC: National Institute of Justice.

Fletcher, G. P. (1995). *With justice for some: Victims' rights in criminal trials.* Reading, MA: Addison-Wesley.

Fletcher, J. (1999, June 14). If crime is down, why is your alarm ringing? *Wall Street Journal,* p. W12.

Foa, E., Riggs, D., Dancu, C., & Rothbaum, B. (1993). Reliability and validity of a brief instrument for assessing post-traumatic stress disorder. *Journal of Traumatic Stress, 6,* 459-474.

Foa, E. B., & Rothbaum, B. O. (1998). *Treating the trauma of rape: Cognitive-behavioral therapy for PTSD.* New York: Guilford.

Foa, E. B., Rothbaum, B. O., Riggs, D. S., & Murdock, T. B. (1991). Treatment of posttraumatic stress disorder in rape victims: A comparison between cognitive-behavioral procedures and counseling. *Journal of Consulting and Clinical Psychology, 59,* 715-723.

Follette, V., Polusny, M., Bechtle, A., & Naugle, A. (1996). Cumulative trauma: The impact of child sexual abuse, adult sexual abuse, and spouse abuse. *Journal of Traumatic Stress, 9,* 25-35.

Forst, B., & Hernon, J. (1985). *The criminal justice response to victim harm.* Washington, DC: U.S. Department of Justice, National Institute of Justice.

Fowler, F. J., Jr. (1993). *Survey research methods* (2nd ed.). Newbury Park, CA: Sage.

Fox, J. A., & Zawitz, M. W. (2000). *Homicide trends in the United States: 1998 update.* Washington, DC: U.S. Bureau of Justice Statistics.

Fox, K., & Gilbert, B. O. (1994). The interpersonal and psychological functioning of women who experience childhood physical abuse, incest, and parental alcoholism. *Child Abuse and Neglect, 18,* 849-858.

Foy, D. W., Sipprelle, R. C., Rueger, D. B., & Carroll, E. M. (1984). Etiology of post-traumatic stress disorder in Vietnam veterans: Analysis of premilitary, military, and combat exposure influences. *Journal of Consulting & Clinical Psychology, 52,* 79-87.

Frank, E., & Anderson, B. P. (1987). Psychiatric disorders in rape victims: Past history and current symptomatology. *Comprehensive Psychiatry, 28,* 77-82.

Frank, E., & Stewart, B. (1984). Depressive symptoms in rape victims: A revisit. *Journal of Affective Disorders, 7,* 77-85.

Frank, E., Turner, S. M., & Duffy, B. (1979). Depressive symptoms in rape victims. *Journal of Affective Disorders, 1,* 269-297.

Frank, E., Turner, S., & Stewart, B. (1980). Initial response to rape: The impact of factors within the rape situation. *Journal of Behavioral Assessment, 62,* 39-53.

Frank, E., Turner, S. M., Stewart, B. D., Jacob, J., & West, D. (1981). Past psychiatric symptoms and the response to sexual assault. *Comprehensive Psychiatry, 22,* 479-487.

Frazier, P. (1990). Victim attributions and post-rape trauma. *Journal of Personality and Social Psychology, 59,* 298-304.

Frazier, P., & Haney, B. (1996). Sexual assault cases in the legal system: Police, prosecutor, and victim perspectives. *Law and Human Behavior, 20,* 607-628.

Freedy, J. R., Resnick, H. S., Kilpatrick, D. G., Dansky, B. S., & Tidwell, R. P. (1994). The psychological adjustment of recent crime victims in the criminal justice system. *Journal of Interpersonal Violence, 9,* 450-468.

Friedman, K., Bischoff, H., Davis, R., & Person, A. (1982). *Victims and helpers: Reactions to crime.* New York: Victim Services Agency.

Frieze, I., Hymer, S., & Greenberg, M. (1987). Describing the crime victim: Psychological reactions to victimization. *Professional Psychology: Research and Practice, 18,* 299-315.

Frieze, I. H. (2000). Violence in close relationships—Development of a research area: Comment on Archer (2000). *Psychological Bulletin, 126,* 681-684.

Garbarino, J., Kostelny, K., & Dubrow, N. (1991). *No place to be a child: Growing up in a war zone.* Lexington, MA: Lexington Books.

Garofalo, J. (1977). *The police and public opinion: An analysis of victimization and attitude data from 13 American cities.* Washington, DC: Law Enforcement Assistance Administration.

Garofalo, J. (1981). The fear of crime: Causes and consequences. In *Victims of crime: A review of research issues and methods.* Washington, DC: National Institute of Justice.

Garofalo, J. (1997). Hate crime victimization in the United States. In R. C. Davis, A. J. Lurigio, & W. G. Skogan (Eds.), *Victims of crime* (2nd ed., pp. 134-145). Thousand Oaks, CA: Sage.

Gauthier, L., Hicks, D., Sansfaçon, D., & Salel, L. (1999). *100 promising crime prevention programs from across the world.* Montreal: International Centre for the Prevention of Crime.

Gelles, R. (1979). *Family violence.* Beverly Hills, CA: Sage.

Girelli, S., Resick, P., Marhoefer-Dvorak, S., & Hutter, C. (1986). Subjective distress and violence during rape: Their effects on long-term fear. *Violence and Victims, 1,* 35-46.

Gleason, W. J. (1995). Children of battered women: Developmental delays and behavioral dysfunction. *Violence and Victims, 10,* 153-160.

Gold, E. (1986). Long-term effects of sexual victimization in childhood: An attributional approach. *Journal of Consulting and Clinical Psychology, 54,* 471-475.

Goodman, L., Koss, M., Fitzgerald, L., Russo, N., & Keita, G. (1993). Male violence against women: Current research and future directions. *American Psychologist, 48,* 1054-1058.

Gottfredson, M. (1986). Substantive contributions of victimization surveys. In M. Tonry & N. Morris (Eds.), *Crime and justice: An annual review of research* (Vol. 7, pp. 251-287). Chicago: University of Chicago Press.

Gove, W. R., Hughes, M., & Geerken, M. (1985). Are uniform crime reports a valid indicator of the index crimes? An affirmative answer with minor modifications. *Criminology, 23,* 451-501.

Graham, E. (1993, October 25). Fortress academia sells security. *Wall Street Journal,* pp. B1, B5.

Green, L. (1995). Cleaning up drug hot spots in Oakland, California: The displacement and diffusion effects. *Justice Quarterly, 12,* 737-754.

Greenberg, J. R., & Greenberg, M. S. (1982). Crime and justice in Tudor-Stuart England and the modern United States. *Law and Human Behavior, 6,* 261-272.

Greenberg, M., & Ruback, R. B. (1992). *After the crime: Victim decision making.* New York: Plenum.

Greenberg, M., Ruback, R., & Westcott, D. (1983). Seeking help from the police: The victim's perspective. In A. Nadler, J. Fisher, & B. DePaulo (Eds.), *New directions in helping: Vol. 3. Applied perspectives on help-seeking and -receiving* (pp. 71-103). New York: Academic Press.

Greenberg, S. W., Rohe, W. M., & Williams, J. R. (1985). *Informal citizen action and crime prevention at the neighborhood level* (Publication No. NCJ-167237). Washington, DC: National Institute of Justice.

Greenfeld, L. A. (1997, February). *Sex offenses and offenders: An analysis of data on rape and sexual assault.* U.S. Bureau of Justice Statistics. Washington, DC: U.S. Department of Justice.

Greenfeld, L. A., Rand, M. R., Craven, D., Klaus, P. A., Perkins, C. A., Ringel, C., Warchol, G., Maston, C., & Fox, J. A. (1998). *Violence by intimates (U.S. Bureau of Justice Statistics factbook).* Washington, DC: U.S. Department of Justice.

Grisso, J. A., Schwartz, D. F., Hirschinger, N., Sammel, M., Brensinger, C., Santanna, J., Lowe, R. A., Anderson, E., Shaw, L. M., Bethel, C. A., & Teeple, L. (1999). Violent injuries among women in an urban area. *New England Journal of Medicine, 341,* 1899-1905.

Groves, R., & Kahn, R. L. (1979). *Surveys by telephone: A national comparison with personal interviews.* New York: Academic Press.

Groves, R. M. (1989). *Survey errors and survey costs.* New York: Wiley.

Guerra, N. G., Tolan, P. H., Huesmann, L. R., Van Acker, R., & Eron, L. D. (1995). Stressful events and individual beliefs as correlates of economic disadvantage and aggression among urban children. *Journal of Consulting and Clinical Psychology, 63,* 518-528.

Gurr, T. R. (1989). Historical trends in violent crime: Europe and the United States. In T. R. Gurr (Ed.), *Violence in America: Vol. 1. The history of crime* (pp. 21-54). Newbury Park, CA: Sage.

Hammarberg, M. (1992). Penn Inventory for posttraumatic stress disorder: Psychometric properties. *Psychological Assessment, 4,* 67-76.

Hanson, R. F., Kilpatrick, D. G., Falsetti, S. A., & Resnick, H. S. (1995). Violent crime and mental health. In J. Freedy & S. Hobfoll (Eds.), *Traumatic stress: From theory to practice* (pp. 129-161). New York: Plenum.

Hanson, R. K. (1990). The psychological impact of sexual assault on women and children: A review. *Annals of Sex Research, 3,* 187-232.

Harrington, N. T., & Leitenberg, H. (1994). Relationship between alcohol consumption and victim behaviors immediately preceding sexual aggression by an acquaintance. *Violence & Victims, 9,* 315-324.

Healey, K. M. (1995). Victim and witness intimidation: New developments and emerging responses. *National Institute of Justice Research in Action* (Publication No. NCJ-156555). Washington, DC: U.S. Department of Justice.

Hellman, D. A., & Naroff, J. L. (1979). The impact of crime on urban residential property values. *Urban Studies, 16,* 105-112.

Helzer, J. E., Robins, L. N., & McEvoy, L. (1987). Post-traumatic stress disorder in the general population. *New England Journal of Medicine, 317,* 1630-1634.

Henning, K., Leitenberg, H., Coffey, P., Bennett, T., & Jankowski, M. K. (1997). Long-term psychological adjustment to witnessing interparental physical conflict during childhood. *Child Abuse and Neglect, 21,* 501-515.

Hermann, D. H. J., Morrison, H. L., Sor, Y., Norman, J. A., & Neff, D. M. (1984). *People of the State of Illinois vs. John Gacy:* The functioning of the insanity defense at the limits of the criminal law. *West Virginia Law Review, 86,* 1169-1273.

Hetter, K. (1993, August 26). Crime victims find counseling on how to cope with the media. *Wall Street Journal,* p. B2.

Hillman, G. R. (1998, January 8). Victims' relatives upset with jury attitudes. *Centre Daily Times,* p. 7A.

Hindelang, M., & Gottfredson, M. (1976). The victim's decision not to invoke the criminal process. In W. F. McDonald (Ed.), *Criminal justice and the victim* (pp. 57-78). Beverly Hills, CA: Sage.

Hindelang, M. J. (1974). The uniform crime reports revisited. *Journal of Criminal Justice, 2,* 1-18.

Hindelang, M. S., Gottfredson, M., & Garofalo, J. (1978). *Victims of personal crime.* Cambridge, MA: Ballinger.

Horney, J., & Spohn, C. (1991). Rape law reform and instrumental change in six urban jurisdictions. *Law & Society Review, 25,* 117-153.

Horowitz, M., Wilner, N., Marmar, C., & Krupnick, J. (1980). Pathological grief and activation of latent self-images. *American Journal of Psychiatry, 137,* 1137-1162.

Hough, M. (1987). Offenders' choice of target: Findings from victim surveys. *Journal of Quantitative Criminology, 3,* 355-369.

Houskamp, B. M., & Foy, D. W. (1991). The assessment of posttraumatic stress disorder in battered women. *Journal of Interpersonal Violence, 6,* 367-375.

Hughes, H. (1988). Psychological and behavioral correlates of family violence on child witnesses and victims. *American Journal of Orthopsychiatry, 58,* 77-90.

Hunter, A. (1985). Private, parochial, and public school orders: The problem of crime and incivility in urban communities. In G. D. Suttles & M. N. Zald (Eds.), *The challenge of social control: Citizenship and institution building in modern society* (pp. 230-242). Norwood, NJ: Ablex.

Jacobs, J. B., & Potter, K. A. (1997). Hate crimes. In M. Tonry (Ed.), *Crime and justice: An annual review* (Vol. 22, pp. 1-50). Chicago: University of Chicago Press.

Jaffe, P., Hurley, D. J., & Wolfe, D. (1990). Children's observations of violence: I. Critical issues in child development and intervention planning. *Canadian Journal of Psychiatry, 35,* 466-470.

Janoff-Bulman, R. (1982). Esteem and control bases of blame: "Adaptive" strategies for victims versus observers. *Journal of Personality, 50,* 180-192.

Janoff-Bulman, R. (1989). Assumptive worlds and the stress of traumatic events: Applications of the schema construct. *Social Cognition, 7,* 113-136.

Janoff-Bulman, R. (1992). *Shattered assumptions: Toward a new psychology of trauma.* New York: Free Press.

Janoff-Bulman, R., & Frieze, I. (1983). A theoretical perspective for understanding reactions to victimization. *Journal of Social Issues, 39*(2), 1-17.

Jensen, G. F., & Brownfield, D. (1986). Gender, lifestyles, and victimization: Beyond routine activity. *Violence and Victims, 1,* 85-99.

Jensen, G. F., & Karpos, M. (1993). Managing rape: Exploratory research on the behavior of rape statistics. *Criminology, 31,* 363-385.

Johnson, M. P. (1995). Patriarchal terrorism and common couple violence: Two forms of violence against women. *Journal of Marriage and the Family, 57,* 283-294.

Johnson, M. P. (2000). Conflict and control: Images of symmetry and asymmetry in domestic violence. In A. Booth, A. C. Crouter, & M. Clements (Eds.), *Couples in conflict*. Hillsdale, NJ: Lawrence Erlbaum.

Johnson, M. P., & Leone, J. M. (2000, July). *The differential effects of patriarchal terrorism and common couple violence: Findings from the National Violence Against Women Survey.* Paper presented at the Tenth International Conference on Personal Relationships, Brisbane, Australia.

Jones, D. A., & Belknap, J. (1999). Police responses to battering in a progressive pro-arrest jurisdiction. *Justice Quarterly, 16,* 249-273.

Kaniasty, K., & Norris, F. (1992). Social support and victims of crime: Matching event, support, and outcome. *American Journal of Community Psychology, 20,* 211-241.

Kaniasty, K., & Norris, F. H. (1993). A test of the social support deterioration model in the context of natural disaster. *Journal of Personality & Social Psychology, 64,* 395-408.

Kashani, J., Daniel, A., Dandoy, A., & Holcomb, W. (1992). Family violence: Impact on children. *Journal of American Academy of Child and Adolescent Psychiatry, 31,* 181-189.

Kaslow, N., Thompson, M., Meadows, L., Jacobs, D., Chance, S., Gibb, B., Bornstein, H., Hollins, L., Rashid, A., & Phillips, K. (1998). Factors that mediate or moderate the link between partner abuse and suicidal behavior in African American women. *Journal of Consulting and Clinical Psychology, 56,* 85-90.

Katz, B., & Burt, M. (1988). Self-blame: Help or hindrance in recovery from rape? In A. Burgess (Ed.), *Rape and sexual assault II* (pp. 151-168). New York: Garland.

Keane, T., Caddell, J. M., & Taylor, K. L. (1988). Mississippi Scale for Combat-Related Posttraumatic Stress Disorder: Three studies in reliability and validity. *Journal of Consulting and Clinical Psychology, 52,* 888-891.

Keane, T., Malloy, P., & Fairbank, J. (1984). Empirical development of an MMPI subscale for the assessment of combat-related post-traumatic stress disorders. *Journal of Consulting and Clinical Psychology, 56,* 85-90.

Kellermann, A. L., & Mercy, J. A. (1992). Men, women, and murder: Gender-specific differences in rates of fatal violence and victimization. *Journal of Trauma-Injury Infection & Critical Care, 33*(1), 1-5.

Kelling, G., & Moore, M. (1988). *Perspectives on policing: The evolving strategy of policing.* Washington, DC: National Institute of Justice.

Kelling, G. L., & Coles, C. M. (1996). *Fixing broken windows: Restoring order and reducing crime in our communities.* New York: Free Press.

Kelly, D. P., & Erez, E. (1997). Victim participation in the criminal justice system. In R. C. Davis, A. J. Lurigio, & W. G. Skogan (Eds.), *Victims of crime* (2nd ed., pp. 231-244). Thousand Oaks, CA: Sage.

Kemp, A., Rawlings, E. I., & Green, B. L. (1991). Post-traumatic stress disorder (PTSD) in battered women: A shelter sample. *Journal of Traumatic Stress, 4,* 137-148.

Kennedy, L. W., & Baron, S. W. (1993). Routine activities and a subculture of violence: A study of violence on the street. *Journal of Research in Crime and Delinquency, 30,* 88-112.

Kenny, D. J. (1987). *Crime, fear, and the New York City subways.* New York: Praeger.

Killer gets maximum—6-plus terms plus 50 years. (1995, March 23). *Atlanta Constitution,* p. A5.

Kilpatrick, D., Acierno, R., Resnick, H., Saunders, B., & Best, C. (1997). A 2-year longitudinal analysis of the relationships between violent assault and substance use in women. *Journal of Consulting and Clinical Psychology, 65,* 834-847.

Kilpatrick, D., Beatty, D., & Howley, S. S. (1998). *The rights of crime victims—Does legal protection make a difference?* Washington, DC: U.S. Department of Justice.

Kilpatrick, D., Best, C., Veronen, L., Amick, A., Villeponteaux, L., & Ruff, G. (1985). Mental health correlates of criminal victimization: A random community survey. *Journal of Consulting and Clinical Psychology, 53,* 866-873.

Kilpatrick, D., & Resnick, H. (1992). PTSD associated with exposure to criminal victimization in clinical and community populations. In J. Davidson & E. Foa (Eds.), *Post-traumatic stress disorder in review: Recent research and future directions.* Washington, DC: American Psychiatric Press.

Kilpatrick, D., Resick, P., & Veronen, L. (1981). Effects of a rape experience: A longitudinal study. *Journal of Social Issues, 37*(4), 105-122.

Kilpatrick, D., Resnick, H., Saunders, B., & Best, C. (1989). *The National Women's Study PTSD module.* Unpublished manuscript, Medical University of South Carolina at Charleston.

Kilpatrick, D., Resnick, H., Saunders, B., Best, C., & Epstein, J. (1994). *Violent assault and alcohol dependence among women: Results from a longitudinal study.* Poster session presented at the annual meeting of the Research Society of Alcoholism, Maui, Hawaii.

Kilpatrick, D., Saunders, B., Veronen, L., Best, C., & Von, J. (1987). Criminal victimization: Lifetime prevalence, reporting to police, and psychological impact. *Crime and Delinquency, 33,* 479-489.

Kilpatrick, D., Seymour, A., & Boyle, J. (1991). *America speaks out: Citizens' attitudes about victims' rights and violence.* Arlington, VA: National Victim Center.

Kilpatrick, D., Veronen, L., & Best, C. (1985). Factors predicting psychological distress among rape victims. In C. Figley (Ed.), *Trauma and its wake: The study and treatment of post-traumatic stress disorder* (pp. 113-141). New York: Brunner/Mazel.

Kilpatrick, D. J., & Resnick, H. S. (1993). Posttraumatic stress disorder associated with exposure to criminal victimization in clinical and community populations. In J. R. T. Davidson & E. B. Foa (Eds.), *Posttraumatic stress disorder: DSM-IV and beyond* (pp. 113-143). Washington, DC: American Psychiatric Press.

Klinger, D. A., & Bridges, G. S. (1997). Measurement error in calls-for-service as an indicator of crime. *Criminology, 35,* 705-726.

Kolbo, J. (1996). Risk and resilience among children exposed to family violence. *Violence and Victims, 11,* 113-128.

Koss, M., Koss, P., & Woodruff, W. (1991). Deleterious effects of criminal victimization on women's health and medical utilization. *Archives of Internal Medicine, 151,* 342-357.

Koss, M., Woodruff, W. J., & Koss, P. (1991). Criminal victimization among primary care medical patients: Prevalence, incidence, and physician usage. *Behavioral Sciences and the Law, 9,* 85-96.

Koss, M. P. (1993). Rape: Scope, impact, interventions, and public policy responses. *American Psychologist, 48,* 1062-1069.

Koss, M. P., & Dinero, T. E. (1989). Discriminant analysis of risk factors for sexual victimization among a national sample of college women. *Journal of Consulting and Clinical Psychology, 57,* 242-250.

Koss, M. P., & Harvey, M. R. (1991). *The rape victim: Clinical and community interventions* (2nd ed.). Newbury Park, CA: Sage.

Kress, J. M. (1980). The spatial ecology of the criminal law. In D. E. Georges-Abeyie & K. D. Harries (Eds.), *Crime: A spatial perspective* (pp. 58-69). New York: Columbia University Press.

Krupnick, J., & Horowitz, M. (1980). Victims of violence: Psychological responses and treatment implications. *Evaluation and Change, Special Issue,* 42-46.

Kulka, R., Schlenger, W., Fairbank, J., Hough, R., Jordan, B., Marmar, C., & Weiss, D. (1991). *Trauma and the Vietnam war veterans' generation.* New York: Brunner/Mazel.

Kyriacou, D. N., Anglin, D., Taliaferro, E., Stone, S., Tubb, T., Linden, J. A., Muelleman, R., Barton, E., & Kraus, J. F. (1999). Risk factors for injury to women from domestic violence. *New England Journal of Medicine, 341,* 1892-1898.

LaGrange, R. L., & Ferraro, K. F. (1989). Assessing age and gender differences in perceived risk and fear of crime. *Criminology, 27,* 697-719.

Lambert, W. (1995, February 27). Victims' rights receive a fresh focus. *Wall Street Journal,* p. B10.

Langan, P. A., & Farrington, D. P. (1998). *Crime and justice in the United States and in England and Wales, 1981-96.* Washington, DC: U.S. Bureau of Justice Statistics.

Latané, B., & Darley, J. (1970). *The unresponsive bystander: Why doesn't he help?* New York: Appleton-Century-Crofts.

Laub, J. H. (1997). Patterns of criminal victimization in the United States. In R. C. Davis, A. J. Lurigio, & W. G. Skogan (Eds.), *Victims of crime* (2nd ed., pp. 9-26). Thousand Oaks, CA: Sage.

Lauritsen, J. L., Laub, J. H., & Sampson, R. J. (1992). Conventional and delinquent activities: Implications for the prevention of violent victimization among adolescents. *Violence and Victims, 7,* 91-108.

Lauritsen, J. L., Sampson, R. J., & Laub, J. H. (1991). The link between offending and victimization among adolescents. *Criminology, 29,* 265-292.

Lavrakas, P. J. (1993). *Telephone survey methods: Sampling, selection, and supervision* (2nd ed.). Newbury Park, CA: Sage.

Lee, L. (1997, April 23). Courts begin to award damages to victims of parking-area crime. *Wall Street Journal,* pp. A1, A8.

Lehmann, P. (1997). The development of posttraumatic stress disorder (PTSD) in a sample of child witnesses to mother assault. *Journal of Family Violence, 12,* 241-257.

Lepore, S. J., Evans, G. W., & Schneider, M. L. (1991). Dynamic role of social support in the link between chronic stress and psychological distress. *Journal of Personality and Social Psychology, 61,* 899-909.

Lerner, M. (1980). *The belief in a just world.* New York: Plenum.

Lerner, M. J., Miller, D. T., & Holmes, J. G. (1976). Deserving and the emergence of forms of justice. In L. Berkowitz (Ed.), *Advances in experimental social psychology* (Vol. 9, pp. 133-162). New York: Academic Press.

Levendosky, A., Okun, A., & Parker, J. (1995). Depression and maltreatment as predictors of social competence and social problem-solving skills in school-age children. *Child Abuse and Neglect, 19,* 1183-1195.

Levine, J. M., & Moreland, R. L. (1998). Small groups. In D. T. Gilbert, S. T. Fiske, & G. Lindzey (Eds.), *The handbook of social psychology* (4th ed., Vol. 2, pp. 415-469). Boston: McGraw-Hill.

Liebschutz, J. M., Mulvey, K. P., & Samet, J. H. (1997). Victimization among substance-abusing women. *Archives of Internal Medicine, 157,* 1093-1097.

Lindsay, B., & McGillis, D. (1986). Citywide community crime prevention: An assessment of the Seattle program. In D. P. Rosenbaum (Ed.), *Community crime prevention: Does it work?* (pp. 46-67). Beverly Hills, CA: Sage.

Liska, A. E., & Bellair, P. E. (1995). Violent-crime rates and racial composition: Convergence over time. *American Journal of Sociology, 101,* 578-610.

Liska, A. E., Lawrence, J. J., & Sanchirico, A. (1982). Fear of crime as a social fact. *Social Forces, 60,* 761-770.

Liska, A. E., Sanchirico, A., & Reed, M. D. (1988). Fear of crime and constrained behavior: Specifying and estimating a reciprocal effects model. *Social Forces, 66,* 827-837.

Lloyd, S., Farrell, G., & Pease, K. (1994). *Preventing repeated domestic violence: A demonstration project on Merseyside.* Home Office Crime Prevention Unit Paper 49. London: Home Office.

Lorion, R., & Saltzman, W. (1993). Children's exposure to community violence: Following a path from concern to research to action. In D. Reiss, J. Richters, M. Radke-Yarrow, & D. Scharff (Eds.), *Children and violence* (pp. 55-65). New York: Guilford.

Luckenbill, D. F., & Doyle, D. P. (1989). Structural positions and violence: Developing a cultural explanation. *Criminology, 27,* 419-436.

Lurigio, A. J., & Mechanic, M. B. (2000). The importance of being sensitive and responsive to crime victims. *Police Magazine, 24,* 22-28.

Maguire, K., & Pastore, A. L. (1994). *Sourcebook of criminal justice statistics—1993.* Washington, DC: U.S. Bureau of Justice Statistics.

Maguire, K., & Pastore, A. L. (1999). *Sourcebook of criminal justice statistics—1998.* Washington, DC: U.S. Bureau of Justice Statistics.

Maguire, M. (1980). The impact of burglary upon victims. *British Journal of Criminology, 20,* 261-275.

Mahoney, P. (1999). High rape chronicity and low rates of help-seeking among wife rape survivors in a nonclinical sample. *Violence Against Women, 5,* 993-1016.

Markowitz, F. E., & Felson, R. B. (1998). Social-demographic differences in attitudes and violence. *Criminology, 36,* 117-138.

Marris, P. (1975). *Loss and change.* Garden City, NY: Anchor/Doubleday.

Martin, S. D. (1996). Investigating hate crimes: Case characteristics and law enforcement responses. *Justice Quarterly, 13,* 455-480.

Martinez, P., & Richters, J. (1993). The NIMH Community Violence Project: II. Children's distress symptoms associated with violence exposure. In D. Reiss, J. Richters, M. Radke-Yarrow, & D. Scharff (Eds.), *Children and violence* (pp. 22-35). New York: Guilford.

Maxfield, M. G., Lewis, D. A., & Szoc, R. (1980). Producing official crimes: Verified crime reports as measures of police output. *Social Science Quarterly, 61,* 221-236.

McCann, I. L., & Pearlman, L. A. (1990). Vicarious traumatization: A framework for understanding the psychological effects of working with victims. *Journal of Traumatic Stress, 3,* 131-149.

McCann, I. L., Sakheim, D., & Abrahamson, D. (1988). Trauma and victimization: A model of psychological adaptation. *The Counseling Psychologist, 16,* 531-594.

McCloskey, L. A., Figueredo, A. J., & Koss, M. P. (1995). The effects of systemic family violence on children's mental health. *Child Development, 66,* 1239-1261.

McDonald, R. R. (1993, October 10). Her attacker walked out of court free. *Atlanta Journal & Constitution,* pp. F1, F5.

McDonald, R. R. (1995, March 20). Son's slaying haunts mom. *Atlanta Journal & Constitution,* p. B2.

McIntosh, S. (1993, October 10). Rape: What you need to know. *Atlanta Journal & Constitution,* p. F8.

McLeer, S. V., & Anwar, R. (1989). A study of battered women presenting in an emergency department. *American Journal of Public Health, 79,* 65-66.

Meichenbaum, D. (1974). *Cognitive behavior modification.* Morristown, NJ: General Learning Press.

Meier, R. F., & Miethe, T. D. (1993). Understanding theories of criminal victimization. In M. Tonry (Ed.), *Crime and justice: A review of research* (Vol. 17, pp. 459-499). Chicago: University of Chicago Press.

Mercy, J. A. (1993). The public health impact of firearm injuries. *American Journal of Preventive Medicine, 9*(Suppl. 1), 8-11.

Messman, T. L., & Long, P. J. (1996). Child sexual abuse and its relationship to revictimization in adult women: A review. *Clinical Psychology Review, 16,* 397-420.

Meyer, C., & Taylor, S. (1986). Adjustment to rape. *Journal of Personality and Social Psychology, 50,*1226-1234.

Miethe, T. D., & McDowall, D. (1993). Contextual effects in models of criminal victimization. *Social Forces, 71,* 741-759.

Miethe, T. D., & Meier, R. F. (1994). *Crime and its social context: Toward an integrated theory of offenders, victims, and situations.* Albany: State University of New York Press.

Miller, L. S., Wasserman, G. A., Neugebauer, R., Gorman-Smith, D., & Kamboukos, D. (1999). Witnessed community violence and antisocial behavior in high-risk, urban boys. *Journal of Clinical Child Psychology, 28,* 2-11.

Miller, T. R., Cohen, M., & Wiersema, B. (1996). *Victim costs and consequences: A new look* (National Institute of Justice Research Report; Publication No. NCJ-155282). Washington, DC: National Institute of Justice.

Miller, W., Williams, A., & Bernstein, M. (1982). The effects of rape on marital and sexual adjustment. *American Journal of Family Therapy, 10,* 51-58.

Mitchell, R. E., & Hodson, C. A. (1983). Coping with domestic violence: Social support and psychological health among battered women. *American Journal of Community Psychology, 11,* 629-654.

Mollica, R., Caspi-Yavin, Y., Bollini, P., Truong, T., Tor, S., & Lavelle, J. (1992). The Harvard Trauma Questionnaire: Validating a cross-cultural instrument for measuring torture, trauma, and posttraumatic stress disorder in Indochinese refugees. *Journal of Nervous and Mental Disease, 180,* 111-116.

Monkkonen, E. H. (1989). Diverging homicide rates: England and the United States, 1850-1875. In T. R. Gurr (Ed.), *Violence in America: Vol. 1. The history of crime* (pp. 80-101). Newbury Park, CA: Sage.

Mulvihill, D., & Tumin, M. (1969). *Crimes of violence: A staff report submitted to the U.S. Commission on the Causes and Prevention of Violence* (Vol. 11). Washington, DC: Government Printing Office.

Murphy, S. (1990). Rape, sexually transmitted diseases and human immunodeficiency virus infection. *International Journal of STD and AIDS, 1,* 79-82.

Murphy, S., Amick-McMullan, A., Kilpatrick, D., Haskett, M., Veronen, L., Best, C., & Saunders, B. (1988). Rape victims' self-esteem: A longitudinal analysis. *Journal of Interpersonal Violence, 3,* 355-370.

Myers, K., Burke, P., & McCauley, E. (1985). Suicide behavior by hospitalized preadolescent children on a psychiatric unit. *Journal of American Academy of Child Psychiatry, 24,* 474-480.

National Organization of Victim Assistance. (1991). *Community Crisis Response Training Institute participant's manual for Pickens, South Carolina.* Washington, DC: Author.

National Victims Center. (1992). *Rape in America: A report to the nation.* Arlington, VA: Author.

Newman, O. (1972). *Defensible space.* New York: Macmillan.

Newman, O. (1973). *Architectural design for crime prevention.* Washington, DC: National Institute of Law Enforcement and Criminal Justice.

Norris, F. (1992). Epidemiology of trauma: Frequency and impact of different potentially traumatic events on different demographic groups. *Journal of Consulting and Clinical Psychology, 60,* 409-418.

Norris, F., & Johnson, K. (1988). The effects of "self-help" precautionary measures on criminal victimization and fear. *Journal of Urban Affairs, 10,* 161-181.

Norris, F., & Kaniasty, K. (1991). The psychological experience of crime: A test of the mediating role of beliefs in explaining the distress of victims. *Journal of Social and Clinical Psychology, 10,* 239-261.

Norris, F., & Kaniasty, K. (1994). Psychological distress following criminal victimization in the general population: Cross-sectional, longitudinal, and prospective analyses. *Journal of Consulting and Clinical Psychology, 62,* 111-123.

Norris, F., Kaniasty, K., & Scheer, D. (1990). Use of mental health services among victims of crime: Frequency, correlates, and subsequent recovery. *Journal of Consulting and Clinical Psychology, 58,* 538-547.

Norris, F., Kaniasty, K., & Thompson, M. (1997). The psychological consequences of crime: Findings from a longitudinal population-based study. In A. Lurigio, W. Skogan, & R. Davis (Eds.), *Victims of crime* (2nd ed., pp. 146-166). Thousand Oaks, CA: Sage.

Norris, F., & Thompson, M. (1993). Victims in the system: The influence of police responsiveness on victim alienation. *Journal of Traumatic Stress, 6,* 515-532.

Norris, F. H. (1990). Screening for traumatic stress: A scale for use in the general population. *Journal of Applied Social Psychology, 20,* 1704-1718.

Norris, F. H., & Kaniasty, K. (1992). A longitudinal study of the effects of various crime prevention strategies on criminal victimization, fear of crime, and psychological distress. *American Journal of Community Psychology, 20,* 625-648.

Norris, F. H., & Riad, J. K. (1997). Standardized self-report measures of civilian trauma and posttraumatic stress disorder. In J. P. Wilson & T. M. Keane (Eds.), *Assessing psychological trauma and PTSD* (pp. 7-42). New York: Guilford.

O'Brien, R. M. (1996). Police productivity and crime rates: 1973-1992. *Criminology, 34,* 183-207.

Office for Victims of Crime. (1998). *New directions from the field: Victims' rights and services for the 21st century.* Washington, DC: U.S. Department of Justice.

Office for Victims of Crime. (2000). *First response to victims of crime.* Washington, DC: U.S. Department of Justice, Office of Justice Programs.

Oglesby, C. (1997, April 18). Widow protests parole of mall killer. *Atlanta Journal & Constitution,* p. F8.

O'Keefe, M. (1994). Linking marital violence, mother-child/father-child aggression, and child behavior problems. *Journal of Family Violence, 9,* 63-78.

O'Leary, K. D. (2000). Are women really more aggressive than men in intimate relationships? Comment on Archer (2000). *Psychological Bulletin, 126,* 685-689.

Osofsky, J. (1995). The effects of exposure to violence on young children. *American Psychologist, 50,* 782-788.

Osofsky, J., Wewers, S., Hann, D., & Fick, A. (1993). Chronic community violence: What is happening to our children? *Psychiatry, 56,* 36-45.

Outlaw, M. C., & Ruback, R. B. (1999). Predictors and outcomes of victim restitution orders. *Justice Quarterly, 16,* 847-869.

Pacelle, M. (1996, July 17). Ugly storefront security gates are bashed by critics. *Wall Street Journal,* p. B1.

Parkes, C. (1975). What becomes of redundant world models? A contribution to the study of adaption to change. *British Journal of Medical Psychology, 48,* 131-137.

Pastore, D., Fisher, M., & Friedman, S. (1996). Violence and mental health problems among urban high school students. *Journal of Adolescent Health, 18,* 320-324.

Payne v. Tennessee, 501 U.S. (1991).

Pearlman, L. A., & Saakvitne, K. W. (1995). Treating therapists with vicarious traumatization and secondary traumatic stress disorders. In C. R. Figley (Ed.), *Compassion fatigue: Coping with secondary traumatic stress disorder in those who treat the traumatized* (pp. 150-177). New York: Brunner/Mazel.

Pease, K., & Laycock, G. (1996). *Revictimization: Reducing the heat on hot victims* (National Institute of Justice Research in Action). Washington, DC: U.S. Department of Justice.

Pennebaker, J. W., & Beall, S. (1986). Confronting a traumatic event: Toward an understanding of inhibition and disease. *Journal of Abnormal Psychology, 95,* 274-281.

Pennebaker, J. W., & O'Heeron, R. C. (1984). Confiding in others and illness rate among spouses of suicide and accidental death victims. *Journal of Abnormal Psychology, 93,* 473-476.

Pennebaker, J. W., & Susman, J. R. (1988). Disclosure of traumas and psychosomatic processes. *Social Science and Medicine, 26,* 327-332.

Pepinsky, H. E. (1976). Police patrolmen's offense reporting behavior. *Journal of Research in Crime and Delinquency, 13,* 33-47.

Perez, C. M., & Widom, C. S. (1994). Childhood victimization and long-term intellectual and academic outcomes. *Child Abuse and Neglect, 18,* 617-633.

Perloff, L. (1983). Perceptions of vulnerability to victimization. *Journal of Social Issues, 39*(2), 41-61.

Phillips, B. D. (1994, June 28). I'm a victim of a crime, but not a statistic. *Wall Street Journal,* p. A18.

Polusny, A., & Follette, V. (1995). Long-term correlates of child sexual abuse: Theory and review of the empirical literature. *Applied & Preventive Psychology, 4,* 143-166.

Pope, C. E. (1977). *Crime-specific analysis: The characteristics of burglary incidents.* Washington, DC: U.S. Department of Justice.

Premises Liability, 62A American Jurisprudence 2d §§ 513-527 (1990).

Prentky, R. A., Burgess, A. W., & Carter, D. (1986). Victim response by rapist type: An empirical and clinical analysis. *Journal of Interpersonal Violence, 1,* 688-695.

President's Commission on Law Enforcement and Administration of Justice. (1967). *The challenge of crime in a free society.* Washington, DC: Government Printing Office.

President's Task Force on Victims of Crime. (1982). *Final report.* Washington, DC: Author.

Put gunman away for life, victims say. (1995, March 22). *Atlanta Constitution,* p. A8.

Pynoos, R., Frederick, C., Nader, K., Arroyo, W., Steinberg, A., Eth, S., Nunez, F., & Fairbanks, L. (1987). Life threat and posttraumatic stress in school-age children. *Archives of General Psychiatry, 44,* 1057-1063.

Pynoos, R., & Nader, K. (1988). Children who witness the sexual assaults of their mothers. *Journal of the American Academy of Child and Adolescent Psychiatry, 27,* 567-572.

Quindlen, A. (1994, October 20). A SANE way to help rape victims. *Atlanta Constitution,* p. A11.

Quinsey, V. L., & Upfold, D. (1985). Rape completion and victim injury as a function of female resistance strategy. *Canadian Journal of Behavioral Science, 17,* 40-50.

Rand, M., & Strom, K. (1997). *Violence-related injuries treated in hospital emergency departments* (Bureau of Justice Statistics special report; Publication No. NCJ-156921). Washington, DC: U.S. Department of Justice.

Randall, T. (1990). Domestic violence begets other problems of which physicians must be aware to be effective. *Journal of the American Medical Association, 264,* 940-944.

Rape victim refuses to help police. (2000, March 31). *Centre Daily Times,* p. 9A.

Reiss, A. J., Jr., & Roth, J. A. (Eds.). (1993). *Understanding and preventing violence.* Washington, DC: National Academy Press.

Rennison, C. M. (1999). *Criminal victimization 1998: Changes 1997-98 with trends 1993-98* (Report No. NCJ-176353). Washington, DC: U.S. Bureau of Justice Statistics.

Rennison, C. M., & Welchans, S. (2000, May). *Intimate partner violence* (Bureau of Justice Statistics special report; Publication No. NCJ-178247). Washington, DC: U.S. Bureau of Justice Statistics, Office of Justice Programs.

Resick, P. (1984). The trauma of rape and the criminal justice system. *Justice System Journal, 9,* 52-61.

Resick, P. (1993). The psychological impact of rape. *Journal of Interpersonal Violence, 8,* 223-255.

Resick, P., Jordan, C., Girelli, S., Hutter, C., & Marhoefer-Dvorak, S. (1988). A comparative outcome study of behavioral group therapy for sexual assault victims. *Behavioral Therapy, 19,* 385-401.

Resick, P., & Schnicke, M. (1992). Cognitive processing therapy for sexual assault victims. *Journal of Consulting and Clinical Psychology, 60,* 748-756.

Resnick, H., Kilpatrick, D., Dansky, B., Saunders, B., & Best, C. (1993). Prevalence of civilian trauma and posttraumatic stress disorder in a representative national sample of women. *Journal of Consulting and Clinical Psychology, 61,* 984-991.

Riggs, D., Rothbaum, B., & Foa, E. (1995). A prospective examination of symptoms of posttraumatic stress disorder in victims of nonsexual assault. *Journal of Interpersonal Violence, 10,* 201-214.

Riggs, D. S., & Kilpatrick, D. G., (1990). Families and friends: Indirect victimization by crime. In A. J. Lurigio, W. G. Skogan, and R. C. Davis (Eds.), *Victims of Crime: Problems, Policies, and Programs* (pp. 120-138). Newbury Park, CA: Sage.

Riggs, D. S., Kilpatrick, D. G., & Resnick, H. S. (1992). Long-term psychological distress associated with marital rape and aggravated assault: A comparison to other crime victims. *Journal of Family Violence, 7,* 283-296.

Rinear, E. (1988). Psychosocial aspects of parental response patterns to the death of a child by homicide. *Journal of Traumatic Stress, 1,* 305-322.

Robinson, J. P., Shaver, P. R., & Wrightsman, L. S. (1991). *Measures of personality and social psychological attitudes.* San Diego, CA: Academic Press.

Rodriguez, N., Ryan, S., Kemp, H. V., & Foy, D. W. (1997). Posttraumatic stress disorder in adult female survivors of childhood sexual abuse: A comparison study. *Journal of Consulting and Clinical Psychology, 65,* 53-59.

Roese, N. (1997). Counterfactual thinking. *Psychological Bulletin, 121,* 133-148.

Rose, D. R., & Clear, T. R. (1998). Incarceration, social capital, and crime: Implications for social disorganization theory. *Criminology, 36,* 441-479.

Rosenbaum, D. P., Lewis, D. A., & Grant, J. A. (1986). Neighborhood-based crime prevention: Assessing the efficacy of community organizing in Chicago. In D. P. Rosenbaum (Ed.), *Community crime prevention: Does it work?* (pp. 109-136). Beverly Hills, CA: Sage.

Rosenbaum, D. P., Lurigio, A. J., & Davis, R. C. (1998). *The prevention of crime: Social and situational strategies.* Belmont, CA: Wadsworth.

Rosenberg, M. (1987). Children of battered women: The effects of witnessing violence on their social problem-solving abilities. *The Behavior Therapist, 10,* 85-89.

Roth, J. A., & Moore, M. H. (1995). *Reducing violent crimes and intentional injuries* (National Institute of Justice Research in Action). Washington, DC: National Institute of Justice, Office of Justice Programs.

Rothbaum, B., Foa, E., Murdock, T., Riggs, D., & Walsh, W. (1992). A prospective examination of post-traumatic stress disorder in rape victims. *Journal of Traumatic Stress, 5,* 455-475.

Rountree, P. W., Land, K. C., Miethe, T. D. (1994). Macro-micro integration in the study of victimization: A hierarchical logistic model analysis across Seattle neighborhoods. *Criminology, 32,* 387-414.

Ruback, R. B. (1994). Advice to crime victims: Effects of crime, victim, and advisor factors. *Criminal Justice and Behavior, 21,* 423-442.

Ruback, R. B., Greenberg, M. S., & Westcott, D. (1981). An archival analysis of victim reporting. *Victimology: An International Journal, 6,* 318-327.

Ruback, R. B., Greenberg, M. S., & Westcott, D. R. (1984). Social influence and crime victim decision making. *Journal of Social Issues, 40*(1), 51-76.

Ruback, R. B., Gupta, D., & Kohli, N. (1988, September). *Normative standards for crime victims: Implications for research and policy.* Paper presented at the Silver Jubilee Symposium on Psychology, National Development and Social Policy, Psychology Department, Allahabad University, Allahabad, Uttar Pradesh, India.

Ruback, R. B., & Ivie, D. L. (1988). Prior relationship, resistance, and injury in rapes: An analysis of crisis center records. *Violence and Victims, 3*, 99-111.

Ruback, R. B., & Ménard, K. S. (2001). Rural/urban differences in sexual victimization and reporting: Analyses using UCR and crisis center data. *Criminal Justice and Behavior, 28*, 131-155.

Ruback, R. B., Ménard, K. S., Outlaw, M. S., & Shaffer, J. N. (1999). Normative advice to campus crime victims: Effects of gender, age, and alcohol. *Violence and Victims, 14*, 381-396.

Ruch, L., Amedeo, S., Leon, J., & Gartrell, J. (1991). Repeated sexual victimization and trauma change during the acute phase of the sexual assault trauma syndrome. *Women and Health, 17*, 1-19.

Ruch, L., & Chandler, S. (1983). Sexual assault trauma during the acute phase: An exploratory model and multivariate analysis. *Journal of Health and Social Behavior, 24*, 184-185.

Russell, B. (1994, July 10). There's no childhood anymore. *Atlanta Journal & Constitution*, p. D6.

Russell, D. (1990). *Rape in marriage*. Indianapolis: Indiana University Press.

Russell, R. (1994, July 10). Growing up should not be this hard. *Atlanta Journal & Constitution*, p. D6.

Ryan, W. (1971). *Blaming the victim*. New York: Vintage.

Sales, E., Baum, M., & Shore, B. (1984). Victim readjustment following assault. *Journal of Social Issues, 40*(1), 117-136.

Sampson, R. J. (2001). How do communities undergird or undermine human development? Relevant contexts and social mechanisms. In A. Booth & A. C. Crouter (Eds.), *Does it take a village? Community effects on children, adolescents, and families* (pp. 3-30). Mahwah, NJ: Lawrence Erlbaum.

Sampson, R. J., & Cohen, J. (1988). Deterrent effects of the police on crime: A replication and theoretical extension. *Law & Society Review, 22*, 163-189.

Sampson, R. J., & Lauritsen, J. L. (1994). Violent victimization and offending: Individual-, situational-, and community-level risk factors. In A. J. Reiss & J. A. Roth (Eds.), *Understanding and preventing violence* (Vol. 3, pp. 1-114). Washington, DC: National Academy Press.

Sampson, R. J., Raudenbush, S. W., & Earls, F. (1997, August 15). Neighborhoods and violent crime: A multilevel study of collective efficacy. *Science, 277*, 918-924.

Sassetti, M. R. (1993). Domestic violence. *Primary Care, 20*, 289-305.

Saunders, B., Arata, C., & Kilpatrick, D. (1990). Development of a crime-related posttraumatic stress disorder scale for women with the Symptom Checklist—Revised. *Journal of Traumatic Stress, 5*, 613-626.

Scheppele, K., & Bart, P. (1983). Through women's eyes: Defining danger in the wake of sexual assault. *Journal of Social Issues, 39*(2), 63-81.

Schlosser, E. (1997, September). A grief like no other. *Atlantic Monthly*, pp. 37-76.

Schneider, A. L., Burcart, J. M., & Wilson, L. A., II. (1976). The role of attitudes in the decision to report crimes to the police. In W. F. McDonald (Ed.), *Criminal justice and the victim*, pp. 89-113. Beverly Hills, CA: Sage.

Schwarz, N. (1999). Self-reports: How the questions shape the answers. *American Psychologist, 54*, 93-105.

Scully, D., & Marolla, J. (1984). Convicted rapists' vocabulary of motive: Excuses and justifications. *Social Problems, 31*, 530-544.

Searles, P., & Berger, R. (1987). The current status of rape reform legislation: An examination of the state statutes. *Women's Rights Law Reporter, 10*, 25-43.

Sebba, L. (1996). *Third parties: Victims and the criminal justice system*. Columbus: Ohio State University Press.

Sedlak, A. J. (1991). *Supplementary analyses of data on the national incidence of child abuse and neglect*. Rockville, MD: Westat.

Seedman, A. A., & Hellman, P. (1975). *Chief.* New York: Avon.

Shaffer, J. (2000). *Offending, victimization, and life-course factors: An examination of probationers.* Unpublished masters thesis, Pennsylvania State University.

Shapland, J. (1983). Victim-witness services and the needs of the victim. *Victimology: An International Journal, 8,* 233-237.

Shapland, J. (1984). Victims, the criminal justice system and compensation. *British Journal of Criminology, 24,* 131-149.

Shapland, J. (1985). The criminal justice system and the victim. *Victimology: An International Journal, 10,* 585-599.

Shapland, J., Willmore, J., & Duff, P. (1985). *Victims in the criminal justice system.* Brookfield, VT: Gower.

Shaw, C., & McKay, H. (1942). *Juvenile delinquency and urban areas.* Chicago: University of Chicago Press

Sherman, L. W. (1992). *Policing domestic violence: Experiments and dilemmas.* New York: Free Press.

Sherman, L. W., Gottfredson, D. C., MacKenzie, D. L., Eck, J., Reuter, P., & Bushway, S. D. (1997). *Preventing crime: What works, what doesn't, what's promising.* Washington, DC: Office of Justice Programs.

Shotland, R. L. (1976). Spontaneous vigilantism: A bystander response to criminal behavior. In H. J. Rosenbaum & P. C. Sederberg (Eds.), *Vigilante politics* (pp. 30-44). Philadelphia: University of Pennsylvania Press.

Shotland, R. L., & Goodstein, L. I. (1984). The role of bystanders in crime control. *Journal of Social Issues, 40*(1), 9-26.

Shotland, R. L., & Straw, M. K. (1976). Bystander responses to an assault: When a man attacks a woman. *Journal of Personality and Social Psychology, 34,* 990-999.

Shuster, B. (1998, August 23). Living in fear. *Los Angeles Times,* pp. A1, A32, A33.

Silver, R., & Wortman, C. (1980). Coping with undesirable events. In J. Garber, & M. E. Seligman (Eds.), *Human helplessness: Theory and applications* (pp. 279-375). New York: Academic Press.

Silver, S. M. (1986). An inpatient program for post-traumatic stress disorder: Context and treatment. In C. R. Figley (Ed.), *Trauma and it's wake: Vol 2. Traumatic stress theory, research, and intervention* (pp. 213-231). New York: Brunner/Mazel.

Silverman, D. (1978). Sharing the crisis of rape: Counseling the mates and families of victims. *American Journal of Orthopsychiatry, 48,* 166-173.

Singer, S. I. (1981). Homogeneous victim-offender populations: A review and some research implications. *Journal of Criminal Law and Criminology, 72,* 779-788.

Singer, S. I. (1986). Victims of serious violence and their criminal behavior: Subcultural theory and beyond. *Violence and Victims, 1,* 61-70.

Skogan, W. (1984). Reporting crimes to the police: The status of world research. *Journal of Research in Crime and Delinquency, 21,* 113-137.

Skogan, W. (1989). The impact of police on victims. In E. Viano (Ed.), *Crime and its victims: International research and public policy issues* (pp. 71-77). New York: Hemisphere.

Skogan, W., & Maxfield, M. (1981). *Coping with crime: Individual and neighborhood reactions.* Beverly Hills, CA: Sage.

Skogan, W. G. (1987). The impact of victimization on fear. *Crime and Delinquency, 33,* 135-154.

Skogan, W. G. (1988). Community organizations and crime. In M. Tonry & N. Morris (Eds.), *Crime and justice: A review of research* (Vol. 10, pp. 39-78). Chicago: University of Chicago Press.

Skogan, W. G. (1990). *Disorder and decline: Crime and the spiral of decay in American neighborhood.* New York: Free Press.

Smith, D., & Visher, C. A. (1981). Street level justice: Situational determinants of police arrest decisions. *Social Problems, 29,* 169-177.

Solomon, Z., Waysman, M., Avitzur, E., & Enoch, D. (1991). Psychiatric symptomatology among wives of soldiers following combat stress reaction: The role of social network and marital relations. *Anxiety Research, 4,* 213-223.

Solomon, Z., Waysman, M., Levy, G., Fried, B., Mikulincer, M., Benbenishty, R., Florian, V., & Bleich, A. (1992). From the front line to home front: A study on secondary traumatization. *Family Process, 31,* 289-302.

Solomon, Z., Waysman, M., Levy, G., Fried, B., Mikulincer, M., & Enoch, D. (1992). Marital relations and combat stress: The wives' perspective. *Journal of Marriage and the Family, 54,* 316-326.

Sorenson, S., Stein, J., Siegel, J., Golding, J., & Burnam, M. (1987). The prevalence of adult sexual assault: The Los Angeles Epidemiological Catchment Area Project. *American Journal of Epidemiology, 126,* 1154-1164.

Soto, L. (1993, October 5). Landlords forced to face crime: Tenants' suits get apartment owners' attention. *Atlanta Constitution,* pp. E1, E6.

Sparks, R. F. (1982). *Research on victims of crime: Accomplishments, issues, and new directions.* Rockville, MD: National Institute of Mental Health.

Stagg, V., Wills, G. D., & Howell, M. (1989). Psychopathology in early-childhood witnesses of family violence. *Topics in Early Childhood Special Education, 9,* 73-87.

Stark, E., & Flitcraft, A. (1988). Violence among intimates: An epidemiological review. In V. B. Van Hasselt, R. L. Morrison, A. S. Bellack, & M. Hersen (Eds.), *Handbook of family violence* (pp. 293-317). New York: Plenum.

Stark, E., & Flitcraft, A. (1996). *Women at risk: Domestic violence and women's health.* Thousand Oaks, CA: Sage.

Stark, J., & Goldstein, H. (1985). *The rights of crime victims.* New York: Bantam.

Stark, R. (1987). Deviant places: A theory of the ecology of crime. *Criminology, 25,* 893-909.

Stets, J. E., & Straus, M. A. (1990). Gender differences in reporting of marital violence and its medical and psychological consequences. In M. A. Straus & R. J. Gelles (Eds.), *Physical violence in American families: Risk factors and adaptations to violence in 8,145 families* (pp. 151-165). New Brunswick, NJ: Transaction.

Stewart, S. H. (1996). Alcohol abuse in individuals exposed to trauma: A critical review. *Psychological Bulletin, 120,* 83-112.

Straus, M. A. (1979). Measuring family conflict and violence: The conflict tactics scale. *Journal of Marriage and the Family, 41,* 75-88.

Straus, M. A. (1999). The controversy over domestic violence by women: A methodological, theoretical, and sociology of science analysis. In X. A. Arriaga & S. Oskamp (Eds.), *Violence in intimate relationships* (pp. 17-44). Thousand Oaks, CA: Sage.

Straus, M. A., & Gelles, R. J. (1990). *Physical violence in American families: Risk factors and adaptations to violence in 8,145 families.* New Brunswick, NJ: Transaction.

Straus, M., Gelles, R., & Steinmetz, S. (1980). *Behind closed doors: Violence in the American family.* Garden City, NY: Anchor.

Sullivan, C., Tan, C., Basta, J., Rumptz, M., & Davidson, W. (1992). An advocacy intervention program for women with abusive partners: Initial evaluation. *American Journal of Community Psychology, 20,* 309-332.

Switzer, G. E., Dew, M. A., Thompson, K., Goycoolea, J. M., Derricott, T., & Mullins, S. D. (1999). Posttraumatic stress disorder and service utilization among urban mental health center clients. *Journal of Traumatic Stress, 12,* 25-39.

Symonds, M. (1980). The "second injury" to victims. In L. Kivens (Ed.), *Evaluation and change: Services for survivors* (pp. 36-38). Minneapolis: Medical Research Foundation.

Taylor, R., & Hale, M. (1986). Testing alternative models of fear of crime. *Journal of Criminal Law and Criminology, 77,* 151-189.

Taylor, R. B., & Harrell, A. V. (1996). *Physical environment and crime.* Washington, DC: National Institute of Justice.

Taylor, S. (1983). Adjustment to threatening events: A theory of cognitive adaptation. *American Psychologist, 38,* 1161-1173.

Taylor, S., Wood, J., & Lichtman, R. (1983). It could be worse: Selective evaluation as a response to victimization. *Journal of Social Issues, 39*(2), 19-40.

Thomas, J. (1997, April 25). Oklahoma bombing trial: Government starts presenting case. *Atlanta Journal & Constitution,* p. A10.

Thompson, M. (1993, April 19). Violence and the verdict. *Wall Street Journal,* p. A12.

Thompson, M. P., Kaslow, N. J., Kingree, J. B., Puett, R., Thompson, N. J., & Meadows, L. (1999). Partner abuse and posttraumatic stress disorder as risk factors for suicide attempts in a sample of low income, inner-city women. *Journal of Traumatic Stress, 12,* 59-71.

Thompson, M. P., & Norris, F. H. (1992). Crime, social status, and alienation. *American Journal of Community Psychology, 20,* 97-119.

Thompson, M. P., Norris. F. H., & Ruback, R. B. (1998). Comparative distress levels of inner-city family members of homicide victims. *Journal of Traumatic Stress, 11,* 223-242.

Thompson, M. P., Simon, T. R., Saltzman, L. E., & Mercy, J. A. (1999). Epidemiology of injuries among women following physical assaults: The role of self-protective behaviors. *American Journal of Epidemiology, 150,* 235-244.

Tjaden, P., & Thoennes, N. (1998, November). *Prevalence, incidence, and consequences of violence against women: Findings from the National Violence Against Women Survey* (Research in Brief). Washington, DC: National Institute of Justice and the Centers for Disease Control and Prevention.

Tjaden, P., & Thoennes, N. (1999). *Extent, nature, and consequences of intimate partner violence: Findings from the National Violence Against Women Survey.* Washington, DC: National Institute of Justice and the Centers for Disease Control and Prevention.

Tjaden, P., & Thoennes, N. (2000). Prevalence and consequences of male-to-female and female-to-male intimate partner violence as measured by the National Violence Against Women Survey. *Violence Against Women, 6,* 142-161.

Tomz, J. E., & McGillis, D. (1997). *Serving crime victims and witnesses* (2nd ed.). Washington, DC: National Institute of Justice.

Tucker, P., Pfefferbaum, B., Nixon, S. J., & Foy, D. (1999). Trauma and recovery among adults highly exposed to a community disaster. *Psychiatric Annals, 29,* 78-83.

Tyler, T. R. (1984). Assessing the risk of crime victimization: The integration of personal victimization experience and socially transmitted information. *Journal of Social Issues, 40*(1), 27-38.

Ullman, S. E. (1997). Review and critique of empirical studies of rape avoidance. *Criminal Justice and Behavior, 24,* 177-204.

Ullman, S. E., & Knight, R. A. (1991). A multivariate model for predicting rape and physical injury outcomes during sexual assaults. *Journal of Consulting and Clinical Psychology, 59,* 724-731.

Ullman, S. E., & Knight, R. A. (1992). Fighting back: Women's resistance to rape. *Journal of Interpersonal Violence, 7,* 31-43.

Ullman, S. E., & Knight, R. A. (1993). The efficacy of women's resistance strategies in rape situations. *Psychology of Women Quarterly, 17,* 23-38.

Ullman, S. E., & Knight, R. A. (1995). Women's resistance strategies to different rapist types. *Criminal Justice and Behavior, 22,* 263-283.

Umbreit, M. S., & Greenwood, J. (2000a). *Guidelines for victim-sensitive victim-offender mediation: Restorative justice through dialogue.* Washington, DC: Office for Victims of Crime.

Umbreit, M. S., & Greenwood, J. (2000b). *National survey of victim-offender mediation programs in the United States.* Washington, DC: Office for Victims of Crime.

U.S. Bureau of Justice Statistics. (1985). *Reporting crimes to the police*. Washington, DC: U.S. Department of Justice.

U.S. Bureau of Justice Statistics. (1987). *Lifetime likelihood of victimization*. Washington, DC: U.S. Department of Justice.

U.S Bureau of Justice Statistics. (1997). *Criminal victimization in the United States, 1994*. Washington, DC: U.S. Department of Justice.

Van den Bogaard, J., & Wiegman, O. (1991). Property crime victimization: The effectiveness of police services for victims of residential burglary. *Journal of Social Behavior & Personality, 6*, 329-362.

Van der Wurff, A., & Stringer, P. (1989). Postvictimization fear of crime: Differences in the perceptions of people and places. *Journal of Interpersonal Violence, 4*, 469-481.

van Dijk, J., & Kangaspunta, K. (2000, January). Piecing together the cross-national crime puzzle. *National Institute of Justice Journal*, 34-41.

Vasu, M. L., Moriarty, L. J., & Pelfrey, W. V. (1995). Measuring violent crime in North Carolina utilizing mail and telephone surveys simultaneously: Does method matter? *Criminal Justice Review, 20*, 34-43.

Verbosky, S., & Ryan, D. (1988). Female partners of Vietnam veterans: Stress by proximity. *Issues in Mental Health Nursing, 9*, 95-104.

Veronen, L., & Kilpatrick, D. (1983). Stress management for rape victims. In D. Meichenbaum & M. Jaremko (Eds.), *Stress reduction and prevention* (pp. 341-374). New York: Plenum.

von Hentig, H. (1948). *The criminal and his victim*. New Haven, CT: Yale University Press.

Walker, E. A., Unutzer, J., Rutter, C., Gelfand, A., Saunders, K., Von Korff, M., Koss, M. P., & Katon, W. (1999). Costs of health care use by women HMO members with a history of childhood abuse and neglect. *Archives of General Psychiatry, 57*, 609-613.

Walker, L. E. A. (1989). Psychology and violence against women. *American Psychologist, 44*, 695-702.

Walklate, S. (1997). Risk and criminal victimization: A modernist dilemma? *British Journal of Criminology, 37*, 35-45.

Waller, I., & Okihiro, N. (1978). *Burglary: The victim and the public*. Toronto: University of Toronto Press.

Warner, B. D. (1997). Community characteristics and the recording of crime: Police recording of citizens' complaints of burglary and assault. *Justice Quarterly, 14*, 631-650.

Warr, M. (1994). Public perceptions and reactions to violent offending and victimization. In A. J. Reiss & J. A. Roth (Eds.), *Understanding and preventing violence: Vol. 4. Consequences and control* (pp. 1-66). Washington, DC: National Academy Press.

Weiler, B. L., & Widom, C. S. (1996). Psychopathy and violent behavior in abused and neglected young adults. *Criminal Behavior and Mental Health, 6*, 253-271.

Weinstein, N. D. (1989). Effects of personal experience on self-protective behavior. *Psychological Bulletin, 105*, 31-50.

Weiss, D. S., & Marmar, C. R. (1997). The Impact of Event Scale—Revised. In J. P. Preston & T. M. Keane (Eds.), *Assessing psychological trauma and PTSD* (pp. 399-411). New York: Guilford.

Whatley, M. A. (1996). Victim characteristics influencing attributions of responsibility to rape victims: A meta-analysis. *Aggression and Violent Behavior: A Review Journal, 1*, 81-95.

White, J. W., Smith, P. H., Koss, M. P., & Figueredo, A. J. (2000). Intimate partner aggression—What have we learned? Comment on Archer (2000). *Psychological Bulletin, 126*, 690-696.

Widom, C. S. (1989a). The cycle of violence. *Science, 244*, 160-166.

Widom, C. S. (1989b). Does violence beget violence? A critical examination of the literature. *Psychological Bulletin, 106,* 3-28.

Widom, C. S. (1999a). Childhood victimization and the development of personality disorders: Unanswered questions remain. *Archives of General Psychiatry, 56,* 607-
608.

Widom, C. S. (1999b). Posttraumatic stress disorder in abused and neglected children
grown up. *American Journal of Psychiatry, 156,* 1223-1229.

Widom, C. S., & Kuhns, J. B. (1996). Childhood victimization and subsequent risk for
promiscuity, prostitution, and teenage pregnancy: A prospective study. *American
Journal of Public Health, 86,* 1607-1612.

Widom, C. S., Weiler, B. L., & Cottler, L. B. (1999). Childhood victimization and drug
abuse: A comparison of prospective and retrospective findings. *Journal of Consulting and Clinical Psychology, 67,* 867-880.

Widom, C. S., & White, H. R. (1997). Problem behaviors in abused and neglected children grown-up: Prevalence and co-occurrence of substance abuse, crime, and violence. *Criminal Behavior and Mental Health, 7,* 287-310.

Willis, I. (1994, July 10). It is a wake-up call to all parents. *Atlanta Journal & Constitution,* p. D7.

Wilson, J. Q., & Kelling, G. (1982, March). Broken windows. *Atlantic Monthly,* pp. 29-
38.

Wilson, M., & Daly, M. (1995). An evolutionary psychological perspective on male sex-
ual proprietariness and violence against wives. In R. B. Ruback & N. A. Weiner
(Eds.), *Interpersonal violent behaviors: Social and cultural aspects* (pp. 109-133).
New York: Springer.

Wilson, W. J. (1987). *The truly disadvantaged: The inner city, the underclass, and public
policy.* Chicago: University of Chicago Press.

Wilson, W. J. (1996). *When work disappears: The world of the new urban poor.* New
York: Knopf.

Winkel, F. W., & Vrij, A. (1993). Facilitating problem- and emotion-focused coping in
victims of burglary: Evaluating a police crisis intervention program. *Journal of
Community Psychology, 21,* 97-112.

Wirth, L. (1938). Urbanism as a way of life. *American Journal of Sociology, 44,* 1-24.

Wisconsin v. Mitchell, 508 U.S. 476 (1993).

Wolfe, D., Jaffe, P., Wilson, S., & Zak, L. (1985). Children of battered women: The relation of child behavior to family violence and maternal stress. *Journal of Consulting
and Clinical Psychology, 53,* 657-665.

Wolfe, D. A., Sas, L., & Wekerle, C. (1994). Factors associated with the development of
posttraumatic stress disorder among child victims of sexual abuse. *Child Abuse and
Neglect, 18,* 37-50.

Wolfe, D., Zak, L., Wilson, S., & Jaffe, P. (1986). Child witnesses to violence between
parents: Critical issues in behavioral and social adjustment. *Journal of Abnormal
Child Psychology, 14,* 95-104.

Wolfgang, M. (1958). *Patterns in criminal homicide.* Philadelphia: University of Pennsylvania Press.

Wolfgang, M. E., & Ferracuti, F. (1967). *The subculture of violence.* London: Tavistock.

Wolfgang, M. E., & Singer, S. I. (1978). Victim categories of crime. *Journal of Criminal
Law and Criminology, 69,* 379-394.

Wortman, C. (1976). Causal attributions and personal control. In J. H. Harvey, W. J.
Ickes, & R. F. Kidd (Eds.), *New directions in attribution research* (Vol. 1). Hillsdale,
NJ: Lawrence Erlbaum.

Wyatt, G., Guthrie, D., & Notgrass, C. (1992). Differential effects of women's child sexual abuse and subsequent sexual revictimization. *Journal of Consulting and Clinical
Psychology, 60,* 167-173.

Yngvesson, B. (1988). Making law at the doorway: The clerk, the court, and the construction of community in a New England town. *Law and Society Review, 22,* 409-448.

Young, M. A. (1997). Victim rights and services: A modern saga. In R. C. Davis, A. J. Lurigio, & W. G. Skogan (Eds.), *Victims of crime* (2nd ed., pp. 194-210). Thousand Oaks, CA: Sage.

Young v. U.S. ex rel. Vuitton et Fils, 481 U.S. 879.

Zawitz, M. (1988). *Report to the nation on crime and justice* (2nd ed.). Washington, DC: U.S. Department of Justice.

Author Index

Subject Index

About the Authors

R. Barry Ruback is Professor of Crime, Law and Justice, and Sociology at Pennsylvania State University. He received a BA in history from Yale University, a JD from the University of Texas, and a PhD in social psychology from the University of Pittsburgh. He is a member of the state bar associations of Georgia and Texas. In 1986 and 1987, he was a Visiting Fellow at the National Institute of Justice. He was a Fulbright Fellow (1985-1986), an Indo-American Fellow (1988), a Fulbright-Hays Fellow (1991) for research in India, and a Fulbright South Asia Regional Scholar (1993-1994) for research in India, Pakistan, and Bangladesh. From 1995 to 1996, he was a Judicial Fellow of the Supreme Court of the United States assigned to the U.S. Sentencing Commission. He has published work on prison crowding and on decision making by victims, judges, and parole boards. His current research, supported by grants from the National Institute of Justice, focuses on the causes, correlates, and consequences of criminal victimization.

Martie P. Thompson, PhD, is Senior Service Fellow at the Division of Violence Prevention, National Center for Injury Prevention and Control, Centers for Disease Control and Prevention (CDC). She received her PhD in community psychology from Georgia State University in 1995. From 1995 to 1997, she was a postdoctoral Fellow in the Department of Psychiatry and Behavioral Sciences at the Emory University School of Medicine, where she received a National Institute of

Mental Health National Research Service Award. She served as an Epidemic Intelligence Service Officer at CDC from 1997 to 1999, before assuming her current position. Her research interests include the application of both psychological and public health knowledge to the study of interpersonal and self-directed violence. She has conducted research on intimate-partner violence, suicidal behavior among women, and family members of homicide victims.